The Year
I Became
a Nomad

The Year
I Became
a Nomad

*A journey through Asia on a quest
for freedom, love and happiness*

Carlos Peñalba

Carlos Peñalba
Calle del Prado 5
Candeleda 05480
Avila
Spain

www.carlospenalba.com

Disclaimer: I have tried to recreate events, locales and conversations from my memories of them. In order to maintain their anonymity, in some instances I have changed the names of individuals and places, and I may have changed some identifying characteristics and details such as physical properties, occupations and places of residence.

Originally written in Spanish. Translation by Carlos Peñalba

Cover Image © Carlos Peñalba
Cover design by Paxton Maroney
Back cover images © Carlos Peñalba
Itinerary map illustration by Carlos Peñalba & José Roldán

Printed in the United States of America
First Printing, 2015

ISBN 978-84-606-6424-6

To my father, who spent a lifetime traveling but only rarely for pleasure, discovery, and fulfillment—as I have been lucky to do, not least of all thanks to him.

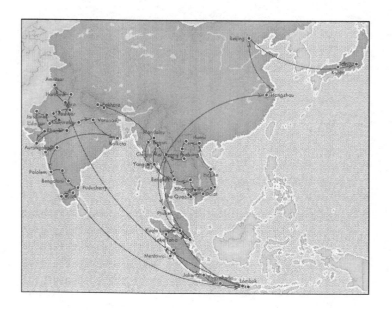

As you read my book, I invite you to travel with me through some of the photos I took during my journey on:

www.carlospenalba.com/photography

Contents

PREFACE

"Twenty years from now, you will be more disappointed by the things you didn't do than the ones you did do. So throw off the bowlines, sail away from the safe harbor. Catch the trade winds in your sails. Explore. Dream. Discover."—Mark Twain

"He who would travel happily must travel light." —Antoine de Saint-Exupéry

In 1996, like many other young Spaniards of my generation, I was suffering from frustration over the inability of my country to absorb the thousands of college graduates it was producing. I was twenty–six, I had completed my business studies and military service and, after having dedicated many years to my education (including postgraduate work), my career had barely begun at an age when in other countries many young men would have been already married and had children. I needed to do something drastic. So I decided to move, in February, from my native San Sebastian, in northern Spain, to London for a year to improve my English, and thus my marketability in a rapidly globalizing economy, before returning to Spain, probably to Madrid, to find a good job, something as much coveted as it was scarce in those days.

Once settled, I found London fascinating. Not only was its cosmopolitan atmosphere exciting, but I was impressed above all by the sharp contrast between the Anglo–Saxon and Mediterranean cultures. English individualism and meritocracy contrasted sharply with the collective family sense of Catholic and Latin Spain. In turn, I had exchanged an adolescent, even childish, democracy for an adult one. I found admirable the seriousness of the British press (not the tabloids, of course), especially the impartiality of the BBC (which, compared to the pro–government TVE in Spain, shamed me), and the freedom with which some politicians criticized their own party, even voting against it in government. To a mind like mine, always attracted to learning, the change was immediately rewarding.

My intended one year turned into eight and a half years, which I spent in London primarily working for a financial software company that gave me the opportunity to delve into both the complex world of investment banking and the exciting field of computer technology, which had just "exploded". Likewise, it gave me, at last, a career, and I was promoted quickly from analyst to research manager.

In the spring of 2004, my company asked me to work in the New York office for three months. As we negotiated the conditions, the request became for a year. The opportunity of living in the Big Apple was too attractive for the inconvenience of the move and the lack of friendships to be insurmountable obstacles. I arrived in New York in late August, and once there, I realized that my stay in London had been too extensive. The last two years had resulted in a stalemate, both professionally and personally, that I did not understand until I was settled in New York. Its energy, Manhattan's compact structure, and Americans' optimism and dynamism hopelessly hooked me and made me forget at a stroke the constant English gray skies and the excessive formality that still prevails in some parts of the U.K. After one year, I asked for my move to New York to become permanent. Once that was achieved, London became the city where I traveled for work several times a year, and where several of my best friends lived (and still live). My career continued to progress in New York, where I was appointed product manager and later director of global operations.

The idea of traveling for a lengthy period had been forged, however, in London and lay dormant for a decade. One of the first aspects I admired about Anglo–Saxons was how many of them travel for months before starting college or their careers. Despite being younger than I was, many of my London colleagues had explored Asia, Oceania, or Latin America for months at a time. By the age I moved to London, many of them had completed their education, traveled the world, and were already on their second or third year working. I, after five years of college, nine months of military service, a graduate course, and a couple of years unable to find an interesting job in my country, felt outclassed by many of my British colleagues and subordinates. Moreover, most of them had left their family homes to go to college (I had spent three of my college years at home and two in Bilbao, not very far away), another reason why I found most of them more mature than I was at their age.

Ironically, I'm sincerely glad about the job crisis I suffered in Spain because I don't know what would have become of me if any of the numerous job interviews I had then had resulted in a long–term job. Would I still be living in San Sebastian, a beautiful city, but small and provincial? Would I have moved to Madrid? Would I already be married and with children? These were evidently unanswerable questions, but interesting to raise because their answers might clarify if indeed, looking back, I might have wished my life to have taken a more domestic route. The answer, however, is a resounding no. Living abroad, particularly in a country with a different culture, makes you open your eyes to new possibilities, to ways of interpreting reality far different from the one you grew up with, and the number of possible paths of your own life multiplies. Despite the difficulties that living abroad brings, emigrating from San Sebastian to London and from there to New York have been two key steps in my personal development, and were key reasons for my decision to travel to Asia for a year.

My resolve to pursue an adventure that I had been daydreaming about for years began taking shape once the chances for career advancement in my company started to dwindle. I had obtained a green card, which would allow me to change jobs, and had saved enough to finance my travels. The arrival of the economic crisis in 2007 gave me the final push: what better time for a long journey than during what seemed the start of a long crisis? I could have asked my company for a sabbatical, but I didn't want to have a specific return date nor a sure thing to hold on to. After almost twelve years in the same company, it was time for another drastic change—as when I left San Sebastian for London with just a few thousand pesetas in my pocket. Now that I had more substantial savings, it was time to break the routine and venture, this time, instead of seeking a new life in a foreign city, traveling across a continent almost entirely new to me. I was free of any anchor: no partner or children, no mortgage to repay.

At the end of April 2009 I became a free man and flew to Spain to spend two months in San Sebastian, to enjoy my city, my family, and my friends, whom I had seen too little of since crossing the Atlantic. I also took time there to start writing a movie script based on an idea I had developed months before.

In July, I returned to New York, and its hot and humid summer, to make travel arrangements. Preparations included purchasing Lonely Planet guides to India and Southeast Asia, establishing a basic itinerary for each country as well as the border crossings I would be using, reading *Vagabonding*, by Rolf Potts (a book with valuable tips on how to be a modern nomad), acquiring the equipment necessary for a long journey through tropical climates, and getting vaccinated against hepatitis B, typhoid, Japanese encephalitis, and rabies, plus acquiring malaria tablets. In August, my fortieth birthday party brought me, besides the good wishes and good company of the vast majority of my friends in New York, a few useful gifts: a map of India and a couple of books on languages I'd find on my trip. Turning forty a month before my departure was pure coincidence; however, some friends interpreted my journey as the result of my arrival, as one friend of mine put it, at "the fourth floor", with the vertigo it represents. I recognize that the attraction many of us feel for the symbolic made me glad my adventure coincided with my new decade; as well, I have to admit that, while my thirties were pleasantly welcomed, my forties were met with a very different feeling. The former is the beginning of a person's settlement into maturity; the latter represents its equator, and with it, the feeling that life is beginning to slip away. Questions about mid–life crisis were put forward repeatedly, and although I felt no crisis at all, I wanted to use my journey to prepare a different life for myself.

Beyond exploring a fascinating continent, finishing the script I had begun, writing a book about my adventure, and immersing myself in photography, I dreamed of a future life outside the corporate world, its stiffness and its infectious politics, and a more creative and flexible existence. The forties represented an ideal time for change.

My passion for photography had started in San Sebastian thanks to a manual Yashica owned by a girlfriend. I learned basic camera technique, and once I was in London, I bought my first SLR, a mid–range Canon plus a 70–200mm Sigma lens, and even went for a few weekends to a composition and lighting course. But it wasn't until recently that I considered making photography a possible career. As for writing, I have always liked literature, ever since my Spanish teacher introduced me to Ernest Hemingway's story *The Old Man and the Sea* when I was only twelve years old. It was my first proper novel and left a deep mark on me, and since then I have continued (although inconsistently) to read good literature. It had probably been a few years since I started to think about writing a novel myself, but my profession didn't allow me the time needed for such a complex and intensive pursuit.

As for the trip itself, the first route I had dreamed of years ago was touring Latin America from north to south, but my first visit to Asia, for a two–week vacation in northern Vietnam in October 2002, and the increasing insecurity in Latin America in the 2000s, made me change continents. Vietnam fascinated me for its scenery, its people, and its culture. Numerous friends and acquaintances had shared with me their wonderful experiences in Indonesia, Cambodia, China, Japan, India, and Nepal. One of the countries that attracted me specially was India, which I'd never considered for a vacation, knowing I would want to have plenty of time to explore it, crossing it from north to south, from west to east, without the constraints of a work break. I planned a minimum of three to four months, to explore it broadly. Before venturing into India, I wanted to visit Nepal, to oxygenate myself in the Himalayas and go rafting down one of its rivers. After Nepal and India, I'd jump to Southeast Asia before ending my adventure with brief visits to China and Japan. I wanted not only to explore the attractive geography of Asia, but also its cultures, its religions and philosophies, so different from those of Europe—all of them, from Hinduism and Buddhism to Taoism and Confucianism, so unknown (ignored would be the more accurate term) in the modern West. In particular, I wanted to go deeper into Buddhism, to understand its history and its evolution as it traveled from India, where it was born, to Japan, where Zen Buddhism remains active, visiting countries as strongly Buddhist as Myanmar and Thailand.

I applied for my Indian visa in New York, knowing that its usual validity was six months. However, the situation got complicated when, after I described my profession, stupidly, as writer and photographer, the consulate insisted on my need for a journalist visa, a profession I had never practiced nor intended to. This was a shorter visa, for three months instead of six, and was twice as expensive, and did not have the option of leaving and re-entering the country in order to extend my stay. This shattered my plans to fly to Delhi via London, using the frequent-flyer miles I had accumulated on Virgin Atlantic, travel to Nepal by land, and return to India after the trekking and rafting. Therefore, I decided to withdraw my visa application in New York and apply for it in Kathmandu, but I did not expect the seal the Indian consulate stamped on my passport stating I had requested a visa there. When I asked for its meaning, I was told it was to indicate I had paid the fees and could reapply there without having to pay again. The explanation didn't seem at all convincing. As I could not enter India without a visa, I had to take an alternative route and bought a flight from London to Kathmandu with Qatar Airways via Doha.

Before leaving my small studio in the West Village at the end of September, I sold my bed, my bedside table, and a couple of lamps to a young man who had just arrived in the Big Apple in search of employment, and my huge leather sofa to a couple of students. I gave my plants to three friends, one of whom also borrowed the coffee table and three bookshelves. I filled several trash bags with clothes I no longer used (it's when you move that you become aware you have more clothes than you possibly need) and donated them to the Salvation Army. The rest—clothes, books, kitchen tools, some small furniture and other objects—were stored in Brooklyn, where a storage room of five feet by five feet cost more than $80 a month.

Being a nomad for a long time is a trip to the past, to a time when humans were not permanently settled in a particular place but in the quest for survival moved constantly in search of food and water. Being a nomad is to cut oneself off from the accumulation of goods that somehow much of the developed world is addicted to today. A nomad carries only what is necessary, hoping to procure the rest along the way. A nomadic contemporary traveler replaces horses and camels with trains and buses, a cart with his own back; traveling light therefore becomes an obligation. For my journey to Asia I carried a forty–two–liter backpack, which contained three pairs of long pants and one pair of shorts, three shirts, three T–shirts, a fleece, five underpants, five pairs of socks, sandals, low boots, flip–flops, a microfiber towel, two bandanas, a silk sleeping bag, a flashlight, and a small health kit. In a smaller backpack I carried my ten–inch Asus netbook, a Canon point–and–shoot camera, a Nikon D700 with three prime lenses (20mm, 50mm, and 85mm) and cleaning accessories and batteries, an external 500 GB hard drive, a couple of notebooks, some pens, and my guidebooks. In total, there were about twenty–four pounds in the large backpack, and about ten pounds in the small one; sufficient to carry everything I needed and to move freely when riding trains, buses, taxis, motorcycles, and rickshaws.

I felt extremely lucky, free, and excited. It had been years since I began to dream about this trip, and months of preparation and waiting. Finally the day my dream turned true arrived, and with it the anticipation of what would befall me: the beautiful places I would visit, the interesting people I would meet along the way. Eliminating, at least temporarily, my need for work and a regular routine, and placing myself outside my comfort zone, I sought to question the tendencies of my personality, my fears and habits, and to take a firm step in reaching a greater happiness. I wanted to capture the entire experience in a book that narrated, not only what happened, but also my reactions and thoughts as I discovered a continent so unknown to me. I committed myself to tell honestly what happened, whether it was positive or not. Would I fall madly in love with an attractive Asian woman? Would I change scenery and move to Asia, the continent with perhaps a better future today than the West? Or despite its novelty and exoticism, would I miss Western culture and its luxuries, even its weaknesses, craziness, evils?

NAMASTE, MOUNTAINS & HOSPITAL

"A journey of a thousand miles must begin with a single step." —Lao Tzu

"A journey is like marriage. The certain way to be wrong is to think you control it." —John Steinbeck

I took off from New York in 2009 and landed in Nepal in 2066. No, I did not travel in a time machine. Nepal has its own calendar, the Samwat Vikram, a lunar calendar whose year begins in mid–April and runs almost fifty–seven years ahead of the Gregorian calendar. Also in use in parts of India, it was established to commemorate the victory of King Vikramaditya over the Sakas, who had invaded the Indian city of Ujjain in the year 56 BC. Most calendars I saw hanging on hotels in Nepal combined the Samwat Vikram with the Gregorian, so the box for each day had two numbers, one for each calendar.

Nepal was my first stop because it offered the possibility of climbing the highest mountains on earth as well as going down the rough waters of its many rivers. I wanted to start my journey in nature, refreshing my body for at least two weeks of trekking and one of rafting, forgetting the urban gym, and replacing New York's lean towers of steel and glass with the Himalayas' massive ones of rock and snow. It would also serve as a brief introduction to India. Nepal is not only predominantly a Hindu country (proportionally, it is the most Hindu of all); it also shares many cultural aspects with its Indian neighbor. My other goals were to explore Kathmandu, its valley, and Pokhara, the quiet town where end, or begin, most of the treks in the Annapurna region.

It was early October, the month that marks the end of the monsoon and the arrival of the dry season, and together with November and spring, the ideal time to approach the Himalayas. It was from a plane that I first saw the highest white peaks on earth, though I almost missed them since my seat was on the right–hand side of the plane, the wrong side to see the albino peaks when traveling to Nepal from the west. At the connection in Doha I tried to rectify my mistake, and Qatar Airways kindly upgraded me to business class on the desired side of the plane, but in an aisle seat. Despite not sitting next to a window, I found it very easy to both admire the spectacular view of the Himalayas and take pictures with my digital compact camera. Thanks to a clear morning, the white peaks strongly contrasted with the blue sky. One of the photos immediately became the one to receive me each day whenever I switched on my laptop, the desktop screen transforming in the blink of an eye into the view from the window of that plane.

I had booked, by email, two nights in a modest guesthouse in Thamel, Kathmandu's tourist area. After obtaining a thirty–day visa at the airport, a hotel employee was waiting outside with a sign bearing my name. "Namaste, Carlos," were his first words. We took a cab to the hotel; the cab was a tiny Maruti Suzuki of the kind I would see repeatedly zipping through the streets of the Nepalese capital. The trip was a brief but accurate introduction to Kathmandu: intense and chaotic traffic accompanied by constant honking, with crowds of people everywhere, some walking, others waiting for a local minibus, and dirt and debris scattered at both sides of the road contrasting sharply with the colorful beauty of the saris worn by most women. I noticed only the saris, red and garnet dominated, with blue, green, and mustard; they made invisible the colorless men.

Usually, after I get to a new city I like to walk the streets immediately, to get a feel for it, both geographically and atmospherically. On this occasion, however, fatigue overcame curiosity, and I immediately went to bed to sleep for a few hours. I decided to dine in my room, and, so brief had my research on Nepal been (I didn't even buy a travel guide), unknowingly I ordered the country's national dish, *dal bhat* (boiled rice, lentil soup, pickles, and vegetable or meat curry), which I ate in a way foreign to local customs. *Dal bhat* is eaten after first pouring the lentils over the rice, mixing them together with the fingers of the right hand (the left is used in the bathroom), adding the curry, and then eating the soaked rice with your right hand. This action is repeated until there are no lentils, rice, or curry left, when you can order everything and start over again. Still ignorant of local customs, I went half way, adding the curry to the rice, but eating the lentils with a spoon, like a soup. The next *dal bhat* I ate was three days later with my guide and my porter at a roadside restaurant halfway between Kathmandu and Besisahar, the starting point of the Annapurna Circuit trek. There, I used a fork instead of my right hand but followed my guide's instructions mixing the lentils with the rice and the curry, although I must admit that my companions' right hands soaked the rice with the lentils and curry more successfully than my metallic "fingers" were able to. During the trek I also learned that most Nepalese eat *dal bhat* twice a day: it's the fuel that keeps the country's heart beating.

I arranged the Annapurna trek in Kathmandu (which, despite being in the Himalayas, is only 4,600 feet above sea level) through an agency recommended by the hotel. There was no group for several days, so I decided to go alone with a guide and a porter. We would leave in two days. I also hired the agency to apply for the Indian visa while I was on the trek, and for a tour guide to the most important temples in Kathmandu and its valley: Kathmandu Durbar Square, Swayambhu, Patan, Bakhtapur, Pashupatinath, and Boudhanath. My guide spoke Spanish. He'd spent three months in Barcelona, and although his name was Mahesh, he had also given himself a Spanish one: Carlos—my Nepalese namesake. When asked about his name choice, he said it was due to a long trek of more than forty days he had taken with a Chilean named Carlos.

First we visited Kathmandu Durbar Square: a spectacular group of temples and palaces in the city center, built at different periods, the oldest from the sixteenth century. Then we jumped into what would be our vehicle for the day, a white Maruti Suzuki, to go to the Buddhist temple of Swayambhu, a stupa at the top of a hill, with spectacular views of the Nepalese capital. A stupa is a Buddhist or Jain structure usually consisting of a square base with a dome topped with a cone surmounted by a disc. It contains saint's relics, and is therefore a goal of pilgrimage. Swayambhu is inhabited by hundreds of monkeys, anything but shy of the many visitors. We continued our Sunday visits to the temples and palaces of Patan and Bhaktapur, both resplendent and more beautiful than those of Kathmandu.

The next stop was the Hindu temple of Pashupatinath. This is situated on both banks of the Bagmati River, which, having an essential role in the ceremonies, runs straight through the partly open–air temple. On our arrival we observed two bodies being prepared for cremation, and others already little more than ash. Most visitors watched the rite from the other side of the river or from the single bridge that crosses it inside the temple. The atmosphere was as quiet as a church during a funeral. Death was in front of us: cremation takes place along the river, in the sight of all. A family had deposited the deceased body, which was covered with a white robe and lying on a pile of logs. Each family member collected water from the river, cupped in their hands and then poured over the body. Mahesh told me that when the deceased is a man, the eldest son is responsible for lighting the pyre, while the youngest does it in the case of the mother. I remembered my brother and myself, along with my uncle and a cousin, carrying my father's coffin to the church on his funeral day.

Mahesh told me that, on one occasion, when he was leading a group of young Americans, they insisted on taking photos of the event, not from the other side of the river, but close to the family and the body. He warned them not to do so, but they, flouting the slightest sense of decency, crossed the river to document the event with close–ups. He warned them that he would return to Kathmandu without them because he could not tolerate being their guide after that behavior. And that's what he did once the group ignored his warning. The tourists returned to the city by taxi and furiously demanded that the agency return their money, unable to understand that it had been their attitude and actions that had been the problem, their blindness the reason for losing their guide.

I liked Mahesh from the start, and after sharing with me

that story I also admired his integrity. He knew he'd lost a good tip, even risked future work with the agency, but he did not hesitate to take the only position that his conscience dictated, and in these difficult times, it is how you react when your ethical values are challenged that shows your worth as a human being.

As curious as I am, at that time I did not want to see fire consuming a corpse. Perhaps it was the unexpectedness of it, the fact I hadn't expected to witness it that day, and so wasn't prepared. Or perhaps it just seemed too grotesque to me to contemplate a body disappearing in the flames. Whatever the deeper reason for my reluctance to witness a cremation, we left Pashupatinath before the pyres were lit.

We ended the tour at Boudhanath, one of the largest stupas in the world, a special place of pilgrimage for Tibetan Buddhists. Buildings of three or four floors, mainly occupied by restaurants and gift shops, surround the stupa. Eating on the roof of one of the restaurants, and unable to look away from the eyes of Buddha watching from each side of the stupa, Mahesh told me that, after losing a girlfriend who ended up marrying another man, he took refuge in vipassana meditation (a form of meditation that I was particularly interested in exploring) and spent three years living in various parts of Nepal as a Buddhist monk. Now he worked as a trek and city guide, usually on his own, thanks to contacts made in recent years. Most guides in Nepal do the same: they try to provide a good service and then be recommended directly to family and friends of previous clients, referrals that get precedence over agency work.

I asked him what he liked most and least in Spain. The most was the cleanliness of the cities; the least, bullfighting and the ability to purchase animals for pure enjoyment, as pets. No doubt he was a true Buddhist, and I fully agreed with him when it came to animals. After the tour, we said goodbye after exchanging email addresses.

Upon returning from the tour, I was told by the agency that the Indian embassy had refused to process my visa due to the stamp on my passport. It wasn't the first time they had known this to happen; they told me the office usually rejected such requests and recommended me to apply in person. I had been suspicious of the stamp the moment I saw it. I tried to forget the setback while preparing my backpack with the essentials for the trek; the rest of my belongings would stay at the hotel.

The next day began the long–awaited trek of the Annapurna Circuit, a popular trek in the Annapurna mountain range. My guide and the porter picked me up early in the morning to catch the bus to Besisahar, where we would spend the first night before hiking to Thorung La (which, at 17,769 feet above sea level, is the highest mountain pass in the world), from which we would descend toward the valley of the Kali Gandaki (Great Black) River, before ending up in Pokhara a fortnight later.

Prahlad, my guide, was a young man of twenty–five whose facial features would not seem foreign in the south of Spain. He seemed ready to start the trek in his mountain boots and hiking pants. The porter, Hari, looked younger than Prahlad despite being three years older. Dressed in slacks, a long–sleeved shirt, and sneakers, he was tall and broad–shouldered for a Nepali. Barefaced, he had a smile as broad as it was white. It reminded me of a young Rock Hudson, and so I would call him during the trek. We exchanged the obligatory *namastes*, the greeting visitors constantly receive in Nepal. A greeting of respect, it's the first word you hear when you are picked up at the airport, when you arrive at your hotel, when you walk into a store or restaurant. The local version, the one usually used by Nepalese people, is *namaskar*, and it literally means "I bow to you." Prahlad told me he never used it with his younger brother but did with his uncle, doctors, judges, and other people of higher status. The police, however, did not receive the salute because the population distrusts them and sees them as corrupt.

When we arrived at the bus station, an area of open land with a few food stalls, we identified our vehicle as a thirty–seater bus that, just twenty minutes before departure, had two men underneath its front axle carrying out some last–minute maintenance. Welcome to road trips in this part of the world! Old and dirty vehicles, usually overloaded with passengers and merchandise, perhaps with poor maintenance, were operated by drivers who moved along the roads honking aggressively at slower vehicles ahead. I soon understood the reason for the honking. It's a very efficient communication system: a vehicle honks to show it means to pass the one in front, the latter giving way as soon as possible. In fact, many trucks carry signs written in English on the back: *Honk Please.* I was reminded of my father, who worked as a truck driver for many years, hard work that made him spend two or three nights away from home each week, mainly in Madrid, Barcelona, and Valencia, cities to which he transported fresh fish caught by Basque fishermen.

Once seated, I realized this was going to be the most uncomfortable bus I had ever ridden. Though I'm not that tall (5′8″), my knees were jammed uncomfortably against the back of the seat in front of me, and the journey was going to take six or seven hours. The German giant from Stuttgart I'd chatted with briefly before boarding the bus sat diagonally, extending his legs into the aisle.

In countries where car ownership is low, transportation is a luxury, and privately owned vans or minibuses often become spontaneous carriers of people (who are, of course, charged for the privilege) between different areas of towns and cities. Along the road, we saw crowds of people, desperate for transportation, who insisted on climbing on vehicles that were already packed. We stopped at a furniture dealer where a wooden dining table and chairs were loaded onto our bus's roof rack. We stopped a few times for bathroom visits, for me to learn to eat *dal bhat* properly, and to release my knees from the pressure of the seat ahead of me.

Seven hours after leaving Kathmandu, we got to Besisahar, where we stayed at a little dirty hotel. Two giant spiders convinced me with their menacing presence to use my bathroom as little as possible. I knew about the similarity between Nepal and India with regards to dirtiness, so I took my dirty room as training for the following months, as exercise to strengthen my immune system. I woke up at six o'clock in the morning. Before cooking our breakfast, the owner opened the door of the hotel to toss several flower petals into the front yard, a Hindu ritual for a prosperous day. I wished the same for ours.

We left at 7 a.m. in search of the Marsyangdi River. The plan for the coming days would be simple: to follow the course of the river in the direction opposite its strong current. In the mountains, rivers are the natural highways to the heart of the most apparently unreachable ridges. As we followed the river, we crossed it several times, seeking the less steep path along the river valley. The crossings were themselves little adventures; they were made across wire suspension bridges, each of which was some 150 feet long. In the whole Annapurna Circuit there are more than twenty such bridges, several up to 100 feet above the river, and although I eventually enjoyed crossing them, during the first one, despite not suffering from vertigo, I experienced a strong sense of temporality and vulnerability. I walked fearfully, suspended by only a few wires and listening to the roar of the wild river under my feet, my body as ephemeral as an insect caught in a spider's web. With each step, and those of my companions, the bridge swayed slightly, accentuating the feeling of walking on air.

At the beginning of the trek in Besisahar, at 2,500 feet above sea level, the humidity was such that after a few minutes' walking, sweat covered my body, particularly my back, because of the backpack with my camera equipment and laptop (which I had brought to avoid a possible robbery at the hotel). The slopes on both sides of the Marsyangdi were covered with green vegetation, and any small space was used to grow rice. Since my first experiences in northern Vietnam seven years earlier, rice fields in the mountains have fascinated me because of the complex harmony between the verticals of the growing crops, the horizontals of the terraces, and the various angles of the slopes. It is an unsurpassed natural geometric spectacle, especially a few weeks before harvest.

We passed the last women I would see wearing saris, since in the high mountains the majority of the inhabitants are Buddhist and their clothes are less colorful and more appropriate to the colder temperatures of the mountains.

Women in saris appeared on the road as wandering flowers gracefully gliding among the green foliage.

After nearly five hours of walking, gaining altitude only to lose it several times, cross the river, and climb back up, we reached our destination, Bahundanda (4,300 ft). My shirt dripped with sweat and even my pants were soaked. After a shower, I sat down to eat just as the rain began to fall unabated for the next thirty hours. Sleeping was not easy because the water pounded angrily against the metal roof of my room and the mattress was very thin, so my bones groaned whatever position I took. I lost count of how many times I woke during the night.

The next day, protected like a Capuchin monk by an orange plastic poncho I bought for fifty rupees, we started under the constant rain towards Chamje (4,700 ft). The monsoon had arrived late that year, so we had to suffer its final assaults. I have always loved water, showering and bathing, swimming outdoors, in sea, river, or lake, and even the rain, with which I grew up in the wet autumns and winters of San Sebastian, with their endless drizzle; but that day, it having rained nonstop since the previous noon, I started to change my mind. The path became a stream. On the steep sections of the path the water flowed over my feet, and it flooded the sections that were flat. Prahlad and Rock Hudson put their boots and sneakers away (the porter had made the entire trek up till then in sneakers) and put on their flip–flops, aware of the impossibility of keeping their feet dry. I, however, helped by the great sense of balance I had because of my soccer–player legs, tried to keep my feet dry by stepping from stone to stone, in a kind of rain dance. Despite my efforts, my boots and feet ended up soaking wet. Hari and Prahlad weren't a bit worried by the danger of leeches, which they had warned me of at the beginning of the day. Prahlad had to remove no less than six of them, while I felt falsely protected by my shoes. After reaching Chamje, while taking a cold shower, I realized that at least two leeches had reached my skin through my thick socks and, still sprouted near my ankles, were sucking my blood.

Once I had dried off and eaten, and as I was enjoying a

tea in the dining room, I felt satisfied with the four–hour brisk walk in the rain. It felt like what I had experienced many times after soccer games played in the rain, which I had enjoyed during my childhood and youth. After an hour and a half of constant effort on a waterlogged field, my socks and boots were just as heavy after my trying to beat both the weather and the opposition. Similarly, this early day of the trek had been a battle against the rain and the mountains. And there, with my tea, wishing the rain to stop, I continued being bewitched by water.

That night in the dining room I met two Australians, father and son, who were going to do not only the Annapurna Circuit but also Tilicho Lake (at 16,000 feet, one of the highest in the world) and the Annapurna Base Camp; a long trek of at least a month. The father was retired and the son had taken a long vacation to travel with him. It was beautiful to see a young man in his thirties traveling with his father across those wonderful places, and I wondered if my father would have ever come with me on a similar journey had he had the chance of retiring. His death had deprived him of that, and of course of much more, and had perhaps deprived me of a moment as precious as the Australian young man was enjoying that evening. I felt glad for him in silence while I remembered my father with an internal smile. After dinner, at last the rain ceased, and everyone left the dining room to look up and smile at the first stars of the night.

The following morning was lit by a beautiful blue sky that became covered with clouds at mid–morning before breaking into more rain early in the afternoon. By then we had reached our destination, Danaque (7,500 ft), and I was grateful for my guide's habit of starting the day early to have more time to rest during the afternoon. After another cold shower (clouds made the solar panels useless), I had lunch and retired to rest in my simple but cozy room, which had a little window onto the rear garden, which reminded me of the garden of my grandparents.

By now we had fully entered Buddhist land. The people of the area are mostly of Tibetan origin, which is obvious not only from their facial features but also from the many posters of Tibet and the Dalai Lama decorating dining rooms and guesthouses. Buddhist flags were ubiquitous. The vertical flags are long, narrow, and rectangular and composed of five parts of equal size and in the following colors: blue, white, red, green, and yellow, representing sky, water, fire, earth, and sun, respectively. The flags were like rainbows coloring rooftops and streets. Every village has either at its entrance or near the temple, a series of metal cylinders that rotate on a vertical axis, the so—called prayer wheels. There can be more than twenty cylinders, usually arranged in double rows, and placed at shoulder height so that worshippers can rotate them with their right hand while praying.

The clear dawn received us with Manaslu (26,760 ft) just behind us. Due to its height, it seemed much closer than it actually was. It was my first sighting from below of a 26,000—foot peak; truly stunning. The rain never came back, and the trek to Chame (8,760 ft, not be confused with Chamje) was very pleasant. At this altitude, the forest was exclusively of pine. In the village I came across the first communist flag, a reminder of the control Maoists had in much of Nepal until recently. Before the king's abdication in 2006, all visitors to the Annapurna had to pay the Maoists 100 rupees a day, a kind of revolutionary tax. Currently, to enter Annapurna National Park it was necessary to request a permit costing 2,000 rupees. The permit had to be presented at various checkpoints that now the police, not the Maoists, controlled along the route.

Rock Hudson was a tireless talker, Prahlad a patient listener. During the trek, common was the picture of Hudson telling stories to Prahlad about his people, his family, his fishing (apparently Hudson was a skilled river fisherman) that I could not share unless Prahlad translated them into English, which he spoke correctly if with some difficulty in pronunciation. Hudson's other addiction was his Nokia, which, except in sections where we lost connection, he often used to talk with his family and friends, though its main use was to play Nepalese and Indian music, so often that the trek had a soundtrack, sometimes folk, sometimes pop, which at first I welcomed but eventually became bored by due to the repetition of many of the melodies. Hudson carried my backpack, which weighed less than 18 pounds, on his back and his own against his chest. Most porters carry two people's luggage, with a weight limit of sixty–six pounds, so Hudson cruised with my light backpack, carrying it slung over his shoulders. Porters serving two tourists can't do the same, so they haul the load in the traditional Nepalese style: a large wicker basket or a big cargo bag carried on the back and held there securely by a band or strap over the porter's forehead. This ancient technique is usual for rural people; they can carry up to 220 pounds this way. One afternoon we saw a man around sixty years of age, and who couldn't have weighed more than 110 pounds, carrying an 82–pound refrigerator this way on his back.

The following day, after a long journey, we reached Manang (11,600 ft), where we would rest for a day to acclimatize to the altitude. The landscape changed dramatically to one populated only by low shrubs. In Hunde, a few miles below Manang, there was a tiny airport that was being enlarged, and a new road was being built up to Manang. I heard several tourists complaining that the road would increase the number of tourists to the area, losing the sense of remoteness and relative calm. It was an extremely selfish attitude coming from many who probably resided in places with highly developed infrastructure. Would these tourists want to live so far from a hospital that their lives would be in danger in the event of an accident, a heart attack, or complications during childbirth?

We arrived late at Manang, at around 3:30 p.m. During lunch in Pisang the porter had suggested reaching Manang instead of spending the night in Hunde, our original destination. I felt strong; the only thing that worried me was the jump in altitude from Chame to Manang. Eventually, we ventured. That day we walked around twenty–one miles and rose almost 4,000 feet. The valley where Manang lies is beautiful, and for the first time I really felt the altitude, not only while walking, but also because of the sight of the shaggy yaks grazing in the valley, and the white peaks, much closer now. In Pisang, we admired Annapurna II (26,040 ft) to the left and the Pisang Peak (19,980 ft) to the right, and in Manang we added to the incomparable view Annapurna III and IV (24,787 ft and 24,688 ft) and the Ganggapurna (24,455 ft). Then I remembered when, a few days earlier, I had sighted at dawn a peak dominating the skyline, I had enthusiastically asked Prahlad for its name. "No mountain," he had answered. He meant it had no name, that in Nepal there are so many peaks above 13,000 feet that many lack one. A peak that anywhere else in the world would have been revered was anonymous in this high country.

Upon entering Manang, exhausted, we learned there were no beds available. Prahlad chatted with other guides to find a solution. A young German from Munich who was going to leave Manang the next day offered to share his room with me. Guides and porters would sleep in the guesthouse's dining room. This is common when rooms are full; dining rooms become dormitories. During dinner two Germans commented on how shocked they were to see swastikas on buses and gates, unaware that the swastika is a symbol with a story that goes beyond Nazi Germany. Its presence in many parts of Asia is ancient, going back several thousand years. A symbol of good luck shared by Hindus, Buddhists, and Jains, it can be seen—its blades facing either clockwise or counterclockwise—on vehicles and buildings, including government ones.

The acclimatization day was taken up on a morning walk to one of the glaciers that advance (perhaps it would be better to write that they are actually receding in this era of global warming) in the valleys between the Himalayan peaks. I spent the afternoon walking among Manang's stone houses trying to capture with my camera the charm of this beautiful village. After the resting day, I felt great hiking up to Thorung La (17,769 ft). The short distance between Manang and Thorung La takes two and a half days to cover, because of the combination of steepness and, particularly, lack of oxygen, but I didn't get too tired physically. It was very important to drink plenty of fluids, about a gallon a day minimum, so I began the day by eating one of the tasty soups prepared by the locals, accompanied by an omelet, some bread, and plenty of tea, continuing with repeated stops to drink water and regain my breath in the steepest sections. Sleeping above 13,000 feet is often difficult, and I woke up briefly and fell asleep again several times during the night. Due to the large number of tourists in that stretch and the difficulty of getting a single room, we decided that Michi (a German I had met on the bus from Kathmandu to Besisahar) and I would share a room the following three nights, and to ensure bed availability, the guide of a Spanish group sent one of his porters every morning to book rooms at the next destination for his group and us. Therefore I not only shared those days with Michi but also with seven Spaniards, from Lugo, a small city in the northwestern Galicia region. It was a happy group who liked to sing (one night they learned a traditional Nepalese song they sang in the dining room to surprise the locals) and play cards.

We spent one night at 13,780 feet in Letdar, the following at 16,158 feet, in Thorung High Camp. On the way to Letdar it started snowing. The snowflakes were tiny and dry, as if powder detergent were being thrown from the clouds. You could take it in your hand and it wouldn't melt or wet you. I feared that if the snowfall persisted, it could hinder, or even prevent, the climb to Thorung La. Fortunately, it did not, and though it snowed for several hours, covering the path with almost ten inches of snow, it did not prevent our ascent; on the contrary, it embellished it. These were days of great excitement, days when I met the same people on the way up and in the dining rooms, everyone excited to have the good fortune of enjoying the Annapurnas' white paradise. Evenings were spent drinking tea (my favorite was mint tea because of the intensity of its flavor), playing cards, and chatting with other hikers. During the trek I met Germans, Spaniards, Canadians, Swiss, Israelis, Ukrainians, Australians, New Zealanders, Lithuanians, Austrians, British…

The day of the climb to Thorung La began at 5 a.m. I didn't sleep much that night and woke up with a slight headache that thankfully disappeared after the hearty breakfast. It was still dark, with a multitude of stars overhead, and with our headlamps on, as if we were entering a mine on the first morning shift, walking slowly and cautiously over the snow. In short time, the dark night woke, the sky turned dark blue at first, and the stars, one by one, were extinguished. Slowly white peaks regained their pristine color and shape in a memorable sunrise. What a beauty! The ascent was slow, very slow. We stopped often to catch our breath and drink water. Some of us rode on the backs of mules; I climbed on foot.

After more than two hours we could finally see the top. What a feeling of fullness to be so close! I stopped two hundred yards from the peak, where the views of the Annapurnas were perfect for filming a video. I asked Hudson to play a traditional Nepali song on his phone, I approached with my camera and started a slow spin on my feet, three hundred and sixty degrees of white paradise accompanied by a beautiful melody to which we danced, first Hudson and I, and then Prahlad taking his place. As I walked to the top, wrapped in the landscape, the emotion of the moment, and the effort of the long climb, my eyes watered slightly.

Once we had conquered Thorung La, we took pictures in front of a board confirming our ascent to 17,769 feet and got ready for the long and steep descent, sometimes icy, that left aches in my knees and toes. At the other side, we were greeted by the mighty Dhaulagiri (26,811 ft), his neighbor Tukuche (22,703 ft), and the beautiful Nilgiri North (23,166 ft), with a line of clouds below us increasing the sense of altitude. What a divine sight!

If climbing undoubtedly required considerable effort, the most complicated part for porters was the steep descent. After reaching Thorung La, we saw a couple of porters slipping on ice (they were unharmed), which was not surprising because they wore sneakers. At the end of the trek, porters, in addition to receiving a tip, often also get clothing from tourists thanking them for their efforts. Therefore it was common to see porters wearing shirts of soccer teams or stars such as Barcelona, Chelsea, Manchester United, Real Madrid, Brazil, and David Beckham; they were true high—mountain athletes. One day, however, I saw a porter wearing a Jennifer

Lopez shirt, and I could only think how much more he would have enjoyed carrying her instead of some tourist's luggage. Rock Hudson, meanwhile, used to wear sweatpants and a blue Adidas jacket; on cold days he covered his head with a Rossignol hat and his neck with a gray Burberry scarf that gave him a distinctive flair.

The hard and long day ended in Muktinath (12,336 ft), a town that has one of the most important Hindu temples in Nepal, so popular that many pilgrims come from India to purify themselves under one of the hundred and eight pipes channeling the cold Himalayan water there. Reaching Muktinath, I heard the sound of an engine behind me, and within seconds a noisy motorcycle carrying two young Nepalese overtook me. The racket it made was a blow to my peace. After leaving Besisahar eight days earlier, I had neither enjoyed nor suffered from the presence of any vehicles; Muktinath represented the return to civilization. I hated the noise of motorbikes sounding there throughout the day. It was not all negative, though; I enjoyed my first shower in three days. During the evening stroll through the village, in a surprise encounter, I met Prahlad and Rock Hudson walking holding hands. Was that a sign of friendship, or did it mean something else?

To the south, where we now journeyed, the geography could not be more different. The white peaks continued to dominate the horizon, but the Kali Gandaki valley, surrounded by barren hills eroded by the monsoon rains, looked like a desert. The river was extremely wide, but the water did not fill even five percent of the riverbed. We did much of the walk from Muktinath to Jomsom by walking in the bed itself. A strong wind usually blows in the valley; we reached Jomsom by about eleven o'clock, when the wind began to rise. The small town, with its long street of low houses, the barren hills on both sides, and a buffeting wind, with dust blowing around every corner, resembled a town in a film about the old American West. There, I said goodbye to my roommate and the group of Spaniards. The latter were traveling by plane to Pokhara the next day; Michi was taking a jeep to Tatopani to save a couple of days of hiking. We continued towards Marpha and, as we walked, were beaten twice over, by the violent wind and the hot sun. To protect me from both, I wore a bandana over my head, another covered my nose and mouth like a bandit, and sunglasses shielded my eyes.

Marpha (8,760 ft) was a pleasant surprise, a stunning village of low stone houses, all painted white, with wooden doors and windows painted in garnet, and protected from the wind by two hills hugging it. On each flat roof, tomatoes, apples, and clothes were dried, with wood stacked around the perimeter, or there was a terrace from which to enjoy the view of the valley, planted mainly with apple trees. I tried the local cider and apple brandy, the former much more enjoyable than the strong liquor. Cider accompanied my dinner and inevitably brought back memories of the *sidrerias* of Astigarraga, a town near San Sebastian famous for its fabulous natural cider, which visitors to the breweries are welcome to taste over a meal served there as well; I had not visited one in a long time, and missed the juicy cod omelettes and tasty beefsteaks usually served there. In the center of Marpha stands a Buddhist temple, reached by long and steep stairs. That evening, the monks played their drums and chanted their mantras across the valley. I woke up next dawn to the same sound: the distant sound of drums woke me up at five. I didn't mind at all because the loud cadence breaking up the night's silence gave me a mystical feeling.

The following day we reached Kalopani (8,300 ft); its name means Black Waters. That day began the Nepalese festival of Tihar (Diwali in India), or Festival of Lights. It's one of three major festivals of Nepal and is celebrated over four days. The first day honors the raven; food is offered to it not to bring bad news. The second day honors the dog, for his honesty; we saw dogs with collars adorned with yellow flowers and the traditional Hindu red dot (*tilak*). The third is the day of the cow, the symbol of prosperity; they also boasted collars on their day. The final day is the day of brothers and sisters, when they exchange gifts. The goddess specially worshiped during all four days of the festival is Lakshmi, goddess of wealth, in whose honor Nepalese gamble at cards. At night the house doors are lit with candles, indicating the way for Lakshmi's arrival.

The next day we arrived at Tatopani (3,904 ft), which means Hot Waters, where there was a small but much—used hot spring where tourists, guides, and porters eased their lower extremities after their treks' accumulated miles (over 110 since Besisahar). As he was bathing in the spring, I noticed that Prahlad wore a rope that hung from his body diagonally from the right shoulder, and was adorned with a small charm. He explained it was a sign he was a Brahmin, one of the upper castes, in charge of guarding knowledge; historically, Brahmins have been priests, preachers, and educators. He was studying to be a teacher of Nepali language and literature, and alternated his studies with work as a guide.

We had been following the Kali Gandaki for three days and had lost over 8,400 feet in altitude since Muktinath, but it was time again to climb up to Ghorepani (9,383 ft), which means Water Horses; an ascent as beautiful as it was hard. The gorgeous mountains, the lush green forest, and the cute, small villages of stone houses alleviated the hardship of the steady rise via steps cut into the stone of the mountainside. Maybe we climbed ten thousand of them. My legs creaked with each one.

The main reason to go to Ghorepani is to reach Poon Hill (10,476 ft) at dawn from which to observe the sun rising over an unparalleled view: the Dhaulagiri, the Tukuche, the Dampus, the Nilgiri, Annapurna I, Annapurna South, and the Macchapuchare, the sacred mountain that cannot be climbed. Once we had photographed that wonderful sunrise, we descended to the village of Hile (4,692 ft), which lies at the bottom of a lovely valley of rice paddies and a narrow river cutting through it. It reminded me of some villages in northern Vietnam. We stopped at a long, narrow, two—storied guesthouse; above were the bedrooms, downstairs the dining room and the family residence.

Prahlad took a drum from the house and showed me some rhythms that I tried to emulate without much success. The young daughter of the house, around twelve years old, with piercing dark eyes, came to practice with me. I'd play a sequence, which she had to repeat. She laughed while trying, but preferred to hit the drum hard at her own pace rather than follow mine. She was a whirlwind of energy, a little crazy, though in a good sense. She stroked my month-old beard and said: "I like it." I was invited into the kitchen and followed the daughters while they prepared dinner. The youngest one remained true to her character, constantly joking around. The laughter of her two older sisters, her parents, and her younger brother was in constant flow. It was the last day of the festival, brothers' and sisters' day, and after dinner, the family put on traditional music, on an old-fashioned radio-cassette player, and started dancing. First Prahlad and the owner danced, and then I joined them with the two younger daughters, plus an English woman and her guide. We danced, rippling our outstretched arms like the wings of birds as we turned on our feet. I will always remember the joy of that family, their kindness, and frank good spirit.

We reached the end of the trek in Pokhara (2,690 ft) after walking from Hile to Nayapul and catching a sixteen-seater van carrying more than twenty-six people in total. It was the end of Tihar, and the road was full of people looking for transport, thus every vehicle was literally packed to, and on, the roof. In fact, we could have parted from Pokhara while riding on the roof of an old bus, but despite feeling very adventurous, I didn't let stupidity compel me to take such a big risk. Knowing the local road conditions and driving style as I now did, I realized keenly that a sudden swerve or braking could end in something much more serious than a simple story to tell.

Minutes before reaching the bus stop we met two young Nepalis holding hands. I did not hesitate to take the opportunity to inquire about it. Prahlad told me it was normal in Nepal, as well as in India, to see young men holding hands in a symbol of friendship, without having any sexual meaning. He asked if we did the same in Spain, and I said no, that men, regardless of their friendship, would never walk holding hands.

In Pokhara I said goodbye to Rock Hudson, who was

eager to return to his village and see his family. I gave Hudson and Prahlad my jacket, gloves, hat, and long johns, to distribute between them, as well as a tip. We shook hands while Hudson said, in English: "Nice to meet you." Prahlad stayed for the night in Pokhara before returning to his studies. He had exams the next month and wouldn't be working as a guide during that time. We went for lunch to a restaurant at the back of the main street, an area almost entirely occupied by restaurants, gift shops, Internet cafes, and travel agencies. The place was empty. It was a long, white–walled space occupied by numerous tables, with a small bar at the entrance. A television showed an Indian soap opera that was being intensely followed by the two waitresses. The young man attending the empty bar wore a shirt of the Spanish national soccer team without a player name or number on it. The only decoration on the walls was a beautiful panoramic photo of Marpha. Both of us ordered *dal bhat*. I took advantage of the silence of the place to ask Prahlad about his marriage plans.

At a dinner during the trek, Rock Hudson, who had married when he was twenty, commented that Prahlad was already late to marry, that at twenty–five he had already missed too many good candidates, and that the more he delayed it, the more difficult it would be to find a suitable spouse (I refrained from asking what he thought of me, forty years old, single, and childless). Prahlad then said he would marry next year despite having no girlfriend yet. And he said it without doubting one bit that he would find the right woman with whom to share his life. It was time to learn about the process in more detail. After eating, he told me his parents would seek a girl of the same caste and from a reputable family, similar educational level, three to five years younger, and if possible beautiful. Parents initiate the search through family and friends, and once a suitable candidate is found, a meeting of ten to twenty minutes is arranged between them. If both respond positively (nobody is forced to marry), parents begin wedding preparations. The wedding day is usually held a week or ten days after the meeting (he told me that one of his brothers married the same day). Until the wedding day, bride and groom do not see each other.

In recent years we have witnessed the propagation of speed dating in Western cities, and Nepal has been practicing speed marriage for centuries. And it seems to work. Prahlad told me that all his family and friends have married following this process, all happy with their choice. It was as if parents were the perfect selectors of sons and daughters' spouses, something entirely impossible to accept in Western society, of which freedom of choice is one of its pillars. I asked about premarital sex, and he said of course it existed, mainly in the cities, but that the new urban generations would gradually end up marrying in the traditional way; he added that many love marriages didn't work, that infatuation is not as strong as the relationship that grows between two people of similar characteristics that enter into marriage with a clear understanding of the hard work it requires. In Nepal, marriage is a relationship based on cooperation rather than romantic concepts, an association between two similar persons who start a family based on common values. The aesthetic, romantic, and sexual aspects are irrelevant. In New York I experienced the opposite; there, first impressions are key, as the patience needed to know a person in depth does not exist. There are so many singles in the city (plus the ones who are not but pretend to be) that dating is part of the daily lives of most New Yorkers. The city is a supermarket of bachelors and, as many studies have demonstrated, the more options on offer, the more difficult it is to choose. Such are the possibilities that, at the discovery of something unsatisfactory, the product is discarded to look for a new one, and so the process is continually repeated, a circumstance that generates more dissatisfaction than people admit to. I had suffered from this dynamic in New York, on both sides, and hadn't managed to be in a stable relationship while living there, a situation that wasn't desperate but that I did want to change.

After walking more than 125 miles over the past two weeks, I had lost a few pounds and gained considerable energy to feel capable of any adventure, a physical sense of fulfillment I hadn't experienced in years. Working in an office sitting for hours is harmful to one's health. Your neck becomes fat, your back arches as your shoulders lose their natural alignment with your chest, whose muscles contract, as do those of your abs; straight alignment of the body becomes an anomaly, a fact most are unaware of unless they stand with head, back, butt, and heels tucked against a vertical wall. For a high percentage of Western adults, the day begins with sitting at breakfast, continues sitting with their arms driving a wheel (or on a train or subway reading), followed by sitting down at a computer with their hands on a keyboard, mouse, or phone, with more sitting down to eat lunch, then back sitting in the office, sitting again in the car, train, or subway, before returning home to sit on a couch, stretching from time to time an arm to take a remote control (some with a laptop on their laps), and finally sitting down to dinner (many do not even change the couch for the dinner table) before bed. It was not surprising that only fifteen days of intense walking would have been enough for my waist, face, neck, and limbs to thin considerably, my whole body lighter and stronger. During my early years in London I had abandoned sport's practice, and the pounds had slowly piled up on my body. I had reached 187 pounds, at least 22 pounds above an acceptable weight for my height and build. I estimate I weighed about 160 pounds after my long walk in the Himalayas.

★ ★ ★

I would have liked to stay more than two nights in Pokhara, but I had to return to Kathmandu to get the Indian visa. Once back in Nepal's capital, I got up early to be one of the first in the visa application office. The young man who checked the documentation saw the stamp and said he could not process it with it on my passport. I asked to speak with someone who could clarify for me the reason for that, and had to wait a couple of hours until the office manager arrived. He told me the stamp was only used when a request had had a problem. I explained I had withdrawn my application in New York because I was coming to Nepal first and had not wanted my three-month visa to begin so soon, discounting the days off since its issue, but the officer did not change his mind and suggested I go to the embassy to talk to the consulate staff in charge of visas. The consular officer repeated the same explanation, adding that only the New York consulate or the Indian embassy in Madrid could void the stamp and process my visa. I asked him to contact the New York consulate to clarify the situation, but he refused, saying that I should do it. I had heard of the inefficiency and arrogant attitude of Indian civil servants, and I was suffering from it even before stepping into the country.

I spent a week in Kathmandu trying to contact via email and phone the Indian consulate in New York. I did not get any response to my emails, and when I called and was connected to the correct extension, the only voice I heard was for voice mail. I returned to the Indian embassy where I got to speak to a more receptive official. He listened to the explanation of my situation in detail, took my passport, and went upstairs to talk to his superior. He then asked me to request a visa normally while he obtained clarification of my situation. Finally some light in the dark tunnel of bureaucracy.

I missed the Himalayas, the daily routine of waking up early surrounded by mountains, walking through the valleys and slopes, breathing its clean air and listening to the reassuring silence. So I ran away from the tedium of waiting in Kathmandu for a weekend elsewhere, as millions do when they fly from their cities after the workweek. I chose Bandipur, a small, old mountain village a few hours from Kathmandu known for its excellent views of the Himalayas. I stayed in a guesthouse at the entrance to the village. My room was on the top floor and shared with another tenant a large terrace with stunning views of the white peaks. These seemed suspended over the horizon, as if someone had stuck them on a blue board, as the mountains beneath the peaks, without snow, were invisible in the distance. During the weekend, I walked each morning for about three hours, then read, wrote, and took pictures of this beautiful enclave.

I returned to the Indian Embassy in the hope that by then

an answer from New York had arrived. Not so. The official informed me of the absolute lack of news. As it could still take a few days, I decided, as planned, to go rafting in the Sun Kosi (Gold River), one of the main Nepalese rivers. The trip would last six days in the company of a group of four Italian canoeists. The daughter of one of them, the guide, two assistants, and I would share a raft, while another guide would be alone in a second raft carrying food, tents, and the rest of our equipment. We started one afternoon in a van for the northeast of Kathmandu after collecting the group of Italians at the airport. It was dark when we set up camp on the bank of the unseen Sun Kosi.

My first experience of rafting had consisted of two adrenaline–spiked days on the Pacuare River in Costa Rica, one of the world's most famous wild rivers. I enjoyed the experience so much I could not waste the opportunity Nepalese rivers offered. I loved being out of dirty and noisy Kathmandu, once again surrounded by beautiful nature, getting carried away by the natural flow of the Sun Kosi. Every time we passed a small village, the children greeted us, fascinated by the colorful boats.

Every evening we camped along the river. I regretted the Italians didn't speak English (we communicated as best we could in Italian and Spanish). Therefore, during the nights I read *Shantaram*, the incredible biography of an Australian who escaped from prison and fled to India on a false passport and lived in the slums of Mumbai working at times for the city mafia. We rafted more than 155 miles, with several grade IV rapids; these are especially dangerous for canoeists, so before facing them, we got out of our boats to give them a close examination. My position on the front right–hand corner of the raft was perfect to anticipate the arrival of adrenaline at the start of the rapids, to feel the motion of the raft and the water hitting my face. On the last day a small spot popped up on the side of my left calf, which I thought was due to the daily friction of the raft. A couple of days earlier I had noticed an irritation in the area and thought that a follicle had got infected. I burst the spot without giving it any thought.

At the end of our descent, two guides and I returned to Kathmandu on a long overnight bus journey of fourteen hours, while the Italian group, with two guides, continued for a couple of days in the rapids of the Arun River. Once back in Kathmandu, the first thing I did was to return to the Indian embassy, to get the same answer: no news from the New York consulate. The official suggested that I phone or send an email to urge a response. The situation was reaching the absurd, almost Kafkaesque. Just an email that included the information and documents required was needed, but it was clear that the problem was not the technology but the human attitude to an unusual situation. I thought the official was seeking a bribe, some easy money from a desperate tourist, but I didn't fall for it.

Living in London I had become interested in Buddhism and subscribed to a correspondence course from the London Buddhist Society. The course explained the basics of Buddhist philosophy, its different schools, and vipassana meditation. The aspect of Buddhism that attracted me the most was the concept of suffering or dissatisfaction (*duhkha* in Sanskrit) and how meditation was an indispensable technique to remove it. The idea is roughly as follows: We stick to what we enjoy, wanting it vehemently, while we anxiously fear what we hate, both of which can paralyze and unsettle us for no real reason. Desire and aversion control our thoughts and our perception of what makes us happy and unhappy, causing dissatisfaction when we don't get what we desire and fail to avoid what we don't want. This is *duhkha*, our constant sense of disappointment. The practice of meditation was supposedly a means of reducing, or even eliminating, *duhkha*.

I had briefly experimented with meditation in London, simply concentrating on my breathing, noticing as the air entered and exited through my nostrils, but indiscipline being one of my weaknesses, my meditation practice was short and sporadic; nevertheless, however brief, it had left a pleasant residue in me that made me want to explore it with more dedication. My journey to Asia was an ideal opportunity to do so. I had planned to attend a course of vipassana meditation in India organized by Professor S. N. Goenka, but the problem of getting my visa forced me to take a course in Nepal instead. And (as it turned out) what better place for such a course could there be than Lumbini, the birthplace of Siddhartha Gautama, known as Buddha?

Lumbini is located in southern Nepal, a little more than twelve miles from the Indian border. I got there a day before the start of the course after a long bus ride of nine hours, with just enough time to go to the hotel, read a while, dine, and unwind. The next day I had to be in the Dhamma Janani meditation center early in the afternoon, so I took the morning to walk around Lumbini. Next to the village is a natural area three miles long by a mile wide that contains the birthplace of Siddhartha Gautama, a number of Buddhist monasteries built and managed by several countries (Nepal, India, Vietnam, Thailand, Myanmar, Sri Lanka, Cambodia, China, Japan, South Korea, France, Germany, and Austria), a library, a research center, and a museum. The idea of creating the current Lumbini came in 1967 after a visit by then U.N. Secretary General U Thant, from Burma (Myanmar), who suggested to the king and government of Nepal the creation of a space dedicated to the study of Buddhism, and turning Lumbini into a place of pilgrimage. UNESCO declared the area a World Heritage Site in 1997. First I visited Maya Devi temple, built on the site where Buddha is believed to have been born, then I walked around the area of the monasteries before going to town for lunch. The Dhamma Janani center is located east of the Flame of Peace, which was brought from the United Nations in New York.

During my weeks in Nepal I had meditated with regularity, but at no time had my practice stretched for more than an hour a day, being usually about thirty minutes. Therefore, the length and structure of the course presented a major challenge. The course lasted ten days and had a severely strict regimen. No electronic devices were allowed, nor any reading or writing materials, and talking was prohibited except with the teacher. Men and women lived separately; only the meditation room was shared, though it was divided in two, one half for each sex. The day began at 4 a.m. and ended at 9 p.m., with meditation sessions of one to two hours, a total of more than ten hours of daily meditation. We stopped during the day for breakfast (6:30 to 8 a.m.), lunch (11 a.m. to 1 p.m.), and tea (5 to 6 p.m.), the food being totally vegetarian. After completing the course, I wanted to use what I had learned so diligently to integrate meditation into my daily life, to make it as much a part of my life as a morning shower, eating, and sleeping. It seemed wise to cultivate the mind (not only purely intellectually) as much as the body, and I wanted to see what effect regular meditation would have on my thoughts, my attitude, and my actions.

Most of the students were Nepalese or Indian. We were shown to our rooms; they were more cells than bedrooms. I shared mine with an Italian with whom I spoke the minimum (we didn't exchange names, and I knew he was Italian because I saw his passport) to facilitate our vow of silence for the next ten days. The cell wasn't much more than seven feet wide and ten long, with a dirty bathroom annexed. The bed was a concrete surface on which rested a thin mattress. I deposited at reception my passport, my cameras, books, and other unnecessary possessions, and I went to the dining room (one for men, one for women) for dinner. The center's director gave a talk in English and Hindi, and what should have been a welcome was more a reminder of the strict rules of the course. It felt like the arrival to a prison or military barracks rather than to a Buddhist meditation center. Then we went to the meditation hall to meet our instructor and meditate for a while before retiring to our rooms at 9 p.m. At the end of the short session, I mentioned to the instructor my difficulty in sitting on the floor in a cross−legged position. He asked one of his assistants to bring a low stool for me, a stool that would remove the pressure on the spot that had resurfaced on my left leg and that, despite its smallness, hurt more than expected.

At 4 a.m. the bell that would dictate our lives for the next ten days rang. The bell, a metal plate hanging from a rope that was hit with a mallet−like a gong, was located between the dormitories. The first meditation session of the morning (of the night, I should say) lasted two hours and was extremely difficult. My body, stiff after sleep, could not sit still. I started noticing a lump on my upper right back that would hinder my meditation in the coming days. The first day of the course aimed to disconnect us from the world outside the center and to calm our minds, as well as adjusting us to the meditation center and its schedule. It was a difficult day, both physically and mentally. To remain seated barely moving for more than ten hours a day is not easy, and trying to concentrate my mind on my breathing for so many hours made me feel really tired at the end of the day. I was able to concentrate on my breath for only a few seconds; my rebellious mind refused to stay in one place, and I became hopelessly distracted.

The second day was somewhat easier in every respect. Persistence is key in improving any practice. My leg was not improving; quite the contrary, it seemed to have gotten worse; a small swelling was evident around the spot. I found an antibiotic cream in my kit and applied it to the affected area with the hope it would be effective. I talked to the teacher about it, and he suggested trying to disinfect it at the center, without any professional medical help. Although dissatisfied with his suggestion, I accepted it, thinking that a tiny spot could not persist beyond a few days.

On the third day, with greater power of concentration, we began to try to feel sensations in the area of the nose and upper lip, any sensations that appeared. In the absence of them, we would continue to concentrate on our breathing. My leg swelling had worsened and now reached the ankle, so I insisted on seeing a doctor. I was informed that there was a nurse among the course participants, and she offered to take a look at my leg. I was relieved to hear that a professional would finally give me an opinion about the infection. After the examination, the nurse asked one of the volunteers to go to a pharmacy to buy some antibiotics as well as suitable material for a proper disinfection. I felt reassured by this and tried to continue with the course without the physical problem becoming a major obstacle.

The awakening on the fourth day was wonderful; the dissipating night was wrapped in a heady morning fog. The first session was my favorite: my body rested, the center silent, without the voices outside of the daily visitors to Lumbini. My leg had worsened despite the antibiotics and the cleaning done by the nurse the night before. I decided if I weren't allowed to see a doctor, I would leave the course to fly to Kathmandu and go to a hospital. After breakfast, the teacher agreed to let a doctor, the nurse's brother, come to the center to examine me. I waited for the doctor with the assurance that the course had ended for me on the day we were going to start the actual vipassana meditation; until then we had practiced anapana, a prelude to the vipassana technique. I sat in a chair outside the reception center, awaiting the arrival of the doctor. I heard the sound of a motorcycle coming, then saw the motorcycle itself through the narrow space between the large metal door and its frame. They were two people on it. The doctor was the passenger, and I immediately understood why he had to be transported: he walked on wooden crutches because his right leg was missing below the knee. Even though I am a highly rational being, I confess I immediately thought it was a warning or premonition. As he approached, walking on crutches, my eyes kept looking at the empty space below his knee, where the fibula, tibia, and foot of the man were missing.

The doctor explored the infected area and advised me to go to a medical facility. I called the airline, changed the time and day of my flight back to Kathmandu, gathered my belongings, and asked for a taxi to take me to the airport. The instructor didn't even come to say goodbye, which did not seem appropriate from someone who was teaching meditation intended to help eliminate human suffering, especially since compassion is one of the pillars of Buddhist philosophy. However, I was neither angry with him nor disturbed by the situation. The more than three days of meditation had had their effect. In the taxi to the airport, with the window open, watching the locals go forth by bicycle or on a cart pulled by an ox, I felt an unusual sense of lightness. I could not remember feeling so light, so relaxed, both physically and mentally. In spite of the setback, with my leg severely infected, I remember leaving the meditation center and the journey to the airport as an extremely pleasant trip, with no worries at all, my mind occupied in simply absorbing reality without distraction, without fear of what might come.

In the airport, I called the emergency number of my travel insurance and asked for a private hospital in Kathmandu. I got two names and jotted them down in a notebook. In the waiting area, I asked a man if he could recommend me one of the hospitals over the other. He said that both were good. I opted for Norvic International Hospital. Until boarding I kept talking to the man, who had been hired by a department of the U.S. government to capture data on child labor in Nepal's carpet manufacturing industry. He informed me that children made up 12 percent of that workforce. He feared the study would push Western governments to pressure Nepal to fight against child labor in favor of schooling, which, according to him, would seriously damage the industry and the economy of many families. It is not easy to try to impose educational values in a country where the main need of the vast majority of its population is not knowledge but basic survival.

Upon entering the emergency room by myself with my two backpacks, a nurse asked me where the patient was. I raised my trouser to show her the infection and swelling, and was immediately invited to sit on one of the beds. The emergency room consisted of four beds divided by a curtain into two sections of two beds each. Soon afterwards, two nurses entered, pushing a gurney with a patient with ventilator support and whose life seemed to be in danger. Several family members standing around the gurney prevented me from seeing if the patient was a man or a woman. The nurses pushed the gurney to the bed next to mine. Facing the crowd and the gravity of the situation, with a feeling of being in the wrong place, and not wanting to interfere or to witness what might happen there in the next few minutes, I got up, grabbed my backpacks and headed for the adjoining section. Compared to the concerns of those who had just arrived with a life held in suspense, my condition seemed insignificant.

The doctor on duty came to examine my leg, asked what had happened, and said he would call a surgeon to take a look. The word surgeon unnerved me. I waited, sitting on the bed with my left leg stretched out on it, the right resting on the ground. A man associated with the person who had arrived a few minutes earlier rested both hands on the metal foot of the bed nearby. With his head down, he not only rested his body on the bed but also all the uncertainty hanging over his loved one. Sometimes he raised his head and looked absently ahead at the hospital−white wall, probably wondering how this could be happening, considering the possible implications of an unexpected loss. Sitting there, waiting for the surgeon and looking at the man, I remembered when my mother called me in London to announce that my father had a tumor in the abdomen. After hanging up, I broke out, mourning uncontrollably, wildly, repeating over and over *no, not my father, no, not my father*, as I walked the long corridor of my apartment, back and forth. Then I had sat on a chair and bent down, with my arms hugging my stomach to try to ease an intense pain I had never experienced before.

The surgeon arrived, examined the leg, asked about the circumstances of the infection, and informed me that I would be admitted to the hospital immediately. After a couple of days lying with my foot raised to force the ankle swelling to go down in the infected area, he would open it for cleaning. Meanwhile I'd undergo intravenous antibiotic treatment. We solved the administrative issues (personal and insurance details), and I waited in the emergency room until the room was ready, a wait that was used by a nurse to take a blood sample and another of the infected tissue for analysis, and to begin immediate treatment through antibiotics given to me intravenously.

I was taken to a private room on the Deluxe floor. The room had international TV programming, air conditioning, and a sofa and coffee table for the nonexistent visitors. I got a scan to determine the depth of the wound. The specialist who performed it, knowing of my six−day expedition in the Sun Kosi, commented on how brave Westerners were, so attracted by adventure. He would never dare to engage in such dangerous activities, the result of too cautious an upbringing. Fortunately, the infection had not reached the muscle tissue.

It was the second time I'd entered a hospital emergency room on my own feet. The first had occurred in London in May 2002, motivated by an arrhythmic tachycardia that began at the end of a soccer game. Once admitted to the cardiology wing, the monitor showed my heartbeat ranging between 150 and 190 beats per minute. A few hours after my arrival, my blood pressure plummeted; my heart was contracting fast but not pumping enough blood. I started to feel a stifling heat and sweated profusely. The arrhythmia had to be remedied without delay, and the only solution was to apply an electric shock to the chest with the hope of stopping it. The procedure, which, given the violence of the voltage, is performed under general anesthesia, was explained to me, and I was informed that, although usually successful in young, healthy individuals like me, it was not guaranteed to work. I signed the consent and waited for a long and agonizing forty–five minutes for the operating room to be ready. Three quarters of an hour of solitude followed, lying in bed, staring at the ceiling, wondering if I would be watching my last minutes of life, if I were to be part of that tiny percentage of failed attempts. Lying there, alone, I tried to be positive, thought of my family and friends, and all the things I had yet to do in life, determined to live against all obstacles.

The descent on a stretcher to the operating room was awful, so much that when one of the nurses noticed the dread and fear on my face she sympathetically said: "Too much to take on." And so it was, as it was for the man leaning on the bed in the hospital emergency room in Kathmandu, or when I got the news of my father's tumor: the unexpected, the sudden and serious situation, was impossible to assimilate. It was real, but I desperately wished it were not. The anesthesia enveloped me softly and inexorably, and for a moment I wanted to hold on, to stay awake, that these would not be my last seconds of life.

Less than an hour later, I woke up in a recovery room with a nurse beside me to reassure me and tell me that everything had gone well. I looked at the monitor, which showed seventy beats per minute, sensed my whole body internally, from toes to head, and felt alive again. Tears began to trickle toward both my temples in a mixture of relief and contained elation. The nurse, expecting this, handed me some tissues.

This time, the severity of my condition didn't seem to reach that of cardiac arrhythmia, but the memories of my days in London's hospital promptly resurfaced.

The Nepalese nurses spoke excellent English and were all very young, probably fresh out of nursing school, attractive, and above all very nice. I thought it must be one of the benefits of being on the Deluxe floor. They visited me frequently to take my pulse and blood pressure, write down what I had eaten, and change the intravenous medication bag when it was empty. One of them had one of the most beautiful smiles I had ever seen, and she showed it at each visit. With very black eyes and hair, her name was Sabina. I loved seeing her smile light up my room as she asked how I was. On the third day I was taken to the operating room, where the surgeon applied anesthetic to my left calf before opening the wound, draining it, and cleaning it thoroughly. I felt no pain at all, but I did notice the surgeon pulling and removing the infected tissue. In just over half an hour I was back in my room, where I spent three days of confinement, reading, watching television, and writing, with regular breaks to eat, medicate, and clean the wound, a process that, despite the painkillers, made me twist in pain on the bed. One day I got to be taken in a wheelchair outside the hospital, where I sunbathed for twenty minutes while the local crowd watched me with curiosity. Six days after my arrival, the doctor discharged me, but I had to return every other day for painful treatments. Before I left, I was given my medical history, with the circumstances of my arrival, test results, medication, and the diagnosis in English: cellulitis with necrotizing fasciitis. The Greek prefix necro scared me somewhat.

That night in my hotel, I looked the diagnosis up on the mighty Google. The research revealed that it's an extremely dangerous condition with a high risk of loss of limb and even death. Early aggressive treatment is imperative, otherwise the infection can spread rapidly throughout the body. It is usually caused by the streptococcus bacteria when it enters the body through a wound, burn, or bruise and infects the fascia, producing a gas in the process that prevents the flow of oxygen to the tissue, killing it quickly. It is rare but on the rise, and not only active in developing countries but around the world; the bacteria are global. Its colloquial English name is flesh—eating bacteria. So scared was I that, despite the time being past 10 p.m., I called the doctor on his mobile. He told me he had not wanted to scare me because I'd arrived early, responded well to antibiotics, and the infection was small and had been completely removed. He assured me that relapse was impossible. However, I sent all the information I had by email to my friend Dyan, a nurse at a clinic specializing in tropical infections in New York, who passed it on to a couple of doctors. Both, fortunately, corroborated the treatment's correctness, which reassured me greatly. Without Dyan my trip would have been cut short just weeks after it began, and I would have gone back to Spain or New York without delay.

The wound, an oval area over an inch long, would take several weeks to heal completely. Therefore, I decided to suspend my trip and stay in Kathmandu to continue being treated by the same doctor. The alternative of going, for example, to Bangkok did not feel attractive. It's true that the Thai capital would be much more interesting than the Nepalese, but besides being more expensive, it's a city I was eager to explore, and I could barely walk. With each step, my bending ankle would pull the injured skin, so I walked, lifting my left leg rigidly, with a noticeable limp. I had to extend my Nepalese visa and delay my attempts to get one for India. I felt totally trapped in Kathmandu, where initially I had planned to stay only the necessary time to arrange the trek and rafting trip and get the Indian visa. Unpredictability is a fundamental part of being a nomad; therefore one should not be too upset with reality but accept it as it comes.

I spent my days relaxing at the hotel, going out to eat and drink coffee, writing, and reading news online. My existence was focused on what made up all of Thamel: two parallel streets lined with shops and restaurants, with tourists walking up and down, and constant offers of pashminas, carpets, flutes, fruits, marijuana, massage, and sex. Every evening Kathmandu underwent a power outage that lasted for at least two hours when shops, restaurants, and hotels, to continue operating, switched on their noisy electrical generators. My guesthouse was one of the few without a generator, so at the arrival of the blackout, its entry and the stairs were lit with many candles. I took advantage of the dark evenings to meditate in my room.

The daily routine was broken by a visit from Mahesh. I had not seen him since he accompanied me to extend my visa before departing for the rafting. He'd had a couple of jobs since as a trekking guide. I invited him for lunch. When I saw him I noticed I wasn't the only one badly injured; his right arm was bent at the elbow and wrapped in surgical gauze. Walking around Kathmandu, a stray dog had attacked him by surprise and locked his right elbow between its fangs. Mahesh had kicked and grabbed it by the neck to get free of it, without success. In the end he had to ask for help because the beast seemed to want to split his arm in two. Once released, he'd had to go to the emergency room to be treated for the wound and vaccinated against rabies. In two days he was leaving for Delhi, where he was to lead a group of Spaniards for more than a week. He could barely move his arm, but he couldn't afford to lose the job. We parted, wishing each other a speedy recovery while smiling at each other on our common misfortune: two maimed Carloses in Kathmandu.

One afternoon I bumped into the Italian I had shared a room with during the four days I spent in the meditation center. We went for dinner, and he described to me the rest of the vipassana technique (focusing on different body parts and observing the sensations that appear without reacting to them, regardless of whether they are pleasant or unpleasant). He confessed that he had also left the course before completion. On the eighth day he decided that, once having learned the technique, he didn't want to carry on practicing vipassana. He did not believe in the process of liberation through meditation. He found the course very interesting, also the technique itself, in order to obtain a higher concentration of the mind, but his rationality prevented him from believing that simply noticing the sensations that bloom in our bodies without reacting to them was the way to get rid of our fears, desires, and attachments.

I was surprised that, after having spent eight days meditating intensely, he had decided not to continue practicing and checking the results before condemning it as a failure. As the professor said during the course, it is more important to experience meditation and its results for yourself than to rationalize about it on a purely intellectual level. And the same should apply to life itself. We can acquire a wealth of knowledge reading, studying, watching documentaries, and listening to others, but nothing beats what we experience as a result of our own actions. In a society saturated with information and entertainment, it is too easy to get hooked on the accumulation of knowledge and fictional experiences (television, movies, video games, novels . . .), when the true way to live is to experience life directly for yourself. I myself had often fallen into that existential trap, to prefer reading, watching movies or television, and leaving aside more direct experiences. No doubt I was now living a new and unexpected situation, and I would certainly learn a lot from it, as I did when I had to confront the crazy tachycardia that had made me experience the worst moment of my life, when I saw my life in danger. I remembered that, after leaving King's College Hospital in London, my first thought was not to waste my life, because it could be more fleeting than I expected, and to follow my dreams. It had taken me a while, but this trip was undoubtedly a result of that experience.

I started thinking about my nurse Sabina; I missed her wonderful smile. The doctor performed the treatments in the emergency room, where it was impossible to see her. A couple of times I went up to the hospital's Deluxe floor, hoping to find her and ask her out for coffee. I didn't succeed, and by the looks of her colleagues, I realized my behavior was considered somewhat inappropriate in a country as conservative as Nepal. I changed tactics. I chose to call and inquire for her next shift. It was not easy, but I managed to get hold of her. When I invited her for coffee, she was so surprised she asked me why. I told her I just wanted to chat; she hesitantly replied before adding that she was busy and had to leave. I asked for her phone number; she hesitated again but didn't give it to me and hung up hastily, as if someone had come or could hear her. It was a little frustrating, but not unexpected, that an innocent invitation was perceived with such surprise.

Between cafe and cafe, restaurant and restaurant, I met a couple of Basque guys who had flown to Egypt with their bikes and from there had biked to Nepal, and Machiko, a Japanese girl who had been working for two years for an NGO teaching women in prison to sew. And I read, I read a lot, as well as working on my script. In Thamel there are several bookstores with a wide range of books in English, both new and second−hand. Once I had finished *Shantaram*, I read several insightful novels: *The Dharma Bums*, by Jack Kerouac, *The Inheritance of Loss*, by Kiran Desai, and *The Life of Pi*, by Yann Martel; *Three Cups of Tea*, a fabulous book about building schools in the mountains of Pakistan by an American mountaineer; *The End of Poverty*, by Jeffrey Sachs, an economist who affirms that the end of world poverty could come by 2025 if the right policies were implemented globally in a coordinated way; *Guns, Germs and Steel*, by Jared Diamond, who explains how geographical differences may be the cause of the disparity in the level of development achieved by different cultures; and *The Art of Living*, a book inspired by the vipassana meditation courses run by S. N. Goenka, which I bought as a consolation for not being able to finish my own ten−day course. I was enjoying reading, which I had unfortunately left aside for long periods because of my profession. Spending long hours in front of a computer screen fatigued my eyes. As a young man, I had been an avid reader, but since I left Spain, except when on vacation, reading had been relegated to a second, or maybe third, place in the list of my leisure activities. My forced inactivity in Kathmandu served to help me regain the joy of reading.

After three weeks of regular treatments, the doctor recommended performing a skin graft to cover the wound.

Going back to the hospital and remaining there for another week did not attract me at all, but the doctor had already warned me it might be necessary, otherwise the wound could take up to two months to close by itself, with the risk of infection involved in such a long period of time. The graft was performed four weeks after the first operation, and three days before Christmas Day, which is not celebrated in Nepal. It consisted of peeling, from my left thigh, a layer of skin that was then stapled onto the wound on my calf, covering it completely. It was performed under anesthesia in both thigh and calf, and took less than an hour. For two days afterwards, I had to stay in bed, with my left leg completely still. Two days later, the doctor removed the calf band to observe the graft and clean it, while the thigh remained fully covered for ten days until the skin grew back by itself. About three–quarters of the graft had been successful; the part covering the wound's perimeter seemed to have failed. The doctor was nevertheless pleased; according to him, the skin in that area would grow under a scab, as a normal wound would.

During the seven days I spent in the hospital, I saw Sabina again, who continued lighting the room with her smile at each visit. However, she never came alone or established a conversation with me beyond what was needed to take my pulse and blood pressure. On Christmas Eve I phoned my mother, who celebrated it with my brother, my uncles, and cousins, to inform her that my progress was favorable. The next morning, one of the nurses gave me a flower and chocolate as a gift, wishing me Merry Christmas. It was a beautiful and unexpected gesture that touched me deeply, and taught me how easy is to give moments of happiness.

One of my best memories of my father happened one Christmas Eve. It was a year in the late '90s, when there were no low–cost airlines, when Iberia and British Airways monopolized the routes between Spain and the U.K., and therefore flight prices during vacation dates were abusively high; this, combined with my lack of enthusiasm for Christmas, encouraged me not to go home for Christmas for the first time. My parents, especially my father, did not take my decision well. As Christmas drew near, I began to regret it, and at the last minute I bought a ticket with the intention of arriving by surprise. The flight cost £350, a fortune for me at the time. I flew to Bilbao, and from there went by bus to San Sebastian. At 7 p.m. on Christmas Eve I rang the bell: my mom's surprise was monumental. My father was enjoying a long nap, but my mother could not contain her joy and went to the bedroom to wake him up and announce my arrival. My father cried when he opened his eyes and I kissed him. I have never invested £350 better in my life.

After being discharged, I had to return in three days to uncover the thigh. There was nothing more to do on the original wound; finally I could leave it uncovered. I started making plans to leave Nepal; I didn't want to stay longer than necessary. I was anxious to depart in search of new experiences because the undesired extended stay in Kathmandu had become altogether too passive a reality. I barely celebrated New Year's Eve. I had dinner at one of the restaurants in Thamel and retired to my room to sleep with the sound of fireworks exploding in the background. That night there was a special full moon: it was the second full moon of the month, something that only happens every two and a half years, and had not occurred on the last night of the year since 1990 (the next will be in 2028). It's called a Blue Moon. Also, a partial lunar eclipse was to take place on the first night of 2010. No doubt, it was the entry to a very special year, one that I would never forget.

On my last visit to the hospital we checked the status of my thigh. The doctor filled out the insurance papers so I could claim the expenses of the two operations (the insurance company paid the hospital directly for the periods I was there). I went to the Deluxe floor and gave two boxes of chocolates, with a thank–you card, to the nurses. Before leaving Nepal, I met with Mahesh* to say goodbye. I gave him my winter shirt, as it would be useless to me in the warm climate of Southeast Asia. He gave me a yellow silk scarf with the mantra, "May God give you long life," which Tibetan Buddhists give to those who leave.

By then I had given up my trip to India. I had not

contacted the embassy again, knowing that nothing would have happened, that my situation was impossible to solve in Nepal. I changed my plans: I would devote the remaining nine months to exploring Southeast Asia, then return to New York in late September to keep my green card, and once I had solved the problem of the Indian visa in New York or Madrid, initiate the second part of my extended trip in India, finishing in China and Japan. My original itinerary, discovering Asia from west to east, involved exploring Nepal and India and learning about Hinduism and Buddhism before continuing the journey eastward to Japan. The new route was a slight inconvenience I had to accept. My original plan had been ambitious; twelve months to visit such a large part of Asia was perhaps insufficient, another reason why I decided to see my unexpected obstacle positively. I was going to extend my trip, thus the cost would be higher than budgeted, but, as they say, you only live once, and I wasn't going to let a physical problem deprive me of my dream adventure.

---

[*] Mahesh was leading a team of four Spaniards and three porters in Langtang when the violent earthquake that shook Nepal on April 2015 struck. All of them are still missing, probably buried under one of the huge landslides the earthquake triggered in the area. He leaves behind his Italian wife and a two year old boy.

MODERNITY & TEMPTATION

"All journeys have secret destinations of which the traveler is unaware."
— Martin Buber

"Without new experiences, something inside us sleeps. The sleeper must awaken." — Frank Herbert

With India temporarily forgotten, my next destination was Myanmar, formerly Burma. Myanmar requires a visa before entering. The tourist visa lasts 28 days, maybe because the Burmese calendar is lunar. I'd apply for it in Bangkok, and from there fly to Yangon, since, to have access to all of Myanmar, I would have to arrive by air (there are a couple of crossings in the west of Thailand that allow access only to two limited areas of the country). I landed in Bangkok at night, and the contrast with Kathmandu was immediate, starting with the airport, which is so modern New York would no doubt be happy to have it for itself, and continuing with the roads to the city, as good as in any European capital. In fact, as we approached Bangkok, the tall buildings and wide roads seemed like those of any American city. It was not until we got into Bangkok's streets that the city's Asian character clearly surfaced, with the sidewalks occupied by stalls selling food, clothes, CDs, DVDs, and souvenirs. Immediately I began to understand the difference between a poor country and a developing one. Kathmandu's dirty streets were badly paved and its traffic chaotic to the point that many vehicles invaded the opposing street lanes, while Bangkok, at least in its central area, looked almost as modern as any Western city.

The bus from the airport carried only one woman tourist that evening; the rest were single men, me the youngest of all, probably evidence of Thailand's notorious sex tourism. The second major contrast between the two cities was the weather in January: cold in Kathmandu, except at midday; very hot in Bangkok even at night. I stayed at a good hotel in the Sukhumvit area, for its accessibility to the Metro and Skytrain. I wanted to enjoy comfort in my accommodations and to have public transport nearby to avoid straining my leg.

The next morning, Friday, I went to Myanmar's embassy to process the visa. I described my job as a consultant. When asked what kind of consultant I was, I said software. The visa would be ready on Tuesday. After my recent experience with the Indian visa, I decided not to buy the plane ticket to Yangon until after the visa had been stamped on my passport. Until Tuesday I spent my time in the Thai capital visiting its splendid palaces and temples, beginning with the Grand Palace and the Emerald Buddha Temple, followed by Wat Pho and its reclining Buddha, which, at 150 feet, is the longest in the country. I then crossed the Chao Phraya River to reach Wat Arun, before ending up in Chinatown with its Golden Buddha. The Great Palace dates from 1782, the year of the accession to power of Rama I, who decided to move the kingdom's capital east of the river, and named it Rattanakosin ("the place of the Emerald Buddha"). The celebrated sculpture was discovered in 1434 in a stupa in the northern city of Chiang Mai when the plaster that covered it started to fall off revealing the original stone. The abbot of the monastery, thinking it was emerald, gave the statue the name it became known by, but it is really carved in green jade.

The first thing that struck me when visiting Buddhist temples was the contrast between the representations of the figures of Christ and Buddha and the different atmosphere of their temples. Buddha exudes calm, his face always smiling. Usually depicted as sitting meditatively, giving a sermon to his disciples, or sometimes reclining at full length, representing the attainment of nirvana, he gave me a feeling of serenity as I stood before him. Christ, however, is almost always depicted as crucified, with blood gushing from his head, torso, hands, and feet, his face in pain, his body lean, suffering, his violent death much more relevant than his generous life. Moreover, Buddhist temples are usually bright, their Buddhas painted in light colors or in gold, radiating luminosity to the visitors. The Christian churches, dark buildings in spite of the art in their interiors, look so sad compared to the happy Buddhist temples, where one receives a clearly positive message.

I wondered what would have become of Christianity if the Romans had not executed Jesus and he had died old, like Buddha, after devoting his life to spreading his message of love and compassion. Perhaps it was his tragic death that facilitated the spread of his message, because we all know how a premature and violent death can help create a myth. Had Christ reached old age, perhaps he would have been ignored, as indeed many others must have been in our history, since neither Buddha nor Christ nor Muhammad have been the only ones, just the most successful, to devote their lives to mankind.

I struggled to get used to Bangkok's humid heat. My left foot ended the day slightly swollen, which worried me a bit, although I attributed it to my passivity of the past few weeks and the temperature. To find relief from the sweltering heat of the streets, I walked into some of the many shopping malls that populate Bangkok, modern and luxurious, huge multi-story areas, air-conditioned oases. I didn't find any difficulty in getting used to the beauty of Thai women. For the first time in more than three months, I saw female body skin, as legs and arms, backs and necklines were bared (in Nepal, long saris and jeans prevented such exposure). Thanks to the hostile heat, Thai women exhibited, to my delight, their beautiful skin.

I asked at my hotel for a good place to get a Thai massage and was recommended to a new spa across the street. The art of Thai massage combines stretching with pressure along the body's so-called "energy channels," mainly in the extremities, and is given on the floor. The masseuse (most are women) uses not only her hands but also her elbows, forearms, knees, and feet. The patient wears baggy pants and a loose shirt to facilitate the movements. I warned the masseuse about the scab on my wound at the beginning of a ninety-minute massage, after which I felt so great that I quickly became addicted.

A few blocks from my hotel was located one of Bangkok's most famous streets: Soy Cowboy, a short street with around twenty *go-go girl* bars that attracts many tourists. I went one night after dinner to experience this part of Bangkok, as characteristic as its palaces and temples. I sat on a terrace in the middle of the street, ordered a beer, and practiced the fascinating sport of observing the behavior of the human race. It was happy hour. Bar girls carried signs with offers to attract tourists, most of them men, some in groups, others alone, many well past their fifties. I saw some curious tourists who didn't dare even stop for a drink (they walked the street as if being watched by their mothers), some businessmen brought by their hosts, and even couples, perhaps motivated by morbid curiosity. The bar where I had parked my own curiosity was called the Suzie Wong, which jostled for customers with other bars in the neighborhood: Midnite, Dollhouse, Afterskool Bar, and Sunshine. The two girls promoting Dollhouse's happy hour carried two big signs with the same wording: "There are probably 20 gorgeous girls, plus many ugly and some fat," which provoked smiles from even the shiest passersby.

Inside the bars, behind those opaque doors and curtains, the shows were held. I saw several men enter the Suzie Wong. Some came out immediately; others seemed swallowed by the velvet jaws. After finishing my beer, and with the excuse of going to the bathroom, I ventured inside. It was a narrow place with a central stage inhabited by eight topless girls dancing to the music and with four long benches on both sides of the stage occupied by only a handful of men. The bar was at the end of the stage, opposite the entrance. The girls, more than dancing to entertain the small audience, were chatting with each other. Despite their youth, beauty, and good bodies, I didn't find it interesting to look at their arrhythmic wiggles; Bangkok's streets were much more attractive. Without being scandalized or feeling any revulsion, I left as when one exits a clothing store without seeing anything interesting to try on.

Bangkok's streets are adorned with photographs of the Thai King, Bhumibol Adulyadej (Rama IX), a harmless Big Brother. On the throne since 1946, Rama IX is the head of state who has been longest in power in the world. In one of my refreshing stops in a mall, I found a great bookstore with an extensive offering of English books, where I bought one about Southeast Asian history and two on Buddhism: *Buddhism, A Very Short Introduction*, by Damien Keown, and *Buddha*, a biography written by Karen Armstrong.

One of the pillars of Buddhism is the Four Noble Truths:

—In life we suffer (*duhkha*, as explained in the previous chapter).

—The cause of suffering is our attachment (*trishna*, literally thirst).

—The suffering may cease if its cause ends. With no attachments we reach liberation.

—To reach nirvana we have to walk the Noble Path.

This path consists of eight practices that are usually grouped into three types:

—Wisdom: Right Understanding and Resolve

—Morality: Right Speech, Action, and Livelihood

—Meditation: Right Effort, Mindfulness, and Meditation

It is necessary to follow the Noble Path in full in order to achieve nirvana. We need an understanding of suffering and its causes, as well as active thought directed to want to end it. Our behavior, both when speaking and when acting, and how we earn our living, should be pure, harmless to others. Finally, we must be aware and present in what we do and feel, and meditate daily to get rid of our attachments without giving up a full life. This is called the Middle Way, the balance between mysticism and hedonism.

On my first night in Bangkok I had dinner at an Irish pub near the hotel (it was already too late to find a better restaurant). There, I chatted with a couple of waitresses and invited them to a drink. Both were from outside Bangkok. One, despite her youth, had a five—year—old son who she had left with her mother in her village while she was working. She told me her mother was suffering from financial problems, so she had to come to Bangkok to work. Two nights later, as I returned to my hotel after dinner at a Korean restaurant (I love Korean food), I stopped by there for a beer. One of them had the day off and with the other I barely exchanged a few words. From the terrace, I was struck by the traffic of young women and men at a neighboring bar with a

Thai name, whose access was down several stairs. It seemed a place for local customers, and without even inquiring about it I went in.

The basement was a large rectangular area with a small bar to the left of the entrance, booths against the walls and an S—shaped bar in the center with stools where people could sit and drink. There were at least 150 young Thai women scattered around the room, most of them leaning against the tables, while men, almost all Asian, roamed the room, looking at them, or drank at the central bar. The girls looked like they were in a formal ballroom, waiting to be asked to dance. However, there was no dance floor and no one was dancing. I ordered a beer and sat on a stool at the central bar to watch. Many young women did nothing, nor did I see any of them approach men, as would have seemed natural; they simply waited in groups to be addressed by the men, who roamed the room in a circle, watching the girls like an exhibition of live sculptures. I was somewhat surprised and confused, because it wasn't like a typical *go—go girls* bar, where the girls sit with you and talk, to encourage you to buy them a drink and generate more revenue for the bar, nor was it like a brothel, where the girls work for the premises and the client chooses one to have sex with. It looked like a normal bar, but one where young Thai women in their twenties and thirties offered themselves, without soliciting, to have sex with a man in his hotel after negotiating the price privately between them. There weren't pimps around, and the girls didn't work for the bar, a place more comfortable and safer than the streets. There they could chat between them, drink, and dine until a client hired them. I found myself, by surprise, without having sought or desired it, in a bar of a kind I didn't even know existed, probably due to my Asian virginity.

To my right sat an Asian man, whom I asked if he spoke any English. He said he did, but very little. He was Japanese and informed me he had been in Bangkok a dozen times. He told me the girls asked two thousand *baht* ($50 to 55), maybe less if you negotiated. The ratio at the bar was perhaps roughly three girls for every man, so I was not surprised that the price could be negotiated. I continued to observe the dynamics of the place with fascination. Most of the girls just stood waiting to be approached, stuck there like stakes, while a few walked around the room connecting their eyes with the men's, launching a visual "What are you waiting for?"

When I finished my beer, I went to the bathroom and on my return sat on a stool next to a pair of girls. They said hello, I introduced myself and asked how much they charged. One of them said 2,000, but her sister's price was 1,500. I was surprised because the sister was more beautiful and sexy. I told her I had never paid for sex (which was true), and she wasted no time in responding to my caution that her sister would do it for 1,000; 2,000 for both of us. What an offer! A 2x1! Then another girl sat to my right, her eyes more slanted and her skin lighter than the two sisters. I introduced myself and asked for her price; 1,500, she replied. When I turned back, the elder sister had moved with a man to the central bar, and her younger sister had moved to the stool closest to me. She stared at me, nodded her head, inviting me to go with her, and I nodded mine without thinking, unconsciously caught in the trap of temptation.

We left the bar and walked to my nearby hotel. Then I realized she didn't speak English, that her sister had led the negotiations (perhaps that was the reason for the discount?), so the ten-minute walk was a time for silent reflection. How could I have hired a prostitute? Would I get excited and enjoy the sex? Or would I end up paying just for walking to the hotel? I palliated my slight remorse with the excuse that there's always a first time and this too was part of my discovery of Asia. At reception, she had to deposit her identity card as a security measure, which I found reassuring; you never know what weapons a strange prostitute may have in addition to her natural ones. In the room, she showered first, then me. Condoms on the table, I lay down with the towel around my waist, hers under her armpits. With diligence, she removed mine before a combined attack of mouth to nipple and hand to penis to provoke my usefulness. Once achieved, and protected, she moved on top. The sex proved to be better than I expected; she willing, me without remorse. I paid as agreed and gave her something extra for the taxi home. I lay on the bed, soaked with sweat, wondering how it had all happened.

Sometimes the unexpected can bring us out of our comfort zone, causing reactions we would never have anticipated. I did not regret the experience at all. It was an area where I had never even thought of experimenting, but once done, it had no greater significance than one more experience to accumulate on my journey and my life. Usually we think we know with certainty how we will react to any new situation however unexpected, but in reality, as several research experiments have shown, it's not the same thing to reason about a possible event, calmly and in the distance, and to be directly affected by it, if only once. In the case of sexual practices, in reactions to acts of violence, in situations of danger, and even with monetary issues, it isn't until we face them that we see our real character, never as static as we think, much more flexible than the rationality of the armchair usually recognizes.

During my stay at King's College Hospital in London, the doctors hadn't found any structural abnormality in my heart. Furthermore, since I didn't take drugs or suffer from stress, and drank in moderation, the cardiologist prescribed me some pills (called beta blockers) for a few months to reduce the risk of acceleration of my heartbeat. Before leaving the hospital, I asked if I'd be able to run to catch the train. The doctor told me not to worry and to lead a normal life, words that were not very reassuring, as who would not be alarmed after suffering such an episode at thirty–two years of age and having had to resort to electric shock to disrupt the cardiac insanity? I started to blame my condition (we always look for possible causes) for my lack of exercise and my slight overweight, and I chose swimming as the best sport to practice in my condition. However, any intense physical activity caused me panic, including having sex. I didn't want my heart to go crazy while making love to a woman, and so I gave up sex for a long period.

The next day was quiet. I got up late, scanned all my medical documents and sent them to myself by email before sending them by mail to New York. An email told me of the impossibility of attending a vipassana meditation course in Thailand; all courses for the next few weeks were fully booked. I was very disappointed. Since the center in Cambodia is not the most active, and Vietnam and Laos (I imagine because of refusal by their communist governments) have no representation in S. N. Goenka's organization, Malaysia was my only alternative. I had to calculate the time it would take me to visit Cambodia, Vietnam, Laos, and northern and southern Thailand, to choose the date of the course. Immediately I filled out the online application for a course in late July (by then, I thought, the World Cup in South Africa, a soccer event I didn't want to miss, would have ended). It was a shame I wouldn't be able to incorporate vipassana meditation into my daily life until much later than I had planned.

I went to Myanmar's embassy to pick up my passport (which I'd had to leave there) with the visa, then, happy to see the visa stamp on my passport, went to a travel agency to buy a round-trip flight to Yangon. I felt great excitement about entering Myanmar, a country I knew very little about and anticipated I'd love discovering. I was eager to resume my journey, to feel again like a nomad after my long stay in Kathmandu.

In the evening I returned to the temptations bar. There was something in the place I hadn't yet understood, and fascinated by it I went back to have a beer and talk to a girl, something I couldn't do the previous night. After observing in more detail, I realized that many of the girls weren't at all interested in the few Westerners there; they seemed more attracted to Asian men, mostly Japanese, maybe Korean. A woman in her 30s, one of the oldest in the bar, sat next to me. I introduced myself, and she immediately asked if I lived in Bangkok or was just visiting. Shortly after knowing my temporary situation, she excused herself to go to the bathroom but did not return and remained on the opposite side of the bar. What kind of place was it where the prostitutes chose their clients? Were some women simply seeking a rich husband or a lover? It was late and my flight to Yangon was first thing in the morning. I finished my beer and left without an answer to my question.

MONKS, SKIRTS & MAKEUP

"I can't think of anything that excites a greater sense of childlike wonder than to be in a country where you are ignorant of almost everything."
—Bill Bryson

"There are no foreign lands. It is the traveler only who is foreign."
—Robert Louis Stevenson

I landed in Yangon, formerly Rangoon, early in the morning, went through immigration and customs without any problems, and took a taxi to my hotel, Mayshan, in the city center, next to Sule Pagoda whose speakers emitted Buddhist chants nonstop. Both the airport and its link to the city were much more pleasant than Kathmandu's, and I began to think at first that Nepal was even poorer than Myanmar, which surprised me. The taxi drove down wide, well-paved roads lined with trees, flowers, and manicured lawns, all of which had been totally absent in the Nepalese capital. It was only when we reached what is known as downtown Yangon that the streets narrowed, the green dissolved, and sidewalks disappeared under piles of merchandise for sale, including fruit and vegetables, clothing, and kitchenware. It was only 10 a.m. and the heat was already relentless.

After sleeping a bit at the hotel, I changed a $100 bill to the local currency, the *kyat* (pronounced "chat"), at a rate of 970 *kyats* per dollar. The rate varied depending on the denomination, a $100 bill being the one with the best rates. Dollars had to be new and crisp; every used bill was rejected because Burmese banks would not take them. In Myanmar there are no ATMs, and credit cards aren't used except in a very few luxury hotels that charge an extremely high commission whether for payments or for cash advances. I had to calculate my budget for the twenty-eight days of my stay and would need to carry all of my money with me all the time. You don't feel too comfortable carrying so much cash. The contrast with New York could not be more extreme. There, even taxis can be paid by card, and many New

Yorkers carry just a few dollars. Fortunately, Myanmar is one of the world's safest countries for tourists, so filling my pockets with over $1,000 didn't entail much danger.

I followed the hotel's advice for my first gastronomic experience. The restaurant was located a couple of blocks away in one of the narrow streets of downtown Yangon, and served the typical Burmese dish: boiled rice, soup, and various curries to choose from (meat, fish, and vegetables). I picked a fish curry and three vegetables to accompany the rice. Women did the cooking while men served customers. The curries were tasty and well seasoned. In the afternoon I walked to Botabtaung Pagoda, on the bank of the Yangon River. The way there took me past the main British colonial buildings, an area that reminded me of Havana, with its faded buildings, the heat of the sunset over the Malecon, the neglected streets full of life. In the pagoda I sat to meditate in one of the rooms with a Buddha. Later, I went to the river to watch the sunset under the warm evening.

I had felt very comfortable in Yangon since I arrived. The contrast with modern Bangkok was substantial. Yangon seemed to be several decades behind, so I found it more interesting and atmospheric than the Thai capital. And I was glad to be active again; after my recent medical problem, it was even more rewarding to resume my exploration of Asia.

Myanmar is visually unique because both women and men wear a long skirt, called *longyi*, a tube−shaped cloth that women attach to the side and men at the front with a bulbous knot, which, by its location if not its form, looks slightly phallic. The feminine skirts usually have floral patterns and light colors while the males' are dark (blue, green, and burgundy are the most common colors). Once accustomed to the skirts, I thought the men, who combined them with elegant, light−colored shirts, were visually more attractive than the women, whose patterns, not only for the skirts but also for their tops, lacked appeal. In addition, women and children wear a makeup called *thanaka* (a kind of facial paint), a natural cream obtained from rubbing the bark of the tree of the same name with a smooth stone that has been lightly wetted. The stripped bark, when mixed with water, forms a yellow paste that is then applied to the face and body. Its properties are sun protection and a fresh scent, with lemon hints. There are women who apply it only on their cheeks; others extend it over their entire face and forehead. Usually it is applied with a brush whose tracks remain after the *thanaka* dries up, and hence are visible all day.

The next day I planned to visit the most attractive monument in Yangon, Shwedagon Pagoda, but before that I went by taxi to Kandawgyi Lake. I walked along the lake's edge with the intention of eating at one of the restaurants in the northwest area. Arriving there, an old man suggested I visit a couple of nearby pagodas. I accepted his invitation and followed him. He spoke good English and told me that once he had been very wealthy, thanks to a successful family business trading precious stones, until the government nationalized all businesses in 1964, two years after the coup led by General Ne Win. Later he spent seven years living as a Buddhist monk. First he showed me the Ngahtatgyi Pagoda and its monastery with over six hundred monks. He asked me the day of the week I was born (Saturday) and led me to a small Buddha with a dragon carved on its base. There he explained that the Burmese horoscope is based on the day of the week on which you were born: the creature corresponding to Saturday is the dragon, to Sunday the eagle, Monday the tiger, Tuesday the lion, Wednesday the elephant, Thursday the mouse, and Friday the rabbit. I was asked to pour ten glasses of water over the head of Buddha to bring me prosperity. I was surprised that Buddhism here was so linked to superstitious practices. Across the road was the Chaukhtatgyi Pagoda, with its reclining Buddha. The old man just showed me the way before asking for a tip for his help. I gave him a dollar, and he thanked me before stating that thanks to *thanaka*, Burmese women smell so good you want to kiss them all.

I had lunch and coffee while waiting for the sun to lose its verticality before going to Shwedagon, a majestic pagoda 325 feet high and of golden splendor. The story says that two merchant brothers, Tapussa and Bhallika, went to India to visit the recently enlightened Siddhartha, to whom they offered some honey cakes. Buddha gave them eight of his hairs for them to take to their hometown, Okkalapa, now Yangon, where the brothers presented the gift to their king, who built the pagoda to a height of sixty–five feet, completing it, it is believed, before Buddha's death; thus it is considered the oldest pagoda, not only in Myanmar but in the world. The pagoda (which in this case, since it contains Buddhist relics, is also a stupa) was rebuilt between the sixth and tenth centuries, repaired in the fourteenth and on several occasions since then until the eighteenth century, when it reached its present dimensions after severe damage suffered in the 1768 earthquake. It consists of ten sections, rising vertically: the base, three terraces, and the levels known as the "monk's food bowl," the "lotus flower," the "banana bud," the "umbrella," the "vane" and the "diamond bud." The last three are decorated with 3,154 golden bells and 79,569 diamonds and other precious stones in a dazzling combination.

Crowds of monks wrapped in maroon robes and nuns in pink ones were visiting Shwedagon. Around the stupa there were numerous enclosures with various Buddha statues for meditation or for worship (although some consider Buddhism more a philosophy than a religion, in Myanmar I soon realized it is practiced as a religion). In all the pagodas I visited, I watched believers making offerings to Buddha in the form of flowers, incense, and water.

Over the head of one of the giant Buddhas there was a huge fan with a long cord so a visitor could pull it and thus prevent Buddha's "melting" from the heat. In another area, a small wooden boat was used to deposit pilgrims' requests before being raised with a rope pulley to the top of the pagoda, where it was deposited. There were bells and gongs visitors could hit with a wooden log to get Buddha's attention and ask for his blessing. A young monk invited me to pour seven glasses of water on a statue of Buddha to protect me during each weekday, and five on the figure of a dragon to protect Buddha, my family, my teacher, my work, and myself. He also gave me a yellow thread to wear as a bracelet for luck and protection.

I could not believe that a Buddhist monk was telling me all this stupidity; that wasn't the concept of Buddhism with which I had come to Asia. My basic knowledge of Buddhism didn't include anything similar; quite the contrary, since its aim is basically to achieve liberation without divine interference or requiring devotion to a particular person or being. It was clear that after more than 2,500 years since its birth, the legacy of Siddhartha had undergone substantial changes. I realized that ignorance still roams in much of the world, superstition still a valid response to many of humanity's doubts and fears. How strange other cultures' superstitions seem, I thought—and how logical our own!

I decided to visit the National Museum and discover the local art forms that could be found outside the temples. In the reception book, I saw I was only the fourth foreign visitor of the day (each pagoda, temple, and museum keeps a record of each visitor's name and nationality). The large building was dimly lit, probably due to one of the power cuts the country suffers for several hours each day. As in Nepal, generators are a must for hotels, restaurants, shops, and businesses, and the museum seemed able to keep on just a few fluorescent lamps. The first floor was dedicated to the Burmese alphabet and calligraphy, the second to ceramics and woodcarvings, the third to paintings (it was so dark I had to almost place my nose against the canvases to see anything), and the fourth to representations of Buddha. Also on the fourth floor was a room devoted to items related to Myanmar's current territorial division and the country's latest infrastructure projects: photographs of the country's military leaders inaugurating bridges, power plants, and schools and voting for the new constitution of 2008. I was amazed at the audacity of the military junta's including itself in the National Museum right next to representations of Buddha.

Walking down the street after leaving the museum, I came across a huge billboard, in awkward English against a pink background, promoting "the People's Desire":

−Oppose those relying on external elements, acting as stooges, holding negative views.

−Oppose those trying to jeopardize stability of the State

55

and progress of the Nation.

    —Opposition foreign nations interfering in internal affairs of the State.

    —Crush all internal and external destructive elements as the common enemy.

I was sure that what the great majority of the Burmese people were really against was a dictatorial regime in place for decades. The most internationally famous Burmese, Aung San Suu Kyi, winner of the Nobel Peace Prize in 1991, was still under house arrest, punished for her fierce struggle against the dictatorship. Her father, Aung San, was cofounder of the Burmese Communist Party, commander of the army, and prime minister after the end of World War II, when the British returned to Burma after the Japanese occupation (1942–1945). On January 27, 1947, Aung San and then British Prime Minister Clement Attlee signed an agreement that guaranteed Burmese independence. In April of that same year, general elections were held, and on July 19, an armed group of paramilitaries linked to former Prime Minister U Saw assassinated Aung San and six of his ministers. On January 4, 1948, Burma was declared an independent republic, and named the Union of Burma, with U Nu as its first president. Democracy's journey ended with the coup in March 1962 by Ne Win, who remained in power for twenty years, followed by a series of military dictatorships up to the present day.

It was time to leave Yangon. I traveled by bus to Kyaiktiyo to visit the Golden Rock, a popular pilgrimage site in Myanmar located east of the city of Bago. There, on top of a mountain, a huge rock, covered with gold, stands on top of a boulder in perfect balance, apparently defying gravity. The story goes that a single hair of Buddha was donated by a hermit to his king in the eleventh century. It is this strand of hair that, according to the legend, prevents the rock from tumbling down the mountainside. Pilgrims stick gold leaves to the rock, which only men are allowed to touch. There was a crowd of people. Many sat with their families on a blanket on the floor to eat and drink; it was a religious picnic.

To get me to Bago, a man with a motorbike waited to

carry me to a hotel that had been recommended in Kyaiktiyo, and despite being a bit far from Bago's city center, it was so nice, with wooden floors, a ceiling fan, and large trees providing shade, that I decided to stay. This entailed hiring the motorcyclist to show me Bago's temples and pagodas over the next twenty–four hours. I agreed to pay him eight dollars, and we started that afternoon, visiting Shwethalyaung, a reclining Buddha 180 feet long; Maha Kalyani Sima, with four standing Buddhas; and Myathalyaung, with four Buddhas, in their usual lotus position. We had dinner, with a couple of Myanmar beers, at a restaurant run by a family of Chinese origin. On the way back to the hotel, my driver asked if I wanted a woman. I declined his offer; the only one I received in Myanmar.

The next day he took me to the main pagoda in Bago, Shwemawdaw, 46 feet taller than Shwedagon in Yangon. The visit ended at the Kha Khat Wain monastery, one of the largest in the country and one of the few open to tourists to witness the monks eating lunch, their only meal of the day: an unusual ritual. We arrived early, about half an hour before food was served at 11 a.m. I mounted my Nikon and entered the kitchen, where several women volunteers prepared the vegetables before cooking them, and a couple of monks were in charge of the rice. Then I turned to the dining room, with its low, circular tables, each seating six, on which shaved monks were placing tea and cups. I was allowed to wander at my leisure, with my camera capturing the whole process. The dining room walls were painted in a faded green pistachio that contrasted perfectly with the monks' maroon robes. As lunchtime approached, the monks began leaving their quarters and made a long, tidy line at the dining room entrance. A couple of Thai tourist buses arrived punctually with pilgrims who had brought food to donate to the monks. The monks accepted the food in silence before passing into the dining room where they served themselves with cooked rice in their bowls, then sat on the floor around the tables where tea and bowls of red curry awaited them. A carpet in the aisle that runs through the middle of the dining room was then the only area accessible to the visitors, and I used it to digitally capture that beautiful room full of hungry, bald monks.

The following stop was Kalaw, a town located at an altitude of 4,330 feet, from which I would reach Inle Lake after a three–day trek. My guide in Bago had introduced me to a friend who worked as a hiking guide in Kalaw. At the bus station in Bago we met and chatted about the trek and his price, and he gave me his clients' most recent recommendations to read. I liked him and hired him. He had to hurry home on his motorcycle to pack because the bus would leave soon. We went together by bus to Kalaw, reaching the town at 4 a.m. under a significant cold snap (around 40 degrees F). I got a room in a new hotel and slept for a few hours (my guide found his own accommodations). Only two–wheeled vehicles run on the streets of Kalaw, population 40,000. After Yangon and Bago, Kalaw's tranquility was wonderfully received by this over–heated traveler. I spent the day visiting a couple of pagodas and a monastery, took a long walk, and had tea on the roof terrace, enjoying the beautiful sunset over the mountains while updating my journal.

The next morning was market day, so I prowled the stalls before breakfast and the start of the trek. With my fleece on, I took my Nikon and explored the market, starting at 7 a.m., for more than an hour. The stalls were being set up; the food unwrapped. Rice, vegetables, fruit, meat, fish, and spices began coloring the streets. I love getting lost in village markets, with my camera ready to capture their color and atmosphere. Many vendors came from surrounding areas to sell their fresh products and wore their traditional clothes, a prelude to what I would see during the trek. I waited for the sun to peek over the tops of the trees, to take pictures of those lucky stalls receiving the first rays, magically making tomatoes appear tastier, vegetables fresher.

We started the trek after leaving my backpack with most of my belongings in the hands of a guide's friend, who would drive to the lake two days later. We went up north on hillsides cultivated with orange trees and tea, to Painepe Pin, a village belonging to the Palaung tribe, where we had lunch at a private home: boiled rice with vegetables accompanied by a soup of pumpkin and yams. As my guide prepared lunch and chatted with our hostess, I wandered through the village, taking pictures, especially of children who came out to greet me, and also of the monastery and the local pagoda. Just as every Spanish village has its church, all Burmese villages have a pagoda or temple and a monastery (though this may be shared with other villages). During the walk a woman gave her daughter two tangerines to share with me. I accepted only one, thanking them for their generosity. It is very beautiful to see how people who barely have enough to survive offer food to a stranger. An elderly woman invited me to her house to sell me bags she had woven herself. I asked if I could take a picture of her, and she immediately dropped the *cheroot*, the local cigar made from green leaves, that she was smoking and posed with a serene look at the camera.

During lunch, Than, my guide, told me that recently his motorbike had been stolen (the one he used now was borrowed from a friend), and justified the fact, arguing that he must have stolen one in his previous life, and it was his time to suffer for it now. The concept of karma, meaning action or its result, is present in most Buddhist and Hindu countries. Since both religions believe in reincarnation, the actions of individuals during each lifetime directly influence their next life. Accumulations of good karma will result in a better life; those whose karma is negative will pay for it in their future lives. On the one hand, this is a practical way to encourage people to act right (as the promise of paradise is in Christianity and Islam), but on the other hand, it can lead to some complacency, when whatever happens is accepted, or justified, without a sense of personal accountability, as if a certain fatality guided our lives. It was an aspect of Buddhism that didn't interest me. I don't believe in reincarnation or eternal life. I believe we are animals that, when we die, spread our atoms in the universe, the only real reincarnation.

After lunch, we resumed our hike until we reached Saty Kone, a Pao village, with its characteristic black–clad women wearing colorful turbans. We had tea at the entrance of a bamboo house. The whole family was there to watch me: the grandfather with deep wrinkles, his wife, his eldest son and his wife with beautiful eyes and tanned skin, and the granddaughters, who were already carrying offspring in their arms. I took pictures of all of them, and they laughed at seeing themselves on the digital display. For them, to be photographed and seeing themselves was an honor, and they posed with pleasure, some so seriously that I had to smile to incite them to smile as well and be more natural.

We walked a total of sixteen miles across four villages, all very basic. Most of the houses were made of bamboo with the typical structure of an open first floor serving as a stable and storage and a second floor consisting of a large common space with a kitchen and a small room on one side. Some new homes of cement blocks and metal roofs had been built recently, although many had only a concrete first floor, with a bamboo second floor and roof. There was no machinery anywhere; buffaloes and oxen were the only "tractors" around. Not every home even had them, and I saw many people plowing the land by hand, using long hoes and carrying water in a couple of plastic containers hung on the ends of a long stick across their shoulders.

During the latter part of the first day we came to a flat and open landscape that seemed surprisingly familiar. I didn't take long to realize that, though we were in mid–January, it looked just like the Castilian fields of early autumn. I thought, if I took a picture and showed it to my mother, she'd believe I was in the south of the province of Burgos, where my father was born, and where we spent part of the summers and some Christmas and Easter holidays. Here, everything had been harvested, the fields rested. Rice, wheat, potato, and ginger were the most common crops cultivated on a vast plain interrupted only by solitary trees with spherically shaped foliage. With the sunset at its peak, a light wind rose, and with it I thought I was hearing the music of the Castilian poplars I'd enjoyed during my teenage summers, but when I looked up, the high and rigid poplars had become flexible bamboo. They were strange moments because of the unexpected familiarity of the landscape and the memories that sprang spontaneously to my mind, memories of adolescent loves, bike rides, and lazy summer afternoons.

We arrived at Kone Lwin, a Danu village, where a group of kids received us excitedly. We stopped at the home of two of the village teachers. Five teachers were responsible for the basic education of 130 children. Almost all primary teachers are female, and the youngest are sent to the countryside for a few years. These two, twenty–six and twenty–nine years old, had already been teaching for three and five years, respectively. They shared a bamboo house with two rooms separated by a common room, and an area at the front where they cooked and ate. The central area was used as a shop, and they sold candy to supplement the meager salary they received from the government, which until that month had been only 27,000 *kyats* per month (about $27). Due to high inflation in recent years, the government had decided to increase their salary by 20,000 *kyats* (to 47,000 *kyats*), a substantial increase but still insufficient, according to them. I liked the fact they thought I was only thirty years old, probably because, in that environment, every man of forty must show much more damaged skin than mine. They couldn't believe that at my age I wasn't married and had no children. Than teased them, saying they were already too old to marry, and advising them to hurry up (both had boyfriends there in the village).

In the Burmese countryside the common practice is to attend school only until puberty, help parents in the fields and learn from them, marry between sixteen and eighteen years old, have children soon, and continue the life cycle. For a Westerner, particularly if, like me, one has lived in London and New York, that life could not be more distant. Fortunately, I had known country life. My grandparents, on both sides, had been farmers, and I used to spend at least one month during the summer with them until I was eighteen. But this was long ago, and now in Myanmar, as when I visited northern Vietnam a few years earlier, I was traveling many decades into the past. That life was hard but simple. It offered no alternatives; to break that life cycle seemed impossible—everything was decided according to a complete fatalism. However, I was myself a good example that the situation could change: In just two generations, my family had gone from being subsistence farmers (my maternal grandmother had been illiterate) to my parents migrating to the city in search of new job opportunities and I, like my brother and some of my cousins, going to college. True, in Myanmar, with its tragic political situation, this seemed a utopia, but as Spain did at the end of the twentieth century, it only required the correct political change to substantially transform a country in a few decades.

After talking with the teachers, we crossed the street to a house where we had dinner and spent the night, the house of former village chief, a widower of seventy—four who lived with his son, daughter—in—law, and three grandchildren. Upon entering, we found the retired chief sitting on the floor watching dinner being prepared, his daughter—in—law cooking while attending to her two youngest children, two boys aged two and five, who were eating on a low, round wooden table. She performed everything while squatting; moving towards the fire to control the cooking of the curry and to the table to check that the children continued eating. Once the youngest finished dinner, he climbed onto her back, where his mom carried him, bound by a cloth. She was young, perhaps no more than twenty—three, and continued to squat, cooking dinner for the rest of the family with her child on her back. At that time, I came to understand the reason for the early formation of families in these areas. The physical demands are extreme, including fieldwork, the transport of water from the river, and children's care. A woman over thirty would have great difficulty performing all those tasks day after day, without even weekends off to rest. Rural women, as my grandmothers did, work extremely hard. The task of the daily care of the children rests solely with them, and considering that most have at least three or four children, it's not difficult to understand the workload they bear stoically. There, sitting on a bench against the wall, I did not cease admiring, and feeling compassion, for that young woman and her continuous and painstaking dedication to her family.

We slept on the second floor, in the open room, the

retired chief and Than along one side, while I was at the center on a thin mat on the floor, a mat too hard to rest on comfortably. The rest of the family slept in the only separate room. While getting used to the hardness of the floor, I thought what a wonderful day it had been. I had witnessed the simple and hard lives of the Burmese country people, their villages devoid of machinery, therefore quiet and harmonious with their surroundings. And above all, I had received the sympathy and hospitality from everyone, especially the lively and smiling children. Besides, my leg had responded well to the long hike, without any swelling. The scab had already gone, but not the clear mark the severe infection had left on my calf. It looked like a burn caused by a hot iron, like a brand on cattle, marked, in my case, by the streptococcus bacteria.

The next day we walked through several villages before reaching Khan Bar Nyi, another Danu village, where we had lunch inside a bamboo house. The heat outside was intense, but the bamboo, miraculously, filtered the air, letting a light breeze through that brought a feeling of freshness to the house. While Than, with the help of a brother and sister, prepared the food, I took pictures and played with the four kids. They loved to see themselves in the camera, and they kept posing, grinning, and laughing. The youngest had an extremely loud laugh for his size, and a terribly contagious one too. I had a great time with them. I loved the children I encountered during the trek, always smiling, waving gracefully, following me curiously, and continually confusing *hello* and *bye—bye*.

Than was single despite his age, already in his forties like me. He seemed to have followed seriously the mantra his father gave him when he was young: "If you kill someone, you'll spend twenty years in jail; if you marry, you'll be in prison for the rest of your life." Some of his brothers were military officers, and one was an official in the land registry and so received "tainted" money (i.e., bribes; $10,000 on one occasion, he told me) that he spent on alcohol, gambling, and women. Win told me that military men, to advance their careers, sought educated women and so, many of their wives were teachers. I asked about the local marriage ceremony. He said the couple received the blessing of Buddhist monks before signing the papers in front of a judge, although this was not required. It took only seven neighbors to confirm a couple's relationship for it to be considered a marriage from the legal standpoint.

At the end of the day, we reached Myaung War Gyi, a Taung Yoe village, and crossed it to reach its monastery, entirely surrounded by bamboo, where we spent the second night. On arriving, we saw a young monk shaving a young novice's head. The monk in charge of the blade had already mowed almost half the locks of the newcomer, who crouched with his head down, patiently watching strands of his black hair fall to the ground around his feet. As part of his education, every male child in Myanmar must spend a week in a Buddhist monastery, taking lessons and living according to the monastic regime. The young novices, who are usually between nine and twelve years old, wear the traditional maroon robes and have their heads ritually shaved. They rise before dawn, pray, and, except when food is donated directly to the monastery by the villagers, go out with their bowls to beg for food. They are not allowed to reject what they are given, nor are they allowed to request something specific. While begging, they go barefoot, their robe covering their entire body except for their head and hands. They have lunch at eleven in the morning and don't eat anything else for the rest of day; the rest of their time is spent taking lessons and cleaning the monastery. Living humbly like a monk—depending solely on the generosity of others—must be a very useful experience in the training of young people. Less commonly, some girls also go to nunneries. Many men return to the monastic life for another week, sometimes more, during their adult lives, even after marriage. I thought how positive it would be to establish something similar in Western schools, such as devoting an entire week (or longer) to charitable work in different fields, such as the environment, education, or health. In the West we have made education's sole purpose the preparation for professional life, ignoring completely educating the whole person—socially, emotionally, culturally—perhaps with the result that recent young generations have become increasingly self—centered and less caring.

The monastery was built in teak, painted maroon and elevated on wooden beams. The main room is very spacious, possibly over a hundred feet wide and sixty—five feet deep. In the central part, opposite the entrance, several statues of Buddha wrapped in monks' robes welcome visitors. There are private rooms at both ends of the main hall: one for novices and one for adult monks, plus a kitchen. Outside stretched a red, dusty playing field, at the opposite end of which stood a crooked soccer goal. Young novices took the hour before sunset to play soccer, an extremely popular sport among youngsters in Myanmar. The monks passed the ball between them, without taking off their maroon robes (although several put their shoes on to kick the ball), and exhibiting much enthusiasm but little ability for the game. I joined them and showed off my skills with the ball through several heel passes, and the monks made sounds of admiration while exchanging looks of astonishment.

During my four weeks in Myanmar, after answering the question where I was from, the most frequent responses I received were, in order of frequency: Fernando Torres, Barcelona, Fabregas, Real Madrid, and David Villa. Nothing about Picasso, Dali, Velazquez, Goya, Cervantes, Zara, King Juan Carlos, or Zapatero. Soccer—especially Spain's recent success at Euro 2008, Barcelona's victories in 2009, and the Spanish stars of the English Premiership—was Spain's best representative, at least in Myanmar. On weekend nights, many bars showed TV matches of the Premier League, the most popular in Asia. Posters of international soccer stars adorned bars and shops all over the country. One of the activities that can be seen during the evenings is a group of four to eight youngsters playing *chinlone*, a game that consists of trying to keep a ball made of rattan off the ground, using not only the inside and outside of the foot but also the knee, heel, and sole; it requires incredible skill.

After playing with the monks, I washed off my sweat with well water, changed, and sat at the very center of the monastery to drink tea while absorbing the peace and darkness that began settling in. During dinner, the young monks, headed by three adults, watched a movie on an old black–and–white television. I was surprised they had a television in the monastery. After the movie, the TV was switched off, novices retreated to their room (a single room, where they all slept on the floor), and the adult monks turned on the radio to listen to Voice of America (VOA), a station owned by the U.S. government that broadcasts in more than forty languages with the objective of promoting freedom and democracy. Along with the BBC, VOA is the gateway of information for those who want to know what is really happening in Myanmar, as the Ministry of Information, in a totally Orwellian way, tightly controls all media in the country.

Monks have been subject to repression by the present government on several occasions, most recently during the 2007 demonstrations demanding democratic change, when a large number of them were stripped of their robes and kicked and beaten by the army. As a Burmese man told me a few days later in Bagan, neither the general population nor even monks and religion are respected by the military. They pretend to be Buddhists, flock to temples, and make substantial donations that appear in newspapers and national television, but in reality, as evidenced by the brutal repression of 2007, all that motivates them is maintaining full control of the country, and benefiting the most they can from it. As a tourist, despite traveling the country for four weeks, I saw no evidence of this brutal dictatorial system. I hardly saw military or police, but I read that there were thousands of secret police all across the country, continually monitoring the conversations of suspected opponents of the regime.

The young monks had prepared my sleeping place next to a window. Before bed, I meditated for a while, as the occasion was unbeatable: rarely was it going to be possible for me to stay overnight in a Buddhist monastery and sleep with beautiful statues of Buddha watching over my dreams. The mattress was thicker than the previous night's mat, so I slept better. The early creaking steps on the wooden floor of the novices woke me out of the deepest sleep before dawn, but it was their prayers by the altar, in the large space where I was sleeping, that eventually woke me up fully. Soon several villagers brought that day's food for the monks. After breakfast, we left the monastery to descend to Inle, the famous lake that is a compulsory stop on the country's tourist itinerary. We ate at a street restaurant on the lake's western side before going by boat to the town of Nyaung Shwe, on the lake's northeast shore, Inle's most important town and where most tourists stay.

On my trek I had made brief contact with some of the various ethnic groups of central Myanmar, the most important ones being those that occupy areas bordering Myanmar's neighbors: Bangladesh, India, China, Laos, and Thailand—areas that are mostly prohibited to foreign visitors. On every journey to these areas, the bus was stopped at a police roadblock, and all travelers had to alight to show their IDs. In the case of foreigners, their passport numbers and final bus destinations were written down in a book. Those trying to leave the central region of the country for areas inhabited by ethnic groups with which the Burmese government has long-term conflicts were usually sent in the opposite direction. In fact, Myanmar has never been a united nation. The population of Burmese origin, dominating the valleys of the great rivers, has always enjoyed political and military control. The Shans, the Kachins, the Karens, and the Chins, to name the most populous of the other groups, have always been suspicious of the Burmese control of the country. This conflict is one of the main features of Myanmar, a situation far more serious than that of its neighbors in Southeast Asia, where most ethnic minorities represent a much smaller percentage of the total population.

★ ★ ★

I decided to plan my exploration of Inle Lake by boat for Sunday, because on that day there would be a market in the village of Maing Thauk that I could visit on the same day. So, on Saturday I rented a bike and went to the town of

Kaungdaing, where I visited a rustic spa and gave a treat to my much—abused and tired legs and feet. The spa had two areas, one for men, the other for women (an example of the conservatism of Burmese society), plus a mixed area exclusively for foreigners. For five dollars one could enjoy three circular pools with different water temperatures. A young receptionist gave me a tour of the spa, and as soon as I told her I was Spanish, she asked me to teach her my language. At first I didn't understand how I could possibly teach an entire language in the few hours I planned to spend there. An hour later, once I had enjoyed the three pools, my lower extremities grateful for the luxury, as I was resting on a chair the young clerk appeared with a notebook, sat down beside me, and showed me a number of phrases in English that she wanted translated into Spanish. They were the phrases she used frequently in her work: good morning, where are you from? what's your name? here are the changing rooms; the restrooms are there. . . I translated all of these while she transcribed my Spanish pronunciation into Burmese so she'd be able at least to pronounce correctly in Spanish the phrases she needed most. Every time I uttered a phrase in Spanish, she, syllable by syllable, would write it out in Burmese, and then pronounce it in full, to see if she had noted it down correctly.

The next day, after failing in an attempt to share a boat, I went out to explore Inle Lake on my own, in a long, narrow motorboat that I rented, piloted by a local. In some respects, this was better; I could stop anywhere I chose and spend more time if I wanted to. The morning mist gave the lake a unique atmosphere. The light reflecting off the water was of intensity similar to the sky's at that early hour. It was an ideal time for photography. When we stopped to watch the fishermen, I took some stunning pictures of them fishing. We also went to the village of Maing Thauk to visit the local market. Then we went to a village of bamboo houses built on the lake, an aquatic village with wide, street—like channels between rows of individual houses separated from each other proportionately. Bamboo stairs sank into the water, with the household's essential boats parked next to them. We ate at a restaurant in one of the towns on the lake whose balcony overlooked one of the canals. From there we left the lake and motored up a river to Shwe Inn Thein, a complex of more than a thousand small pagodas. The main section of the complex contains a large number of stupas, all with tiny bells at their summits; the wind made them sing a soothing melody. Finally, back on the lake, we passed the floating gardens of Kela, where tomatoes and other vegetables grow, before stopping at the Nga Phe monastery.

During the Annapurna trek I had taken some good photos, I felt, but it wasn't until my days in Myanmar that I really started to enjoy my new photographic equipment. The monastery in Bago, where I had to act fast to capture the food preparation, the arrival of the monks, and their lunch; the morning exploring the market in Kalaw; the two days through the Burmese countryside; and now the beautiful Inle Lake, with its fishermen and their houses on the lake had resulted, with the particular bright colors of Myanmar and its people, in some photographs that I really loved. I'd had the opportunity to portray monks, children, peasants, and fishermen, to capture some of the country's beautiful landscapes, monasteries, and temples. I still had a lot to learn, but the last two weeks had been very fruitful.

Mandalay was my next destination; the night bus journey there took ten hours. I was lucky not to have a seatmate, so I was able to stretch my legs or rest them on the empty seat to sleep. The bus's TV showed Burmese music videos with lyrics, a moving karaoke. My rear seat neighbor knew most of the songs as he sang the lyrics with ease. Upon stopping for dinner, we began the descent from the mountain area to the central plain of the country, at a walking speed down a dusty, twisting road that managed to silence the spontaneous singer, since he began to vomit. It's singular that, although most of Myanmar's vehicles have their steering wheel on the right side of the vehicle, as in most Asian countries, the Burmese government, under the pretext of eradicating the British colonial heritage, forces people to drive on the right—hand side of the road, with the result that drivers' visibility is seriously impaired and the safety of passengers put at risk whenever they have to get on and off buses, which as a result of the irrational rule, is on the side of traffic, in the middle of the road. Once again, it was evident that the welfare of the population was not among the priorities of the Burmese military junta.

We arrived in Mandalay at 4 a.m. A motorcycle took me downtown from the bus station. Since I was alone and traveling fairly light, motorcycle taxis were the best option to avoid spending much money or wasting time (for those who might be wondering, the driver wedged my large backpack between his legs, and I wore the small backpack on my back). The fresh air of incipient dawn woke me up from my sleepiness as we moved towards the center of Mandalay through its deserted streets. Despite the early hour, I had no problems finding a room, and still caught part of the night to sleep.

My first visit was to the Royal Palace, located at the center of a large square area more than a thousand yards long, the area's walls surrounded by a wide moat. The palace is just a reproduction of the original, which was destroyed during battles between the British and Japanese armies during the Second World War. Mandalay was the country's capital from 1857 until the British victory in 1885 in the so−called Third Anglo−Burmese War, which incorporated all of Burma into the British Empire. During the reign of King Bagyidaw (1819−1837), Burma invaded Bengal, conquering the Indian states of Assam, Manipur, and Arakan. In response, the British army attacked the country's south, taking Rangoon in 1826, which resulted in the Treaty of Yandabo, by which the British regained the lost Indian states, plus Tenasserim, a southern province bordering Thailand. The Anglo−Burmese War, which began in 1852, was caused by British troops without the approval of London, and ended with the annexation of Pegu province, renamed Lower Burma. Following the establishment of the capital of Burma in Mandalay by King Mindon, his son, Thibaw Min, decided to side with the French, the British rival for the control of Southeast Asia, forcing the Third Anglo−Burmese War, which led to the aforementioned total annexation of the country.

After the palace, I took a rickshaw to the base of Mandalay Hill, where I visited the Atumashi monastery, Samdamuni pagoda, which contains the largest iron Buddha in the world, and Kuthodaw pagoda, containing the largest book on the globe, 729 vertical slabs of stone, each three and a half feet wide and five feet tall, inscribed with Buddhist scriptures. These were the result of the Fifth Buddhist Council, organized during the reign of King Mindon (1853–1878) in order to revitalize Buddhism in Burma. In nearby Kyauktawgyi pagoda lies one of the most spectacular Buddhas I had seen: the Big Marble Image, a Buddha carved from a single piece of pale green marble from a quarry twelve miles from Mandalay. It is said that it took more than ten thousand men and thirteen days to transport the stone from the Ayeyarwady (Irrawaddy) River to the pagoda. Later, I climbed Mandalay Hill, walking up the 1,729 steps to admire the two standing Buddhas that can be seen, one half way up, the other almost at the top, pointing his finger toward the city. The views of the Ayeyarwady River at sunset were fabulous.

The next day I rented a bicycle to go to the south of the city, to Shwe In Bin monastery, built of teak in 1895, a beautiful building open to tourists. In the afternoon, I went to the most important pagoda in Mandalay, Mahamuni, which has the most admired "golden" Buddha in the country. Brought to Mandalay in 1784, it is believed to have been sculpted in bronze in the first century. As with the Golden Rock, only men were allowed to approach it, to paste gold foil sheets onto the effigy. My second day of cycling was devoted to Amarapura, which, with Inwa, Sagaing, and Mingun, is one of the ancient cities near Mandalay. Located seven miles from the old capital, Amarapura was itself capital of the country for two brief periods (1783–1823 and 1841–1857) and is now famous for having the longest teak bridge in the world, U Bein, which is 1,300 yards long across the Taungthaman Lake and holds almost two hundred years of history. Several monasteries and pagodas stand along the lake's perimeter; one of them, Ganayon Monastery, also allows tourists to watch the monks prepare and take their lunch. In the afternoon I went to look at Sagaing across the river, where the view of Sagaing's hills, all dotted with white and golden pagodas, was spectacular. Having gone back to the U Bein bridge to see the sunset, I saw many tourists and monks walk and stop on the bridge to watch the descent of the orange sun; others rented boats to witness it from the river. It is an idyllic, beautiful, and serene spot.

After two days of cycling, which I loved, my last day in the area was dedicated to Sagaing and Inwa. I took a pickup to Sagaing. Five women sitting in the pickup smiled at me as soon as I got in. People were very charming in Mandalay, they said hello on the street often, always smiling. One of the women in the pickup, in limited but good English, asked me where I was going, where I came from, and if this was my first visit to Myanmar. While on our way, she took out her phone and took a photo of me. In Sagaing, I took a rickshaw to visit three pagodas and go to its highest hill, where another pagoda dominates the city, the river, and the plain to the west. After lunch at a restaurant down the street, I jumped onto a motorcycle to cross the bridge and visit the ruins of Inwa, formerly known as Ava, capital of Burma between 1364 and 1841 (excluding the years Amarapura had that privilege). I visited two monasteries, Bagaya, with 267 teak pillars, and Maha Aungmye Bonzan, as well as the tower of Nanmyin, which still stands despite the inclination that gives it the nickname "the leaning tower of Inwa." The surroundings were extremely beautiful, with green rice fields and palm trees adorning the buildings.

That night there was a full moon, a celebration for which is usually held in the Mahamuni Pagoda. At the hotel I ran into a young Korean I had met the day before, and we agreed to go to dinner with a young Austrian and a Taiwanese who also were staying there, and then join the celebration. Across the street from the hotel, we sat on plastic stools at a *chapatis* restaurant. It was a place as simple as the food was greasy. We then took a taxi to Mahamuni, which was already closed when we arrived. Nevertheless, a cheering crowd shopped and ate at the many stalls. We were the only foreigners there.

I saw a man dressed as a woman in a beautiful green dress showing his thin calves, which would be unusual for a Burmese woman, who are always covered with the *longyi*. With him was a man (dressed as a man), and they were lost in the crowd before we could observe them in more detail. Minutes later, we passed two men dressed as women, and one looked me in the eye and smiled with playful flirtation. I smiled back, while the young Austrian congratulated me on my conquest. Until then, everyone in Myanmar had seemed very conservative, and seeing three men dressed as women in one night took me aback. We discussed among ourselves that maybe the full moon, as it did with the man who turned into a wolf, made some Burmese men become women without much fuss.

The boat to Bagan left at 6 a.m., still dark, under the light of the full moon, still anchored in the west, opposite the pier. I took some pictures of the moon's reflection in the water from the deck, where I sat on a bench waiting for the sunrise. An Asian woman sat next to me as the boat headed south towards Sagaing. Her accent was distinctly American; she was from California but of Korean origin. Her family had immigrated to the United States when she was a little girl. She had just completed a three-week vipassana meditation retreat in one of the monasteries of Sagaing, and was going to Bagan with two fellow meditators. She worked as a psychoanalyst and had been devoting more and more time to meditation with the aim of incorporating it into her patients' treatment. The emergence of the sun above the trees on the horizon was glorious, and soon we saw the heights of Sagaing, with its hills and dozens of pagodas, softly illuminated by the rising sun. All of the travelers took photos of the sunrise from the deck. In response to the hazardous concentration of passengers to port, a crewman asked us to distribute ourselves more equally around the deck. In the shallow stretches, a crewman at the bow sank a stick marked with different colors to measure the river's depth. A couple of times we had to head back and steer carefully through the narrow navigable stream during this, the dry season.

At noon, with the sun beating down, I went to take my

seat inside the boat for a nap. As I entered the row where my seat was my located, one of the German–speaking tourists, abruptly, almost aggressively, warned me that the seat was taken. Her attitude and tone carried me back for a brief moment to the aggressiveness we sometimes experience in large Western cities, an attitude that often makes you respond in the same manner. However, that stupid woman was not going to alter my state of mind, and I quietly showed her my ticket and, ignoring her, took my seat and got some sleep.

Later, back on deck, looking at the tourists, most of whom were from the wealthier parts of Europe, I suddenly felt uncomfortable. The boat represented luxury, and perhaps influenced by the unpleasant encounter, I felt totally out of place. Obviously, I too was an example of Western wealth, but having enjoyed in recent weeks an existence without many possessions, in the simplicity of a nomadic traveler, I thought I might be pulling away, perhaps slowly, perhaps inevitably, from the obsession with accumulating things that dominates life in developed countries. It was a question that remained, lingering, in my mind, and only the advance of my trip and the answers my experiences would bring might help me find a resolution and an answer.

When we docked at Bagan, Myanmar's main tourist destination, it was not surprising that we were awaited with anticipation by a large group of children trying to sell us postcards and souvenirs. A young woman offered me a copy of the novel *Burmese Days*, by George Orwell, a work inspired by Orwell's own experiences during his stay as a policeman in British Burma. The Burmese say that Orwell wrote not one but three books about Myanmar, affirming that both *Animal Farm* and *1984* were inspired by their country. Bagan, known as Pagan in antiquity, was the capital of the ancient Burmese empire for long periods, beginning in 874 and reaching its zenith during the twelfth and thirteenth centuries, when the city was one of the world's main religious and cultural centers. In 1287 it was invaded by the Mongols, who then controlled China under the Yuan Dynasty (1271–1368), an event that marked the beginning of its decline. In an area of about twenty–five square miles, there are currently more than two thousand pagodas and temples; it's estimated there were over five thousand in its heyday. The powerful earthquake that struck the area in 1975 severely damaged many buildings and "beheaded" many sculptures of Buddha: I could see scars on the necks of many of them, where they were repaired. Unfortunately, the government's overall efforts at repair have not been executed with the quality required to name Bagan a UNESCO World Heritage Site, an accolade it certainly deserves.

After the enjoyment of two days cycling around Mandalay, I decided my exploration of the temples and pagodas of Bagan was also going to be on two wheels. The distance I would have to cover was ample, but the terrain was flat, and the roads and trails in good condition. I began by pedaling to Old Bagan, and along the way stopped to visit one of its main pagodas, the dazzling Shwezigon, completed by King Kyansittha around 1090. Although it has been repaired many times, it retains its original structure and served as a prototype for later pagodas, including Shwedagon in Yangon, with which it competes in the amount of bright gold adorning it. I stopped at a couple of temples on the way to Old Bagan before reaching the city's second architectural star, the great Ananda temple, dedicated to Buddha's faithful servant. Also completed by King Kyansittha, this is a building in the form of a Greek cross, at the center of which stand four gigantic golden sculptures of Buddha gazing toward the four cardinal points down four long, nave–like halls, instead of the usual one found in smaller temples. It is an impressive building in the dimensions of both the structure itself and its towering Buddhas.

I stopped to eat at a vegetarian restaurant near the temple. Soon came the Korean–American with two of her meditation–retreat companions. We chatted a while with a Burmese man who told us he thought our way of traveling appropriate because our money went to local businesses rather than to the more luxurious ones, which attracted what he called "monkey tours"—tours that mainly used expensive hotels, restaurants, and luxury coaches, all belonging to a few families close to the junta. He ended his speech criticizing the materialistic attitude of the ruling Burmese, adding that the dead have no pockets. I spent the afternoon visiting various temples in Old Bagan, including Thatbyinnyu, the tallest of Bagan's temples. To end such a pleasant day, I enjoyed the sunset from the Shwesandaw temple, with its fabulous, 360–degree view across the plain on which stand most of the temples of Bagan. Sellers of souvenirs and antiques thronged, aware of the number of people attracted by the sunset. I perceived the aggressiveness of some tourists with children who were among the sellers, which was totally undeserved because all of the children were very polite and not very pushy in their attempts to earn some money. I used to smile at them before I immediately warned them I would not buy anything. They were always very nice to me. I cannot understand the attitude, devoid of all empathy, of some tourists who react with so much upset at a simple, needy approach. During my three days of exploration I visited over forty temples and pagodas, noting down on my map the order in which I saw them, so I would know which monument corresponded to the numerous pictures I took. Besides those already mentioned, I loved the Upalithein frescos, the Buddhas and the reliefs on the walls of Mahabodi, the smiling, long–eared Buddha in Ywahaunggyi, and the reclining and vertical Buddhas in Alonyi.

For my last days in Myanmar I wanted to enjoy the beach. The country's most famous beach is Ngapali, difficult to access, so tourists fly there. I wanted to travel by ground, which left two choices: Chaungtha and Ngwe Saung, both in the southwest and reachable by bus directly from Yangon, via Pathein, the Ayeyarwady River delta's main city. I opted for the extensive Ngwe Saung beach (ten miles long). Taking the bus there from Bagan through Yangon, when seen on the map, didn't seem at all attractive. Bussing from Bagan to Yangon took thirteen hours; there I had to change bus stations, and from Yangon to Ngwe Saung was another seven hours on the road. Adding exchanges and waiting hours, it took almost twenty–four hours to reach the idyllic beach from arid Bagan. The effort, however, was worth it.

I stayed in one of the hotels along the beach, in a bamboo

bungalow between coconut trees. The sand was white, the water clear and warm. Since it looked west to the Bay of Bengal, the sunsets were glorious. My plan for the next four days was to walk on the beach in the mornings, write, read, meditate, and unwind from the recent bustle. And that's what I did every day. I walked along the beautiful beach for two hours before the sun rose in a glorious excess of light. I hardly saw anyone, just some locals on their motorcycles going from one end of the beach to the other. The hotels were almost empty; some had recently closed and were in a state of neglect. The ones that seemed to suffer most were luxury hotels. One day I went to one to access the Internet (the only place offering it to the public, but at an exorbitant price) and saw there only employees, diligently cleaning the lobby.

To eat, I usually went to one of the restaurants on the road or in town. The fish was fresh and the smell of the sea invited me to order it grilled. In one of the restaurants on the road I was welcomed with joy due to the scarce activity. I was shown a couple of fish caught that night and chose one to be grilled with chili sauce. The young waitress kept glancing at me sheepishly, as if not wanting to be caught by the owners, a couple in their fifties. I wasn't sure if she was their daughter or an employee. She paced in front of my table, sometimes just stopping in my field of vision. Our eyes met several times, the first time something like this had happened to me in conservative Myanmar. She was attractive, of clear complexion and slanted eyes instead of the usual bronzed skin and round eyes, which made me think she was from one of the minority tribes. I thought about saying something to her, maybe suggest meeting outside, but the proximity of the owner stopped me. It was my first day there, so I decided to go back and try again. I walked past the restaurant every day but never saw her again.

It was February 5, 2010, a day that should have been my dad's seventieth birthday. I would have found a booth to call and congratulate him, but it now made nine, the birthdays of his that we had missed. In October 2001 I was supposed to travel to Thailand on my first trip to Asia, but a week before my departure, I received a call from my mom informing me of my father's illness, an advanced tumor in his abdomen. I canceled my vacation and flew from London to San Sebastian immediately. My father died five weeks later. To experience the brutal damage suffered by a person such as my father, who had always been physically so healthy, was an unforgettable shock almost impossible to process.

My last hours in Yangon were devoted to buying a monk's robe and taking pictures of the city at sunset. When I went for dinner to 50th Street Cafe, the bar's TV began showing the deferred transmission of the Super Bowl. An enthusiastic group of Americans were waiting for the start. I would never have expected to watch the Super Bowl in Myanmar with the usual background noise of Americans screaming. Undoubtedly, the world is getting smaller.

The military junta spoke of general elections in the autumn, but no Burmese I spoke with was very hopeful at the announcement. Some doubted they would be held at all, others simply considered it cosmetic. Everyone thought that corruption would taint either the conditions of participation or the count; in either case, the junta would prevail once again. However, I thought the economic development of all of the country's neighbors, including Thailand, India, and China, would finally push the junta to make a controlled transition towards a more open, less corrupt and repressive system. I wanted to be right, and for such a transition to occur as soon as possible for the sake of the country's wonderful population.

Myanmar had captivated me. The four weeks of intense exploration of the country's most visited parts I had enjoyed to the fullest, especially after my weeks of forced sedentary existence in Kathmandu. Its landscapes, its people, its temples and monks, its unique atmosphere, a mixture of poverty, economic backwardness, humility, and compassion, will remain forever etched in my memory. Myanmar is a beautiful old jewel kept in a wooden box, a classic precious and beautiful stone. Its light will dazzle anyone who takes the trouble to open the box that contains it so tightly.

PROSTITUTION & NATURE

"A traveler without observation is a bird without wings." —Saadi

"Though we travel the world to find the beautiful, we must carry it with us or we will not find it." —Ralph Waldo Emerson

I spent a few days in Bangkok, from where I sent to my friend Carmen in New York (my legal address while traveling) the monk's robe I had bought in Yangon with some maps of Myanmar that I wanted to keep; I also enjoyed a Thai massage and did my tax return online. And I fell into the temptation of going for the third time to the bar that had managed to break one of my moral barriers. I sat with a beer and looked into the eyes of the girls, some timid, even elusive, others direct and flirtatious; at the groups of young Japanese men, who walked around the bar as though they were at a shopping mall, stopping to talk to girls here and there before boldly pursuing their examination of the available supply; at the shy single men who, like me, sat on a stool with a drink, maybe waiting for a hint of flirtation from one of the Thai women; at men who invited a girl to sit at a table for a drink and a chat to justify the subsequent transaction; at the girls who, as soon as they came into the bar through the back door, went, first thing, to the small shrine attached to the wall and bowed to Buddha with their palms together, perhaps asking him for protection or a fruitful night; and at the Western men who, although tempted by the girls on offer, seemed content to just watch and consume beer instead of female bodies. I tried to talk to a couple of girls with no luck; they ignored me either because they didn't speak English or because they were just interested in Asian men.

While I was exploring all that fascinating activity from the central bar, a brunette with penetrating dark eyes fixed them on mine. We smiled in unison, and I invited her to come closer. Her English was very good, which I appreciated. I liked talking to her; she had a good sense of humor. Obviously, she was not there just to chat, so she insisted on my taking her to the hotel where I was staying. I agreed because I really liked her company. If my first encounter was the result of the visceral masculine impetus, this time it was motivated by rationality. The experience was 50 percent more expensive, and the result less satisfying. Having finished the service, she stayed for a while, chatting on the bed before leaving. She was divorced and had an eight–year–old daughter who lived with her grandmother outside Bangkok. Until a few months ago she had worked as a shop assistant in a friend's store, but the current economic crisis had affected the business, she lost her job, and it hadn't been easy to find another one. She told me that from 70 to 80 percent of her customers were Japanese who lived in Bangkok or were visiting on business or vacation. The girls—some students, some single mothers, others looking for additional income to their daily jobs—preferred Japanese customers to Westerners because the girls could charge them more, and also because they were smaller and ended sooner. She loved my straight nose. She said many Thai women inserted silicone to redraw their flat nose. She asked about my life and my plans after Bangkok before dressing up and going to dinner with a friend.

After my brief experience with prostitution, I found it clearly unsatisfactory, which wasn't a big surprise. Paid sex would never reach the satisfaction achieved when both parties really are into it; sex practiced as part of a loving relationship was clearly superior. Knowing a little about the girls' life and their financial problems made me more sympathetic toward them. It's too easy to give moralistic sermons from the pulpit of economic wealth. My position on prostitution, as with drugs, has always been in favor of legalizing and regulating the consumption of both. That way, it would help to end the underground world in which many women live, as well as the mafias that control the production and trade of narcotics. At least the Thai women who regularly or sporadically went to that bar did so without coercion and were the sole beneficiaries of their work. If it hadn't been that way, my little adventure would have never happened. Sexual slavery is disgusting; in theory it's in the hands of men to end such slavery, but, while admitting there will always be men who put their sexual desires ahead of the welfare of their sexual partners, the legalization of prostitution would be a big step in the fight against that plague.

Weeks later, in Cambodia, I bought an interesting book by Louise Brown: *Sex Slaves: The Trafficking of Women in Asia*. Although perhaps lacking the rigor an investigative book requires, the information gathered there is without doubt of great value. I summarize here the author's main points:

−Despite the great attention that sexual tourism gets, the main consumers of prostitution in Asia are local men.

−Families themselves often sell their daughters to traffickers to get rid of a mouth to feed, get needed cash, and receive money from the sold daughter in the future.

−A large network of people benefits from the trafficking: recruiters, transporters, brothel owners, their managers, the police, and even doctors.

−Many of the slaves are still children; virginity is demanded and has a corresponding price. Others are raped as a prelude to forced prostitution.

−Prostitutes have, with their work, to repay the debt incurred by the brothel owner (the cost of the girl, transportation, bribes, medical treatment), which involves years of slavery.

−Their living conditions are extremely harsh, and they suffer from lack of privacy (some are chained and stacked in rooms without freedom of movement) and poor hygiene.

−The traffic moves young Nepalese to India, Bangladeshis to Pakistan, Burmese to Thailand, and Filipinos and Thais to Japan (they enter with entertainers visas).

−Japanese men are major consumers of prostitution due to the unhappiness of a high percentage of their marriages. The relationship with their wives is many times closer to a maternal one than one between partners.

−There is a correlation between societies that value virginity as a condition for marriage and prostitution. The inability to have sex before marriage with socially acceptable marriage partners induces young men to get sex by paying for it.

I used the Thai railway network for the journey from Bangkok to Ayutthaya, the ancient capital of the kingdom of Siam. In Southeast Asia few countries have railroads, and after the endless bus trips in Myanmar, the change was welcome. The train was old and wooden, with windows that opened fully and blinds to shelter from the sun. We left Bangkok Central Station at a slow pace, and stopped at various stations in the suburbs. With the air coming through the windows, the train ride was as it was in the past in Europe. The new trains are more comfortable and efficient, but deprive us of the unique feeling of a train journey, of being so close to the environment. Departing from Bangkok, the train passed so close to the houses of the suburbs I feared a naughty kid would give me a slap, or an object would come through the window thrown from a kitchen in a domestic fight.

After getting off in Ayutthaya, I took a small boat to cross the river to the old part of the city, which is on an island at the intersection of three rivers: Chao Phraya, Lopburi, and Pa Sak. I stayed at Bann Kun Pra, a beautiful guesthouse built in teak that overlooks the river and has a good restaurant open to it. I had dinner there before retiring to meditate in my room. I turned off the light and sat on the bed when I noticed a light from downstairs through a gap wider than normal between the wooden floorboards. My curiosity pulled me to bend forward from my meditative sitting position and see what was happening. I could clearly see a young woman with fair hair and skin in her underwear getting ready to go to bed. I watched for a moment as she gathered her clothes and folded them in her backpack. Then she picked up a digital camera to review some pictures. I sat straight again, closed my eyes while still watching her, and plunged into meditation. After half an hour the heat in the room was stifling. The fan wasn't able to relieve the accumulated heat in the room. I went down to reception to buy a cold bottle of water, which I had run out of. When I returned and switched off the light, I again saw the light coming from the room below mine. I bent forward a second time and saw the woman on the bed with her naked partner (she was in her panties). Intertwined, they spoke French while stroking themselves in that peculiar way when both want more but prefer the other one to take the initiative, both needing the confirmation of the other's desire. I became an accidental voyeur. I thought they might have not been long together, both still somewhat shy before making the final assault. After several minutes of confusing caresses, the burning male desire overcame the feminine patience. How uninteresting it was to watch a couple making love! I closed my eyes to continue with my meditation.

The next morning, I awoke to noise coming from the next room. The dividing wall was so thin I could hear a Thai couple making love. Their passion hit their bed against the wall, and even slightly rocked mine. I was surrounded by loving couples, which emphasized my loneliness in such a romantic guesthouse. Life can sometimes be extremely cruel. Perhaps it was the result of my recently accumulated karma: two nights with prostitutes in Bangkok resulted in having to suffer from two couples making love around me. It was a magic touch warning me not to fall again into the temptation of materialistic sex and to focus on finding a woman to love, something that has become so complicated in recent years. I could not in any way presume that my stays in London and New York had been fruitful love—wise. After a several years of a long relationship that began in San Sebastian and ended in London, there followed an extended period of desired bachelorhood that seemed to have recently become, against my will, endless. Traveling solo periodically intensified this unpleasant sensation.

I rented a bike to visit the old temples found both in the old part of the city and outside the island. Ayutthaya, whose name comes from the Indian city of Ayodhya, birthplace of the god Rama, succeeded Sukhothai as the second capital of the kingdom of Siam; a title it held from its founding in 1350 until it was destroyed by the Burmese army in 1767. It is believed it once had a population of one million in the early eighteenth century, and thus, at the time, was one of the largest cities in the world. After the defeat, the capital was moved to Bangkok.

To reach the entrance of Khao Yai National Park, considered one of the most beautiful in Southeast Asia, I traveled by train from Ayutthaya to Pak Chong. In the station a couple of young women waited for tourists, with offers of accommodation and tours of the park. I chose the cheaper of the two, and the young Thai took me in her car to the outskirts of town, where her parents had a one—story building with a dozen rooms. I purchased a tour of two and half days. Half a day was spent visiting a monastery and witnessing the departure of three million bats from a cave before sunset. It takes them about an hour to get out (it looked like black smoke pouring from a chimney), and they fly ten miles to Khao Yai each evening, looking for a hearty meal of insects. After the night hunting, once having satisfied their vampire appetite, they return to the cave individually.

The two full days were reserved for exploring the park. A guide picked me up after breakfast to go to Pak Chong Khao Yai, twenty miles away. He wore camouflage pants and military boots, carried at his side a large knife in a sheath, and drove a pickup. At the entrance of the park we saw a couple hitchhiking, and the guide asked me if we could take them; I said of course, and the couple climbed in the back (I was in the front seat). I knew they were Spanish by their accent when they spoke English with my guide, and when we got to the visitor center I introduced myself. Their plan had been to rent bikes to visit the park, but Khao Yai unfortunately didn't offer that amenity. I suggested they spend the day with me in the pickup, sharing the expense. They agreed, and I sat with them in the back as we approached the first area to visit. Iosu was from Pamplona, Ana from La Rioja, both park rangers, he in Navarra, she in Aragon. They were passionate about nature, especially animals, and often used their vacation time to visit parks around the world.

We took a couple of walks that day before going to watch the sunset from the highest point in the park. On the way there, we stopped where several groups of visitors stared silently into the thick forest. A wild elephant was about thirty yards away in the dense jungle. We could distinguish its tail and its right ear, slightly moving. It was eating; we could hear the leaves and branches rustle as it moved. It shifted slightly to the right, and with a slight twist, we could catch a glimpse of one of its tusks. It was amazing to be so close to a wild elephant, yet never be able to see it completely. Wild elephants were the stars of the park; it is so populated by them that their excrement is scattered over the entire park (in huge balls that look like coconuts). After sunset, on the way to the campsite, with our jeep's headlights illuminating both sides of the road, I saw an elephant standing by the road, waiting for us to pass. It was a vision of less than a second, as if a flash had gone off in total darkness, more a vision of a ghost than of a living animal, its silhouette slightly reflected against the black background. I hit the side of the pickup to alert the guide. Iosu also saw it, and we urged the guide to turn around to see if it was still there. He quickly turned back, but the ghost had disappeared into the darkness of the jungle.

The next morning, after sleeping in tents, we woke up early to go to one of the park's watchtowers with the hope of seeing wild animals, but just enjoyed seeing some birds and an otter swimming in a pond. Later on, we reached a place of shallow water where hundreds of butterflies fluttered above the puddles. They were green, yellow, blue, some with spots, large and small, dark and bright. On one of the rocks there were many in what looked like military formation, over thirty "soldiers" in green uniforms. Iosu, using his Nikon mounted with a telephoto lens, excited as a child with his favorite toy, began portraying those subtle beauties. It was supposed to be my last day in the park, but its immense beauty made me stay one more night, so I sent the guide in his pickup home, and rented a tent and a sleeping bag to spend my second night in Khao Yai.

As those who go camping or hiking well know, the feeling of having with you everything you need is really liberating. I know that many people would stress out just thinking about spending so long with few belongings. However, the saying "less is more" is definitely true. Not only is there the practical aspect of greater mobility; there is also the psychological impact, the realization that we do not really need as much as we think we do. It's true that living in a city brings the social obligations of work, family, and friends, each with its load of expectations, style, sense of belonging, and social status to maintain or conquer. In London and New York I had met many people obsessed with apartments, cars, clothes, electronic gadgets, vacations—all symptoms of the wrong way to achieve happiness. Several studies have confirmed that once a certain economic level has been achieved, happiness does not depend on the accumulation of greater wealth. As already noted by psychologist Abraham Maslow in his famous hierarchy of needs, after ensuring physical survival, what matters is friendship, love, self–esteem, and creativity. While there certainly exists a natural tendency to accumulate as a defense against possible future shortages, it can become a burden when it's no longer a survival strategy but a comparison obsession. Our natural predispositions, born of our animal condition (accumulation of food, risk aversion, fear of the unknown, need for a secure social identity . . .) can easily turn negative for our happiness when uncontrolled. Greed, passivity, tracking prevailing norms (religious, family, social . . .) can easily limit our search for happiness, to achieve a rich and interesting life.

A trip like the one I'd started was a great opportunity to break with the habits acquired during a hitherto sedentary and, compared to most of the world's population, opulent life. I had very few belongings with me, but I didn't miss anything. The warm weather made necessary only a few clothes, and the simplicity of the local dress didn't encourage wearing anything ostentatious. Food was not only cheap but also very easy to find; however small a village was, it always had a restaurant. I decided not to take my iPod, to resist the temptation to isolate myself from what was happening around me, and I had not regretted my decision for a moment. I lived each day as it came with no expectations or desires for something specific to happen. The itinerary for each country was more or less decided in advance to make the most of the days available in each country, but if I loved a place I did not hesitate to alter my plans and stay longer to enjoy it. Routine didn't exist. Each day was different. For this reason, and perhaps also because of meditation, my mental process had been altered substantially. Instead of constantly planning the order to which each day was subject while I was working (getting up, breakfast, subway, the workday with all its tasks to complete, the gym, shopping, cooking . . .), my mind only had the obligation to absorb what was happening in front of me, to be swayed by the senses rather than by reason; I had a magnificent sense of lightness and spontaneity. Of course, my current situation was the result of many years of well−paid routine work, and I was well aware of its temporary nature. Nevertheless, I had still plenty of time to keep enjoying my new mental state, my substantial freedom, and my incredible privilege.

I was woken up at midnight by the sound of an animal running around outside my tent. I looked out the window and saw two porcupines, one chasing the other. Two others sniffed around the tent, sometimes so close I could hear their breathing clearly. They were huge, with black and white spikes over thirty inches long. When I got up, a couple of macaques greeted me with a good morning, knowing there would be some food at that early hour at the campsite. I also sighted a couple of hornbills, big birds with long curved beaks that live in tropical areas. I left the campsite, walking down the road towards the visitor center, located about eight miles away. The morning silence helped in the sighting of numerous animals: several colorful birds, some playful squirrels climbing a tree, a wild rooster proud of its colorful plumage, a blue pheasant among the foliage, gibbons screaming from the top of the trees to their compadres across the forest, a herd of deer, lapwings, two hornbills, an eagle... A wonderful hike.

I tried to walk one of the trails from the visitor center through the jungle but was informed there was no guide available because overnight poachers had killed an elephant to get hold of its prized tusks, and all the park's rangers were trying to hunt down the murderers. I rode on a Thai minibus that picked me up when they saw me walking down the road. Outside the park, I missed the last bus to Pak Chong, so I had to hitchhike back to the hotel. A pickup driven by a woman with her old father stopped to invite me in. During the twenty—mile journey, I felt really free, riding in the back of the pickup, enjoying the view and the wind. As a child, during school holidays, I always made at least one trip with my father in his refrigerated truck loaded with fresh fish. I was so small that my father had to help me climb the steps to get into the cab, where I felt like a king on a chariot. The view of the road and the scenery from the top of the truck was very extensive for a small being like me. Going down some mountain road, my father allowed me to operate the electric hand brake. He said one, two, or three, and I moved the lever on the right of the steering wheel to the correct position. Then I sat on the truck's engine, and felt the warmth of the old Pegasus on my buttocks and legs. One night, while we unloaded at the fish market in Barcelona, I sat in the driver's seat (maybe I was kneeling) and played being the driver as I turned the giant steering wheel to and fro and manipulated some of the levers. I even decided to push a black button, and the engine started and the truck began to move. Panic broke out in the building. My father ran out and climbed into the cab to stop the truck. I was petrified on the seat.

I arrived in Nakhon Ratchasima (a.k.a. Khorat), Thailand's second city, with the intention of staying a night before arriving in Cambodia; however, a Thai man engaged me in conversation while drinking a beer in a bar and insisted passionately that I visit Phimai, a town forty miles away with a group of temples, he said, as interesting as those of Angkor in Cambodia. Although it was not on my itinerary, I decided to stay an extra night in Khorat and spend the next day in Phimai. Its temples didn't disappoint and were an excellent introduction to the architecture in Angkor. Its main temple, Prasat Hin Phimai, from the tenth century, was started by the Khmer King Jayavarman V when much of Thailand was part of the great Khmer empire.

During the European arrival to the area in the nineteenth

century, Thailand, however, was the only Southeast Asian country that wasn't colonized. The British began their Asian conquest in India before expanding to Burma, Malaysia, and Singapore. The French, meanwhile, arrived to the east, in Cambodia first, then Vietnam, their main target. Thailand was in a complex situation as a country sandwiched between the British and the French. Its fear of being devoured by one of the two European powers made the Thai king give ground to both in exchange for maintaining independence; a difficult position to hold onto that its king, Chulalongkorn Rama V, successfully managed to handle with great diplomatic skill.

BAGUETTES, TEMPLES & GENOCIDE

"The world is a book and those who do not travel read only a page."
—St. Augustine

*"Traveling is like flirting with life. It's like saying 'I would stay and love you,
but I have to go, this is my station.'"* —Lisa St. Aubin de Terán

I entered Cambodia from the west, in Poipet, a town
bordering the Thai town of Aranya Phratet. I crossed the
border on foot, the first border I had done so, with my big
backpack on my back, the small one in front. It took a while;
there was a long line to exit Thailand and another of equal
length to get into Cambodia, whose 30–day visa can be
obtained at the border. After the paperwork, I took a free bus
from the border to a station where I could take a bus to
Battambang or Siem Reap, the two main destinations from
Poipet; I, however, had decided to spend the night in
Sisophon, on the road to Siem Reap, to visit a couple of old
temples located near the town. A storm of wind and rain as
unexpected as it was violent entertained us while we waited
for the bus. The rain beat against the roofs of the houses
opposite the station and the cars parked nearby puddles
sprouted within seconds, and several naked children came
running over the puddles, chasing each other, rejoicing in the
cool water.

The bus to Siem Reap left after the storm receded.
Immediately upon leaving the station, the honking concert
started. After Thailand's silence, I had come to the conclusion
that a country's development status could be measured by the
level of honking on its roads. Although we were traveling on
a good road—people had waited many years for a decent
overland connection from Thailand to central Cambodia—
the bus drove ahead too slowly, as if it were still driving
down the old dusty road instead of the new, paved one, or
maybe the rain made the driver slow down. After an hour's
ride, I got off in Sisophon, the only tourist to do so. Under a
light rain, I asked a young man on a motorcycle to take me to

a guesthouse recommended in my Lonely Planet. Inside, two women waited for customers while lying on a wide lounger. The room I was shown to was as spacious as it was simple. It lacked air conditioning; a fan would be responsible for clearing out the heat overnight. The room was cheap, only $5.

After cooling down under the shower, I asked the women for the price to go to the Banteay Top and Banteay Chhmar temples. They barely spoke English, but I understood they had called a driver to come by. As I waited for him, a young tenant came out of her room and sat in front of me to talk in her decent English. She was twenty years old, already married, and heading to Poipet with her husband for a business meeting. She was very friendly, and beautiful, with a wide smile. She liked to practice her English, which is very common among young people in Southeast Asia, and was curious about my travels and my life. As on many other occasions, she asked about my age and marital status, and once again, my age surprised her as much as my bachelor status. The driver arrived, a tall and burly young man, unexpectedly for a Cambodian, who are usually small and spare. He spoke good English and took me on his motorbike to dinner at a local restaurant where we negotiated the price to visit the temples. These are forty miles north of Sisophon, a city of over a hundred thousand inhabitants with few tourists, who rarely venture to visit the temples due to their remoteness. The temples are reached by a dusty and bumpy road, so it takes all day to go, visit them, and return.

We left by motorbike the next morning after a breakfast of black coffee, strong and thick, with a baguette spread with pâté and jam. Baguettes and pastries are found throughout Cambodia, a legacy of the French colonial era. Cambodia came under French governance in 1863 when their king, Norodom I, fearing a possible invasion by the country's Thai and Vietnamese neighbors, asked the Gallic country for protection. With the exception of the Japanese invasion of 1941–45, the French occupation lasted until 1953; when faced with difficulties in Vietnam, the French government decided to withdraw from Cambodia and Laos to concentrate on its Asian gem.

About two hours was the estimate of my driver to reach Banteay Top, the first of the temples to visit. The consequences of the previous day's storm were still evident: the road was still slightly wet, so the way there wasn't dusty at all. The road, however, was dotted with potholes, so it was necessary to drive at a moderate speed. I had to grab tightly the bar behind my seat with both hands because the potholes my driver wasn't able to avoid were deep enough to make me jump out of my seat. The bouncing was constant, as if the road were being shaken by an endless earthquake. My brain seemed to be inside a shaker; I wasn't sure how my neurons would end up after four hours of stirring like this. Hopefully, the shaker would pour out new and imaginative ideas. Often, after an unavoidable bump approached the bike's front wheel, and my driver braked heavily to reduce the impact, my head collided with his like a woodpecker pecking a tree. Had it not been for the closed helmets we both wore, I would have ended the trip with a flat nose, my driver with a hole in the back of his head.

Banteay Top is a small temple in ruins. Large stones scattered from the ruins of its four towers occupy most of the area. I walked around, trying to decipher the temple's original shape (the site had no reference map), and from stone to stone to access the temple's former interior. Some children were playing on the rocks. Ten miles away is Banteay Chhmar, a temple that really is worth the journey's effort. Its towers had also collapsed; I had to walk on the stones, well above the original ground level, above the height of the temple's windows, their lintels beneath my feet. The temple was surrounded by a wall with carvings and a moat filled with water, a structure typical of many temples of the Angkorian era. Its impressive carvings show the battles between the Khmers and the Chams. Famous is a spectacular carving of Avalokiteshvara, with thirty−two arms. Avalokiteshvara is the bodhisattva of compassion, and is sometimes depicted with many arms as a symbol of his dedication to help anyone in need. Bodhisattva is the generic term given in Buddhism to anyone who is on the path to nirvana.

We returned early to avoid a possible afternoon storm. The prospect of facing potholes filled with water, a heavy rain without shelter, and the resulting mud wasn't an attractive adventure. However, we had to suffer, not just the inescapable potholes, but also dust gusting from traffic, now that the moisture had evaporated from the road. We arrived at the guesthouse exhausted from our fight against the bumps and coated in red dust, like two human croquettes. I wiped and washed under the shower before lying on the bed to help my body reconquer tranquility. Once recovered, I went for a walk in Sisophon, dined on a terrace next to the road, the city's main street, and returned to the guesthouse, where, stretched out on the floor, my driver, the two women who had welcomed me the day before, and another man were eating small, edible shells, with chili sauce and beer. I sat down with them to talk. The driver, the only one who spoke English, was extremely curious about Europe and the United States, their women, my travels, and my life in general. He insisted on commenting on how lucky I was to be able to travel as I was doing; he was dying to leave Cambodia and get to know other countries, other worlds. And he was right; I certainly had had good fortune. A large part of the world's population never leave their country, many not even their villages, their vision and experiences limited by geography. They finished eating the shells and all lay down in different parts of the room to sleep, which they seemed to do frequently in downtime.

Then a couple of young Cambodians arrived by motorcycle. My guide told me the girl worked at a karaoke where men came to drink and sing in the company of young women. If a man wanted sex during the women's working hours, the fee was divided between the woman and the karaoke, but it was possible to hire the women at the end of their shift, probably at a lower price. In the present case, the girl had the day off and wasn't working. The driver asked me if I would like to go to a karaoke, but I declined. He told me local customers visiting the guesthouse on business trips had repeatedly invited him. As a sideman, he was invited to drink with the girls. These were usually very young and didn't like to go with European customers because they were too big for their small bodies. Candidly, he told me he had only a little more than five inches, which seemed short, given his tall, strong body. He said this, showing some insecurity about it. He was twenty—eight, had no girlfriend, and didn't want to marry yet despite his age. He had decided that thirty—two would be a good age for marriage. Until then, and given the difficulty of premarital sex, he had to wait, or perhaps have occasional fun on his visits to the karaoke with customers.

Battambang, Cambodia's second largest city, is located on the banks of the river Sangker an hour south of Sisophon. I stayed at the hotel Chhaya, very central and with spacious rooms, air conditioning, and refrigerators. A young motorcyclist who helped me take my bag to my room offered to drive me to the most attractive temples in the area. He was young, friendly, smiled easily, and spoke good English, so I hired him. That afternoon we went to see Wat Ek Phnom, a temple in ruins from the Angkorian era. It's located ten miles north of the city, and the way there is beautiful; first, by a narrow road lined with wooden houses between coconut and palm trees, then, in the countryside, through farming villages. My driver was twenty—three and liked movies so much he blew out phrases unknown to me from films like *Die Hard* and *Crocodile Dundee*. Films were his English teacher. When asked if he had a girlfriend, he replied, "No money, no honey", an expression so popular it's printed on shirts for sale in many shops.

Next day my motorist picked me up at 9 a.m. to go to Wat Banan temple, located on a hill that comes out of nowhere in the middle of the plain. I had to climb 359 steps to reach the top, where the views were spectacular. Later we went to Phnom Sampeau, better known as The Killing Cave. It's at the top of a hill and has a skylight in the ceiling. The Khmer Rouge established a prison there and killed approximately 10,000 people by hitting them on the head and throwing them through the skylight to the bottom of the cave, about 65 feet below. Anyone who still remained alive was then finished off. In the cave there are many skulls and bones of those killed; a reclining Buddha has been placed there as a result of the killings. I asked my guide if someone in his family had died during that period: he said his mother witnessed her brother and sister's murder, an uncle and aunt the young guy never had the chance to meet. He said his mother barely spoke about it because sadness and weeping took possession of her whenever she did.

I asked the driver to pick me up at 9 p.m. to go to the only club in town, Sky. While dining at Smoking Pot, a restaurant popular with tourists for its cooking classes, I met Brian, a young American who was also staying at Chhaya. I invited him to come to Sky, and we arranged to meet in the hotel lobby. From there we went out in the local style: the three of us on a bike. We went into the club without paying, sat at a high table with stools, and ordered three Angkor beers. It was Wednesday, and gradually the place filled up, surprising for the day of the week. The clientele was young; few were over twenty–five. As usual, there were more men than women, but surprisingly, males were more active on the dance floor. There were also some *lady–boys*, exaggerated in their hairstyles, makeup, and movements so there wouldn't be any doubt they were really women. Western pop music alternated with Asian, with some hip–hop and rock in between. With midnight there also arrived half an hour of ballads so that couples could slow dance. None of us danced, although Brian and I tried unsuccessfully to push our young driver to hit the dance floor. On leaving the club we saw two attractive local women we had spotted dancing inside. I asked my driver to talk to them and ask them where they were going. Everything was closed already, but I insisted on his getting their phone numbers.

The next day I had planned to rent a bicycle and leave Battambang towards the Ek Phnom temple, to enjoy the beautiful Cambodian countryside. Before leaving, I went to the central market to repair the zipper on one of my shirts. In Asia everything that breaks can be repaired easily: shoes, clothes, bicycles, any machinery. Once inside the market, in the area where the seamstresses sew dresses, I showed my shirt to a woman who was putting together a wedding dress with her sewing machine. She glanced at the zipper and sent one of her two employees to buy a new one to sew onto my shirt collar. I sat on a bench to watch the women sew. The opposite stall was a ladies' hairdresser, who was washing a lady's hair; the sink was a large plastic drum. A stocky man approached with a thick wad of old money in his hand. All the stalls were handing him money, which I later learned were the daily market—cleaning fee. The collector asked me, in correct English, what I was doing there. He was friendly and chatty, and named Yam. He said the youngest of the seamstresses thought I was very handsome. I appreciated the compliment as she smiled, blushing. She was just eighteen. While playing with the notes, he invited me to his home for lunch, something he said he did from time to time with tourists. I hesitated but eventually accepted. He would pick me up at one of the market's exits at 11:30 a.m.

After picking me up, he drove me on his bike across the river to his home in Battambang's Muslim neighborhood. He had married a young Buddhist despite his parents' opposition, who in protest didn't attend the wedding. He told me he hardly visited the mosque; he wasn't very religious and drank alcohol regularly. His house was a simple wooden building, with an open floor for cooking and storing tools, and a wooden platform to sit and eat on. The surrounding houses were so close that the concept of a neighborhood was given a new dimension. External stairs reached the first floor, where there was a main room and a bedroom. The neighboring Muslim children came to see me. Some girls covered their hair with scarves; a boy wore a Muslim cap. All were extremely friendly and curious. Yam's wife was young, twenty—three. He was thirty—six, and they had a three—year—old boy who was with his grandparents, and another child was on the way: Yam's wife was seven months pregnant. Yam liked soccer so much he'd named his son Wayne Rooney, after the excellent striker for Manchester United. At first I thought this was a nickname, but the father assured me it was his son's legal name. Yam and I ate a fish soup and a delicious beef curry with rice on the wooden flooring downstairs. His wife remained on the top floor.

Later, he took me on his motorbike to see the ruins of a

small temple about twenty minutes away amidst the beautiful countryside. On the way back, we stopped to watch three men fishing with their hands in a pool a foot deep. It is said that, during the rainy season, Cambodia when viewed from the sky looks like a huge pool full of fish. After the rains, as the rivers recede, many ponds are left behind, forming natural pools ideal for fishing; therefore, it's common to see Cambodians fishing with their hands in those opaque ponds. In a little more than ten minutes, the fishermen threw four large fish at our feet. A woman and her daughter rushed to pick them up and place them in a bag before their frantic shaking could return them to the pond. Yam decided to buy three fish for his parents. It was up to me to carry the fish in a tied plastic bag while the still—living animals were trying to escape their fate. I met Yam's parents, his sister, and also Wayne Rooney, who, fully naked, had a small plastic truck between his feet instead of a soccer ball. After we greeted them all and I gave them the bag with their night's dinner, Yam dropped me off at my hotel but insisted I have dinner at his house. He was very persistent, always in a friendly way.

At the hotel I saw my young driver and asked if he had called the girls we met the previous night. He said that one of them had called earlier, saying she had to work that night in a bar he didn't know but believed was a karaoke. She had invited us to stop by, but the proposal didn't attract me too much, so I preferred to stick with the plan to have dinner with Yam. He picked me up on his motorbike. On the way home I asked him to stop to buy some drinks for dinner—a beer for me, two soft drinks for him and his wife, as in her presence Yam didn't drink alcohol. We had dinner inside, sitting on the floor with the TV on showing a Korean soap opera. This time his wife joined us, but as she didn't speak any English, she concentrated on the TV. Yam told me she was serious because she knew he had another girlfriend. He had met a young girl of twenty, who lost her parents very young, and was very poor. Although she worked as a waitress in a restaurant, she barely made enough to survive. In fact, she was homeless and slept in the restaurant. According to him, he was with her to help her out of pity, and that once committed he could not leave her. At that point I didn't know what to think of him, whether he was being a true Good Samaritan or was just excusing himself without remorse.

When we finished dinner, he said he would like to introduce me to a woman. He told me she was not only beautiful physically but as a person too. I said, of course I would love to meet a woman with those characteristics. She lived nearby but that night was having dinner at a friend's house. It took us a bit to find the address. Once we did, we were invited in to have a beer. Five people—a couple on vacation, the woman I was to meet, and two others—sat on the floor around the remains of a feast. The woman's friend and her husband had just arrived on vacation from the United States, where they lived in California. The woman Yam wanted me to meet was called Sokun, pretty and tall, of dark complexion, with round eyes, high cheekbones, and a wide white smile. She spoke enough English without difficulty. After the beer, we said goodbye, and Sokun escorted us to the bike. Yam asked what I thought of her, if I liked her. I said yes, and we agreed to meet the next day in the afternoon.

We jumped on the motorcycle to go to Sky. On the way, Sokun called Yam to make sure I'd like to see her the following day, and to apologize for not coming with us for a drink. She said she was too drunk to venture out. In Sky we just had a beer, and afterwards I asked Yam to take me to the hotel. On the way, he swerved and stopped at a "massage" place where several scantily dressed women sat outside, waiting for customers. I told Yam I was not interested, but he seemed to want one, and maybe thought I would pay for it. I stood firm and left the women without a customer and Yam dissatisfied. My opinion of him was deteriorating.

Sokun called Yam and agreed to meet up at 6:30 p.m. in the park by the river. She preferred to meet in a public place but after dark so her appointment wouldn't be too visible. Sokun arrived on her motorbike, and we sat on a bench watching a group of women who gathered daily at the park for an aerobics class. We talked about going to dinner together. I exchanged Yam's bike for Sokun's. The restaurant was a large place with live music: a woman brightened up the night with her songs. We sat down and Yam went to talk to a waitress; he had brought us to the restaurant where his young friend worked. We had eel soup, rice, and beef with vegetables. Yam's girlfriend reluctantly sat down to dine with us. She had a sweet and humble smile with a mixture of tenderness and sadness. The image of Yam's wife, seven months pregnant, sitting alone at home worried about her husband's whereabouts didn't stop flashing in my head. I didn't feel guilty about the situation, his being there with me dining with Sokun and that girl instead of his wife—if not me, someone else would have been his excuse—but the memory of that young woman left at home when she needed him the most was souring my dinner. Afterwards, Sokun and I left Yam in the restaurant and went to one of the street bars along the river.

Sokun was thirty–six years old, divorced for twelve years, and had two children, a boy of thirteen and a girl of eleven. She had married at twenty–one, as arranged between her and the groom's parents. She had accepted it, as millions of women in many parts of the world have done and still do. Once married, she suffered tremendously as her husband spent his money in bars and on women, didn't show her any respect, and even beat her regularly. Sokun had decided to divorce him while pregnant with the girl. She cried every day, unhappy, looking at the difficulties that awaited her, a young woman of twenty–four with two children, alone in a country where a divorced woman would probably remain so for the rest of her life. Her husband, as it happened, had not expected the divorce, repented, and came home, asking for forgiveness, crying for her to return. He knew it would be very difficult, if not impossible, to find another woman after the divorce and the bad reputation he would get, in addition to losing the services of a housewife. She, however, could not contemplate being with him, preferring to deal with the difficulties of a dignified solitude. Now she worked at a guesthouse, cleaning and cooking six days a week, for which she earned $100 a month, a salary that had to feed her, her children, and her mother, with whom they lived.

We had just met, but she wanted to know my intentions. The physical attraction between us was obvious, but it seemed that she already harbored dreams of something more than a temporary affair. Honestly, I said that I liked her, but I was going to continue with my travels and couldn't see something serious emerging between us. She received my answer with a face that said, "What an idiot I am, what can I expect from someone who is just passing by and who in a few weeks will be in Vietnam to continue his tour of Asia and then go back to New York." With the record straight, we continued chatting amiably. She took me to my hotel on her motorbike. As I got on she asked me to get closer to her, our bodies perfectly assembled like two puzzle pieces. Before I had the chance of inviting her to come to my room, she asked if she could come up with me. We sat on the bed and I started kissing and caressing her. She withdrew from my advances without any conviction, just retreating an inch, inviting me to follow her. She was in the eternal dilemma between passion and duty. Her body thanked my touches and my kisses, her head tried to neutralize them. I stopped so my desire didn't seem uncontrolled, and waited for her reaction. She got closer to me. She told me how handsome I was and stroked my beard saying she liked to see it but not to touch it. She asked me not to go to Siem Reap the following day as I had planned. I'd already told her I could change my plans and stay an extra day in Battambang; she required certainty that it wouldn't be our only day together. I started kissing her again, this time removing her top. In doing so I found a rope with some ornaments around her waist. She explained that many women carry it; a Buddhist monk had given it to her for protection. That night it also served as a chastity belt because she didn't allow me to continue undressing her. Her mother was waiting for her, and she had to get up early to go to work, reasons that made her leave. After she left, I lay awake on the bed thinking what to do, but decided to stay one more day and see her again.

It was Saturday; I got up late and did little. Sokun worked until 3 p.m., so I called her after lunch and she came to pick me up at the hotel. She was hungry so we went to eat something at White Rose, where they serve the best fruit smoothies I had ever tasted. Then we went to visit her uncle, who lived with his family not far from the hotel. On the way, it started to rain and we got slightly wet on the motorbike. We stayed at her uncle's until the rain eased. Sokun gave some money to her cousin's kids. I suggested going to the Riverside Balcony, a bar on the second floor of a wooden house overlooking the river from a balcony with a balustrade. The rain came back accompanied by a raging wind as we sat at a table by the balustrade. It's a lovely place for enjoying a drink with a beautiful woman. Sokun was very affectionate with me. She kept saying she was going to miss me when I left, wondering if we would ever see each other again, and even suggested coming with me to Siem Reap. Although I enjoyed her company, I realized that the more time we spent together the greater the differences between us would appear. Our worlds were so far apart that, after the mutual discovery phase, the relationship would lack a natural path for development. After the drinks, she took me shopping. I felt she wanted to take advantage of my presence to get a gift. She needed some pants and we stopped at three stores, but she found none that convinced her. However, she fell for a long-sleeved top with a V neckline and fitted waist that suited her. We bargained with the shopkeeper to lower the price, and I bought it for her.

We had dinner and went to the hotel. She called her brother to tell him she'd be spending the night at a friend's house and to avoid talking to her mother, who the previous night had earnestly inquired about her whereabouts, since she had gotten home so late. Sokun behaved like an inexperienced teenager, timid and embarrassed in the nude. Despite her age, she didn't seem to have enjoyed sex, and confessed it'd been an eternity since her last time. Since her divorce she hadn't been interested in any man. She said Cambodian men treated their women badly and therefore were not worthwhile. She looked like a woman so damaged by her disastrous marriage that she mistrusted all men. Her scar was deep, and she had been unable to stop looking at it in the mirror every morning. I felt sad for her, such a beautiful woman and good person stuck in the past without giving herself a second chance in life. Perhaps for that reason, she took this unexpected encounter as her last chance and romanticized it so quickly, almost tinged with despair. The boat to Siem Reap departed at 7 a.m. Sokun helped me fold my clothes and collect my belongings strewn around the room. I gave her $40 to help with the cost of her kids' schooling. We said goodbye in the hotel lobby. She asked me to call her from Siem Reap; I thought best to leave it with the beautiful memory of our only night together.

★ ★ ★

In the dry season the river does not carry enough water for the large boats that make the journey to Siem Reap, so I got on a smaller boat, long and narrow, with around twenty seats occupied almost exclusively by tourists. As we left Battambang behind, we observed those who live in boats on the river enjoying the first swim of the day, brushing their teeth, washing their clothes, or taking water to cook breakfast. Children waved at us while shouting *bye–bye* or *hello*. We couldn't stop taking pictures, fascinated by the aquatic morning routine. Later we encountered fishermen throwing nets in search of their livelihood. When the river narrowed, the boat had to slow down so much that bicycles along the riverbanks passed us by. We saw families living on bamboo platforms raised off the ground, with roofs of cloth or plastic. Later, the river widened, and we passed floating villages of wooden houses. We stopped at one of the villages to have lunch at a small restaurant. After more than five hours, the boat entered Tonle Sap, the largest lake in Southeast Asia. It's actually a lake and a river: During the dry season its depth is drastically reduced and it flows into the Mekong River, with which it is connected. During the monsoon the current changes direction, running from the river into the lake, filling it up. It's a little over a foot deep during the dry season, thirty feet during wet months, when its waters are rich in fish. Because of its importance, UNESCO declared it a Biosphere Reserve in 1997.

Siem Reap is a city dedicated to tourism, thanks to the nearby temples of Angkor, so its city center is packed with hotels, restaurants, cafes, bars, gift shops, and *tuk–tuks* to ferry tourists around. That night I bought a good map of the Angkor temples, and with the help of my Lonely Planet I established a chronological journey to explore them, starting with the Rolous Group, at the first location of the capital of the Khmer Empire in the ninth century. One–day ($20), three–day ($40), and seven–day tickets ($60) were on sale; as I wanted to take my time exploring the temples, I opted for the last. Once purchased, I headed by *tuk–tuk* to see the three major temples in Rolous: Lolei, Preah Ko, and Bakong, dedicated to Lord Shiva and the most imposing, with its five–level central pyramid flanked by eight towers.

The Khmer Empire was founded in 802 when King Jayavarman II created a single kingdom at Angkor and declared himself a god–king. It was a Hindu kingdom in which the figure of Shiva was worshiped. During the reign of Suryavarman I (1002–1050) various elements of Mahayana Buddhism were added to the Hindu worship that had prevailed until then, therefore many of the temples I later visited incorporated Buddhist elements. The next two days I explored Angkor on bike. The first day I visited the east of Angkor, around the vast *baray* (pool of water), but before getting there I approached the southern gate to admire one of the splendid entrances to the central complex, with its bridge lined with statues of warriors. The second day was dedicated to the core of the temple complex, known as Angkor Thom, and the temples around it. I loved Banteay Kdei, which I saw caressed by the morning light. The popular Ta Prohm is spectacular thanks to the giant tree roots that entwine the structure like tentacles climbing the walls and roofs. So full of tourists was the temple that it was almost impossible to take a photo without any of them in it.

Before lunch I got to Baphuon, a gigantic building that was being restored. The west wall is itself a gigantic reclining Buddha, 230 feet long and made of thousands of stones. The sweltering heat was taking its toll on me after several miles of biking and exploring the temples on foot. I arrived at one of the restaurants located within the temple area, not only exhausted but also dehydrated. I ordered a mango smoothie immediately followed by another, then a third, which I gulped down to the surprised look of the waitress.

I waited there for the sun to fall a bit before continuing my visit. The star of the afternoon, and all of Angkor, was Bayon, a temple without equal in the world, with its fifty–four stone towers; the base of each tower is formed of four giant, smiling faces, each facing a different direction: 216 huge, smiling faces that some consider represent King Jayavarman VII, some the bodhisattva Lokesvara (the most widely accepted interpretation nowadays). It was hypnotic to enter Bayon under so many serene gazes, to walk between the towers up to the different levels in order to admire the imposing faces. It's a stunning and unforgettable temple, one of the most amazing places I had ever visited. Before I left, I walked around its outside wall, almost a mile of carvings in low relief, resplendent in their quality. To end the long day, I went to Phnom Bakheng to watch the sunset. It was full of tourists, too many for serene enjoyment.

After the exhausting couple of days on two wheels, I took a rest day in Siem Reap. The following day, I hired a *tuk–tuk* and visited Angkor Wat, the largest religious building in the world, the building that all visitors come to see. Built in honor of Vishnu by Suryavarman II (reigned 1112–1152), its three–level central structure and its tower 180 feet high as well as its bas–reliefs on the outer wall are exquisite. I spent most of the afternoon, when the sun embellished them with its warm softness, photographing the reliefs in detail. As the sunrise over Angkor Wat is one of the experiences there not to be missed, I arranged for a *tuk–tuk* to pick me up at 5:30 the following morning. I arrived at the temple in time for breakfast: an omelet sandwich and coffee at one of the many stalls that welcome the sleepy tourists. I caught the sunrise with the silhouette of the temple between the nascent sun and my camera. After sunrise, I visited two spectacular reliefs: the Terrace of Elephants and the Leper King, and one of the temples that struck me most: Preah Khan, a vast complex of well–preserved buildings thought to have been a Buddhist university.

Zhou Daguan, the Chinese envoy to Angkor in 1296, said it was the richest city in Southeast Asia. The empire encompassed not only current Cambodia but also much of Thailand, Laos, and southern Vietnam. Its success was not based on international trade but on agriculture and a series of canals and water reservoirs that formed a complex irrigation system, including the use of the water–level rise of Tonle Sap during the wet season that allowed up to three harvests per year. At its peak, between the eleventh and thirteenth centuries, it is estimated that Angkor had a million people at a time when London had barely fifty thousand. The empire collapsed when some regional leaders questioned the king's supreme authority, thus damaging its economy and making it vulnerable to military attacks from Thailand.

On the way to Phnom Penh, I decided to stop in Kampong Thom and visit a number of ancient temples from the seventh century that were precursors of the glorious Angkor. I stayed in a guesthouse near the market and hired a driver with his motorbike to take me to the temples the next morning at 6:30, to avoid the heat and return in time for a shower before taking the bus to the Cambodian capital. The afternoon I arrived was spent walking around the market, next to which I had dinner at a popular restaurant. Beside my guesthouse stood a hotel of the same name and owner on whose top floor was a karaoke. It was time to visit one and find out what was cooking there. I went up the elevator, the only one in town, to the fifth floor. I was hoping to find a bar with people drinking, young women accompanying clients or waiting for them to arrive, and a reserved area for karaoke; however, what I found was a corridor with doors to rooms, as on any hotel floor, with a couple of long benches on which a score of young Cambodian women were chatting or watching television, and a tiny desk with a man behind it. There was no bar, no music, and no customers in sight. It was immediately clear that the only option was to choose a girl and go with her to one of the rooms.

When I got off the elevator, all eyes rested on me without surprise or interest. All the women paused in their conversation for a few seconds to see who had landed, but once they saw me, they ignored me as though I was invisible. When I told the man behind the counter that I just wanted to have a beer, he, looking surprised, asked me if I didn't want a girl. I said no, and he gave me a can of Angkor beer, which I paid for instantly, then went to the balcony behind the main room. On the balcony, several girls chatted in the cool of the evening breeze. Most of them wore very short skirts or pants, their faces had on too much makeup, and their hair and wrists were adorned with clips and bracelets, all in bright colors. Although impossible to be certain, I feel sure many were underage. Due to their youth, small size, and clothes, they didn't seem more than little girls who wanted to be women ahead of their time. I didn't talk to any, nor did they seem interested in me; it was a place for local clientele. I drank the beer in twenty minutes, enjoying the breeze, and left. When the elevator doors opened, a couple of youngsters with blond hair and light eyes appeared; I was not the only curious tourist in Kampong Thom that night.

In Phnom Penh I stayed in one of the hotels overlooking the Tonle Sap River, the tourist area of the city. I visited the National Museum, where what attracted me the most were the Angkorian sculptures of Buddhas and Hindu deities. From there I went to the Royal Palace with the Silver Pagoda, which was somewhat disappointing after having visited Bangkok's, more splendid in all respects. At night I took a couple of drinks in the fabulous Foreign Correspondents Club, on the second floor of a corner building with windows open to the promenade and the river, where I chatted with a Spanish couple who were going to Vietnam on a boat on the Mekong. The most interesting visits, however, had nothing to do with art or religious buildings, but with the brutal atrocities committed by the Pol Pot regime during the control of the country by the Khmer Rouge between 1975 and 1979. I went first to the Tuol Sleng prison, known at the time as S–21, which is now a museum dedicated to the memory of the genocide. Days later I bought the book *Voices S–21*, by David Chandler, who had access to the prison records. Much of the information about S–21 I got from his book.

Tuol Sleng is a former elementary and middle school that was converted into a detention and torture center, the most important of the Pol Pot regime, on the same day as the communist victory: April 17, 1975. It is 650 yards long and 440 yards wide, and totally enclosed. Inside its walls there are four three—story buildings accessible at the front by walkways covered with wire to prevent prisoners from committing suicide by jumping. Building A, used primarily for those accused of resistance to the regime, was converted into a series of torture rooms with glass windows to keep the sounds of torture from reaching outside. Each room had a bed, a blanket, a pillow, and a metal bucket or plastic container as a toilet. Buildings B, C, and D contained the prisoners' cells. The original classrooms on the first floor had been divided into narrow brick cells, the second floor classrooms into wooden cells. The rooms on the top floor were not even divided into cells, and prisoners were crowded into them and slept lying on the floor next to each other in two opposite rows, their heads against the wall and their feet fastened to metal turnstiles to prevent movement. In the courtyard a wooden pole used before by students for physical exercise became an instrument of torture. Prisoners were attached to it, their hands tied behind their backs, and hung upside down until they lost consciousness. Other torture practices, besides lack of food and the general conditions of the prison, included beatings, cigarette burns, electric shocks to various body parts, nail removal, needle sticks, water immersion, plastic bag suffocation, water drops on the forehead, and being forced to eat excrement and drink urine. The number of prisoners was 154 in 1975, 2,250 in 1976, 2,350 in 1977, and 5,765 in 1978. The prisoners at S—21 usually stayed there between two and four months, between six and seven if they were political prisoners. Every day, ten to forty prisoners were mounted on trucks and taken to Choeung Ek (known as The Killing Fields), where they were murdered. Of all the prisoners who passed through S—21, only seven survived. The head of the prison was Kang Keck Iev, known as Comrade Duch, who in early 2010 was being tried by a court in

Cambodia with the support of the United Nations. Duch was sentenced to thirty-five years in July 2010.

To end the visit I sat on one of the patio benches. Where, decades ago, children and youngsters had played during recess, their cheerful voices had turned into inaudible shouts of despair in a deserted city. A school where the skills needed to thrive in the future were acquired, where teachers taught history, science, and language to their students, became, for a few dark years, the opposite, a center of terror, suffering, and cruelty, where human life was worthless, where instead of laying the foundations for a successful life, everyone who arrived there saw their existence disappear into despair. It was my first time at such place. I have never visited the former Nazi concentration camps in Europe, so the visit to Tuol Sleng produced in me a feeling of disgust towards the human race. How is it possible that humans can commit such atrocities? It seemed impossible that while I went to school and played on the playground with my friends, thousands of Cambodians were transported to that school, their lives exterminated after intense torture. It seemed unreal that this had been happening while I was enjoying a happy childhood.

A couple of days later, to end my exploration of the Khmer Rouge's terror, I went to Choeung Ek, located about nine miles southwest of Phnom Penh. Leaving my hotel, I hired a man with his motorbike to take me to The Killing Fields. It's estimated that around 20,000 people were executed at Choeung Ek. Inside it, 129 mass graves were found. Prisoners who arrived there were ordered to squat or kneel next to one of the graves blindfolded and with their hands tied behind their back, before being beaten with an ax or a hoe in the head. Their throats were slashed with a knife afterwards to ensure death. Bullets were too expensive. When the place was discovered after the defeat of the Khmer Rouge at the hands of the Vietnamese army, an open pit was found there containing 450 bodies, another with more than a hundred headless bodies, a third one was full of naked women's bodies. Alongside the last pit there was a tree against which women's babies were killed. The executioners took the babies by their feet and smashed their heads against the trunk. When The Killing Fields were found, there were the remains of babies' hair and brains embedded in the tree's bark. Today there's a memorial containing about 9,000 skulls and a small museum memorializing the barbarism committed there.

On the way back to Phnom Penh, the driver told me how, when he was ten years old, he saw the Khmer Rouge kill his father not far from where we were. He, in terror, hid, afraid of being executed too. After arriving home, he returned with his mother to look for his father's body but couldn't find it. His mother believes that one of the skulls at Choeung Ek is her husband's, and they go there once a year to remember him. A few days later I bought the book *First, They Killed My Father*, by Loung Ung, a fabulous and painful memoir of the Khmer Rouge period. Nine years old when terror took up residence in Cambodia, she recounts the odyssey of her family in forced flight from Phnom Penh, the living conditions in agricultural communities, the execution of her father, and her escape to the West via Thailand. I burst into tears on more than one occasion while reading it. I at least had many memories of my father, many and good; both the driver and the writer didn't have time to accumulate more than a few.

It was time to forget the Khmer Rouge's terrible vestiges by taking a trip to the Cambodian coast. I went by bus to Sihanoukville, where I stayed on Serendipity Beach. The next day I went by boat for a couple of days to Koh Russei (Bamboo Island), a tiny island with only two places to stay. On the western side of the island there are a number of basic bungalows, a dormitory for twelve people, plus a bar and restaurant. The bungalows were already booked so I had to sleep in the dormitory. Koh Russei is a beautiful island where there is nothing to do but swim and relax. It's so small you can barely walk more than half an hour before you have two choices: turn back or go searching for Davy Jones's locker. It was an effective antidote to the pain the visits in Phnom Penh had inflicted on me. A swim in the ocean, drying out on the beach under the sun, reading in a hammock, dining outdoors. How wonderful a relaxing day could be! The beautiful and peaceful sunset appeared almost without my realizing it.

During the afternoon I devoured in one go *The Diving Bell and the Butterfly*. I had seen Julian Schnabel's film based on it and recalled the story, but I bought Jean–Dominique Bauby's book to read his thoughts during his terrible disease. The story, as a film, had been excellent. Reading it, you fall in love with life. I believe those who have had to deal at an early age with the loss of a loved one or a serious illness tend to value life more than those who have never suffered anything similar. Perspective is needed to evaluate our existence, and unexpected suffering can be a magical reference, to be used daily. Those insignificant problems that paralyze many are seen as so many minor stones in our shoes, and a proper weight is given to most issues. Maturity takes years to settle in fully (if it ever does), but experiencing those tragic life events can provide an effective shortcut to it. In my case, the memories of both the tachycardia and my father's death remind me that life can change drastically at any time.

Thanks to the air conditioning in Phnom Penh, I had gotten a sore throat a few days earlier that reached its zenith during my first night in Koh Russei. With it, a tiny, almost imperceptible cyst that had been accompanying me on my right sideburn for two years had gotten infected and grown in size. This was the last thing I wanted after my experience in Nepal. I had some antibiotics in my health kit that I started taking twice a day, hoping it would help improve both my throat and the erupting cyst (the only shadow over my paradise stay of two days of total relaxation).

Before going to Vietnam, I made two final stops in Cambodia, the first in Kampot, an interesting town of French colonial buildings, some abandoned, others in restoration, and the capital of the province of the same name, famous for its excellent black pepper. It was really pleasant to stroll through the streets by the river, although the heat of the day was hardly inviting. The town offers many cute restaurants and bars, perhaps too many for the few people there. My throat had substantially improved with the antibiotics, but not the infected cyst. I considered going to a doctor, but decided to continue with the antibiotics and seek medical care in Ho

Chi Minh City.

My last stop in Cambodia was Kep, a place created by the French to enjoy the seaside. More than a village, Kep is a meeting point with the sea, a place where low green mountains complement the sea's beauty. Many of the old French villas were still standing. With the arrival of the Khmer Rouge they were abandoned, then sacked. Some have been replaced by new villas, and many plots had been enclosed by stone walls without any obvious construction going on inside. Apparently, the plots belonged to men in the military and the government who were waiting for growth in the area before selling them at high prices. Undoubtedly, Kep is a place to develop. In the future yachts will dock at a modern marina, expensive restaurants and bars will entertain wealthy customers, and large villas will host rich Cambodians. Maybe it'll be a while for all of that to arrive, but Kep is set fair to become an opulent seaside resort.

The western walk I took along the beach reminded me of the Paseo Nuevo, my favorite place in San Sebastian, although the lack of roughness of this sea allowed me to enjoy it closer than I ever could the Bay of Biscay at home. Unconfined by any protective seawall, the small waves splashed my feet. I sat on the sidewalk, my feet hanging over the rocks, to watch the sunset. A young couple did the same, a family arrived with their dinner in plastic containers, and others simply walked or passed by on their bicycles or motorbikes while the fishing boats left the harbor. It was a simple but beautiful moment, perfect to be thankful for being alive.

MOTORBIKES, CAFES & COMMUNISM

"A good traveler has no fixed plans and is not intent on arriving." —Lao Tzu

"The earth belongs to anyone who stops for a moment, gazes, and goes on his way." —Sidonie-Gabrielle Colette

The southernmost border crossing between Cambodia and Vietnam links the towns of Prek Chak and Xa Xia. The bus from Kep carried only seven tourists to Vietnam that morning, and, having no authorization to operate in Vietnamese territory, it stopped on the Cambodian side of the fence marking the border, where we got off and crossed the border on foot. After receiving a Cambodian exit stamp, we walked towards Vietnam. Halfway across, a high, wide gate with yellow letters on a red background and a mast displaying a red flag with a yellow five-pointed star welcomed us. We had to fill a form about our health status, to identify possible symptoms of swine flu. The officer in charge demanded $1 per person, and although I smiled sarcastically when he asked for it, I ended up paying, as it was not worth jeopardizing entry into the country for such a tiny amount. The notes ended up in one of his pockets. The officer responsible for stamping our entry visas was at lunch. While we waited for him to come back, Cambodians and Vietnamese crossed the border on their motorbikes and bicycles without any formality. After our passports were stamped, a van waited to take us to Ha Tien pier, from which we departed at 1 p.m. by fast boat to Phu Quoc, Vietnam's largest island, even though, ironically, it stands closer to the Cambodian coast than to Vietnam's.

In Phu Quoc we docked at a 500-foot-long pier occupied by an army of motorbikes waiting for passengers. A van picked us up to cross the island from east to west, to an area south of Duong Dong called Long Beach, the most popular beach in Phu Quoc, where I stayed in a bungalow near the sea. To explore the island I rented a motorbike for five dollars a day, one of the typical 125cc Honda models seen all over Southeast Asia. I had never ridden a bike with gears before. Shifting gears was done with the left foot, though a clutch was not needed. Adjusting the accelerator and controlling the speed in the busiest stretches took a little getting used to, but once I crossed Duong Dong, the journey was easy, despite a dirty track. I came first to a charming fishing village. After that, I reached a long, deserted beach, where I stopped for a swim. No one was there: a paradise almost a mile long, all to myself. The water was warm, the slope so gradual I had to walk out far to reach deep waters. It was wonderful to be in such a beautiful place alone, with no more noise than the sea, and the only distraction the beauty surrounding me. I continued with my motorized expedition to the next cove, where another beach of similar size welcomed me: another stop on the beach to abandon myself to the sumptuousness of the blue sea. It was a day of adventure on the bike and relaxation on the beaches. I wondered how long it would take those two beaches to become populated with noisy hotels and tourists. A resort was being built nearby, and the main road from Duong Dong was being prepared for paving. I felt fortunate to have enjoyed it before it was fully developed.

I went back to Duong Dong before sunset, coated in dust from head to toe. I parked the bike next to the sea inlet, crossed one of two bridges over the river, and walked through the market. The heat and light from the sun beat gently against the stalls looking west, tanning them with a warm tone ideal for photography. I mounted my Nikon with the 85mm lens and shot uninhibitedly the stalls, their vendors, the goods, and the customers. These last came on motorbikes, didn't get off to place their orders, collected their shopping, and paid the shopkeeper before accelerating away. The street was narrow and long, following the river, and I had to be careful not to be run over or hit a biker with my backpack. In the evening, after washing off the dust under the shower, I returned to Duong Dong for dinner at one of the restaurants that are mounted along the streets daily at sunset. I ordered shrimp and clams on the grill, with a beer. Delicious dinner, wonderful day.

My cyst was still infected. Perhaps the swelling had diminished slightly, but it was clear I had to see a doctor. I read my Lonely Planet's section with information about healthcare in Vietnam, and decided to continue my exploration of southern Vietnam, then, in a few days, go to a medical center in Ho Chi Minh City.

I left Phu Quoc by fast boat, heading to Rach Gia, and from there by bus reached Can Tho, the largest city in the Mekong Delta, where I wanted to visit a couple of floating markets on the famous river. In Can Tho, I got a room in the Tay Ho Hotel, which faces a tall, standing statue of Ho Chi Minh that dominates the river walk. With the fall of the sun, the promenade flooded with people, both locals and tourists, and street restaurants sprouted quickly under the mild temperature. I had dinner at one of them: grilled calamari that I cooked myself. The waiters brought me a bowl of burning coals with a tray of metal rods on which to cook. The squid was seasoned with a chili sauce. It was fabulous to dine outdoors along the river. I liked the charm of Can Tho.

The next morning a woman on her motorbike waited for me at 6 a.m. to take me to the pier to board a boat and visit two floating markets and the delta canals. I shared the long narrow boat typical of the area with two young women, one Canadian, the other Turkish, both based in Geneva. The driver let his two daughters board as well. We reached the first and largest of the floating markets, Cai Rang, where we were received by a small boat with a couple selling breakfast, a nautical coffee. My companions ordered a couple of coffees and bought drinks for the girls. There were all kinds of boats selling fruits and vegetables. The floating markets were once essential for people who lived on the river (there are some that still live on boats on the river) or with houses facing the water and far from villages, but due to economic development, they would certainly wane. We visited another market a few miles to the south, located at the junction of two rivers. We bought a watermelon while waiting for the tide to rise to get into one of the narrower canals of the delta. Once in the canal, we got stuck and the pilot had to step down into the water to release the propeller from the mud.

Before arriving in Ho Chi Minh City (which is sometimes shortened to "Ho Chi Minh"), I spent a night in the delta countryside near the town of Ben Tre. In the guesthouse I hired a boat to tour the canals. A young man of eighteen was my guide. Just a few meters from the house there was a canal hidden between the thick vegetation and the boat tied up waiting. As soon as we parted, we entered a tunnel of beautiful palm trees outlining the direction the boat was taking. Images of Vietnam War movies with soldiers walking in water up to their chests and their arms raised above their heads came to my mind. We visited the beautiful and peaceful Turtle Island, a small hidden paradise of little houses, fruit trees, and flowering shrubs, where I walked for nearly an hour on a path that circled it. I asked my guide where he was from and if he had a girlfriend. He told me he lived in Ben Tre with his aunt, although he was from Ho Chi Minh, and that it was impossible to have a girlfriend because he was poor. His work earned him just $30 a month, so he could not buy a motorbike, a phone, or the clothes young Vietnamese women demanded today. The Cambodian "no money, no honey" was also valid in communist Vietnam.

The next morning I rode a bicycle to explore the fields of the delta. First I stopped at a stall to have *pho bo*, the traditional noodle soup that almost all Vietnamese have each morning. Three children turned up, with charming smiles, saying "Hello. How are you? Nice to meet you. What's your name?" The three went home and returned with their English books. I helped them say a few basic words and phrases, and photographed them posing with their books, proud to say a few things in English to a tourist.

After the communist victory in the Vietnam War, Saigon was renamed Ho Chi Minh City in honor of the victorious communist leader. A city like Saigon has much more history than the most charismatic person, no matter how important, therefore renaming it made no sense. Saigon continues today to be called Saigon except in official documents. Imagine the British renaming London *Winston Churchill City*, or the French calling Paris *Ville Charles de Gaulle*. What are you doing for Easter? We're going shopping to Winston Churchill City. How are you celebrating your wedding anniversary? Romantic weekend at Ville Charles de Gaulle. Absurd. A landmark like the Parisian airport named in honor of the general was appropriate; a city with its great history wasn't. Therefore, I will use the name Saigon hereinafter to refer to Ho Chi Minh City, as I did while in Vietnam.

The entrance to Saigon was spectacular, through a long avenue flanked by towering trees of naked trunks and rounded foliage at their tops dwarfing the surrounding buildings, and motorcycles dominating the streets, moving in droves to protect themselves from the increasingly present cars. The latter had to adapt to the law of the majority and circulated carefully, honking to move through the swarming motorbikes whenever they found a breach. They moved like hippos surrounded by gazelles. The van that brought me from Ben Tre finished its journey some distance from the city center, so I jumped onto a "gazelle" to take me to Pham Ngu Lao, Saigon's backpacker area, where I intended to stay. The driver deftly slipped his vehicle through the dense traffic. Accurate braking, lateral movements as smooth as unexpected, crossing recklessly in front of cars, left and right turns ignoring traffic lights. Riding on a motorbike in Saigon is an adventure that every visitor must experience.

I went by motorbike to the International Medical Centre, next to Notre Dame Cathedral. The waiting room was almost full. I had to sit on a stool with my back against the wall. While waiting to be called, I started reading *Catfish & Mandala*. Its author, Andrew X. Pham, a Vietnamese who immigrated as a child with his family to the U.S. after the unification of Vietnam, recounts his experiences when he returned to Vietnam for the first time, with a plan to cross the country by bike, visiting the places of his childhood. *Viet Kieu* is the name given to these exiles when returning to Vietnam; the Vietnamese consider them rich (they expect gifts from them), but also traitors for fleeing, and, of course, they are viewed with suspicion by the communist authorities. The glimpse of a woman's long legs in blue jeans arriving on a motorcycle lifted my eyes from the book where I was sitting in sight of the door, which was open to the street. As she entered, I looked at her, she looked at me, turned left to go to the bathroom, and turned her head back to me as she walked away. She was not very pretty but had a great figure.

Back in the waiting room, she crossed it entirely to sit on the stool closest to mine despite others being free. Noticing the lump on my face, she said that maybe we had the same condition, and she showed me a slight swelling on the left side of her face. She seemed to suffer from an ear infection. She spoke English with a slight French accent. She was married, had a boy five years old and a girl of one. She didn't work and devoted her time to her children's care, but was studying English and French in order to compete with younger workers once she was ready to return to the workforce. Her husband was engaged in the food export and import business, mainly rice and coffee. She was from Hanoi, where the rest of her family lived. She told me that there they were more traditional than in Saigon. Her parents, always thinking about saving for their children, didn't even dare to take vacations. Saigon is the city of business, Hanoi the city of political power. Southerners are more open, always ready to have fun and spend money, than the conservative northerners. Like many I met during my trip, particularly women, she was surprised I was travelling alone. Don't you get bored? Don't you feel lonely? Don't you have any friends? She'd be lost without her husband. When she learned I lived in New York, we talked about successful women who focus on their careers instead of starting a family, and how some end up alone, too late to conceive, making it difficult to get a life partner. She said that, thanks to the television series *Sex and the City*, she knew how some American women thought. She even knew a woman like that in Saigon. She confessed she wanted her son to learn to play the piano, but he wanted to be a rapper. How difficult, sometimes impossible, to get children to inherit their parent's dreams! The doctor called my name and she joked: "Shouldn't women go first?" I enjoyed talking to her. She was friendly, interesting, attractive, honest, and with a good sense of humor. If she hadn't been married, I would have asked her out without hesitation.

The doctor was French and spoke a little Spanish. After listening to my explanation about the evolution of my infection, he sent me to see a maxillofacial surgeon at the Franco—Vietnamese Hospital without charging me for the brief consultation. On leaving, I wished my waiting companion a speedy recovery before going to the hospital, of course on a motorcycle. The hospital was in the south of the city, a very modern hospital with a bright lobby accompanied by a charming cafe. I checked in at reception and was given a patient card before seeing the specialist. How effective! The surgeon was Vietnamese and spoke French better than English, and like most of the staff, sported a blue, white, and red flag on his chest as proof of it (the hospital was founded by French doctors). The surgeon confirmed the diagnosis of infected cyst, prescribed antibiotics for four days, and scheduled me for Friday to remove it. The operation would take place under general anesthesia, and I might be ready to leave the same evening. Then they took a scan of the lump and extracted a blood sample. I spoke to the anesthesiologist, also to the finance department to go over my insurance, and finally went to the drugstore to buy antibiotics. I had to put down a deposit to secure the operation and bed availability. I spent almost the whole day there. My memories of the hospital in Kathmandu were still very fresh, and on the way back to my hotel my mood dived. My new obstacle was not as serious, and I seemed to be in a much better hospital, but the thoughts of the general anesthesia for a couple of hours, the chance of infections and complications, and the insurance paperwork didn't lead me to feel euphoric. At least Saigon seemed much more interesting than Kathmandu.

Until the day of the operation I visited the most important places in the city. I started with the Reunification Palace, where the last government of South Vietnam was located, and which has been maintained as it was on April 30, 1975, after the capture of Saigon by North Vietnamese forces. It is an interesting building with its meeting rooms, the offices of the president and his office staff, as well as rooms where the president and his staff followed the evolution of the war, with displays of maps, phones, and radio sets that were in use at the time. The next day, I went to the Remnants War Museum, a museum about the history of the Vietnam War, which provides detailed information on the end of the Second World War, the withdrawal of Japanese troops after their surrender as a result of the atomic bombs at Hiroshima and Nagasaki, the declaration of independence by Ho Chi Minh, the French effort to recover their Asian colonies, American aid to France to stop communist expansion in the region, the 1954 Geneva declaration agreeing to elections throughout Vietnam in July 1956 to create a single state, opposition to them by the government of Ngo Dinh Diem in the south of the country, and the consequent escalation of the war until the communist victory in 1975. I visited sections devoted to the consequences of the genocidal use of bombs with napalm and Agent Orange, the total volume of bombs dropped on Vietnam and Cambodia by the U.S. military, the total number of troops used, as well as the war's total cost.

The museum was really interesting for its extensive information, but something was missing. As the name clearly states, it's a museum about the war and its consequences, but information on the communist government's crackdown after the unification of Vietnam was completed on those who had supported or worked for the South Vietnamese government or the Americans was absent. As recounted in *Catfish & Mandala*, the author's father, like thousands of Vietnamese, was jailed for being considered a supporter of the former regime and put to forced labor. He survived thanks to his wife's family connections in the communist army. Despite the lack of data, some people estimate that at least 100,000 southern Vietnamese were killed immediately after the communist victory, to which we should add all those who perished in the re−education camps, where between one and two million Vietnamese were sent, plus those who died trying to escape by sea from the communist ferocity. The museum, with impunity, ignored this other legacy of war, perhaps not surprisingly since history is usually written by the victors.

Friday arrived, and although the operation was scheduled at 9 a.m., I had to be in the hospital at 6 a.m. The insurance letter guaranteeing payment of the procedure hadn't yet arrived despite my numerous calls. It was the Easter holiday, which seemed to complicate things, so I had to pay the entire cost of the operation. I settled in a double room shared with a Vietnamese man. He was called on time; I had to wait until 10 a.m. to be taken to the operating room. Once again the strange and dreaded trip, staring at the ceiling of the corridors of a hospital, those moments of fear, hope, and vulnerability, a trip that was short but intense. The operating theater was packed with modern machines, in contrast to Kathmandu's, so basic and bare. The doctor examined the lump and made marks on it with a marker. A nurse pierced one of the fine veins of my left hand. The anesthetist appeared to place an oxygen mask on my face at the same time the knockout fluid entered my body. An excruciating pain in my left forearm came as a surprise. The anesthesiologist told me this was the result of irritation in my vein on contact with the anesthesia. Soon I felt groggy and then . . . I woke up slowly in a recovery room. My consciousness was short–lived, it came and went; I wanted to wake up, but it wasn't yet time.

Fully awake, already back in my room, I felt tired, so I took a three–hour nap. Later, I turned my phone on and saw a couple of messages from my friend David. He and his wife, Lisa, should have arrived in Saigon a couple of days before as part of their vacation in Vietnam. The previous day I had sent an email telling him about my medical situation. The first message from David said they had come to see me at noon, the second that they were now on their way. I met David (a Madrileño who says "güigki" instead of "whiskey") in London where he'd arrived as a result of a job transfer by Air France, the company he worked for in Madrid. In Air France's London office he met Lisa, a charming, petite Swedish blonde who followed him to Paris when he was transferred to Air France's headquarters a few years later. They married in the outskirts of Stockholm in the summer of 2005, a wedding I keep in very fond memory. My gift had been an album of black–and–white photos I had taken of the most emotional moments of the wedding.

In addition to his passion for his wife, David has two

main passions: soccer and the band U2. Two of my strongest memories of him are precisely related to these passions we share. In 2000, while both of us were living in London, there was a Champions League match between Manchester United and Real Madrid at Old Trafford. As on many soccer evenings, several friends went to watch the game in the Walkabout, a huge bar behind the Temple tube station. On those occasions, Walkabout is filled with hundreds of professionals fleeing nearby offices to drink a few pints of beer with colleagues, watching the game. Fernando Redondo, Real Madrid's fabulous Argentinian midfielder escaped to the left flank, a place totally foreign to him, and when cornered there, he invented a heel pass that got the ball behind Manchester's defender without his seeing it. Then Redondo ran to the goal line and put the ball on a plate for Raul to score. David, a Real Madrid supporter (his father had actually played for Real Madrid) climbed onto a chair, and there, in the middle of the huge English crowd, he began shouting ecstatically: *Toma! Qué Golazo! Qué Golazo! Toma ya!* And so he went on, for an eternity. I also celebrated the goal, but with my feet on the floor and quietly, since the English can be somewhat belligerent in soccer matters, especially after a few pints. If looks could kill, David would have fallen, struck down by the sudden–death glares of those English eyes, because practically the whole bar had turned towards the crazy man from Madrid. Unforgettable. One of the last memories I have of my father is also of a soccer match of Manchester United in the Champions League at Old Trafford, this time against Deportivo La Coruña. The Spanish team deployed their high quality to beat the mighty English team 3–2. My father followed the game from his hospital bed while I sat on it at his side. On the one hand, I enjoyed a great game of soccer as I had done many times with my father; on the other, I had a sense of deep sadness because I knew it would be our last one together.

As for U2, after my move to New York I got two tickets to their concert at Madison Square Garden in October 2005. It was the Vertigo Tour, and when I invited David, he didn't hesitate for a moment to take a couple of days off and fly free on Air France to New York, even though he had already seen the concert twice, in Paris and Madrid. The start with "City of Blinding Lights" and the vertical curtains illuminated by thousands of bulbs recreating the streets of New York was unbeatable. We had a great time singing and jumping all night. That's David, a spontaneous and passionate guy, and a great friend.

We agreed that I would pick them up at their hotel the following day to go to dinner after they returned from their day trip to the Mekong Delta. I spent the night in the hospital, which meant the insurance would pay for the operation directly and the hospital would reimburse me for the cost. I left the hospital after breakfast and went by taxi to my hotel. The stitches would adorn my face for six days. Meanwhile I had to disinfect them twice a day with a solution that, in turn, I flushed with another solution before covering the stitches with Vaseline.

When I arrived at their hotel, only David came down; Lisa was suffering from a slight fever and preferred to rest at the hotel before they were to spend a few days at the beach. David and I had dinner on a nearby terrace. After a couple of drinks, we went looking for a night bar with good atmosphere. We stopped at a couple of them before being recommended to go to Apocalypse Now, a popular bar and disco. The place was packed; it was Saturday night. We had to fight to reach the bar, in true Spanish style. While David went to the bathroom, a young Vietnamese girl came by, saying she wanted to spend the night with me. I asked her for how much; she was as interested in money as she was direct, and asked me for $100. Very expensive! I don't pay for sex. How much you give me? Sorry, I do not pay for sex. And she disappeared as quickly as she'd come. I mentioned it to David, and we began to look in more detail at the women in the bar. Many of them were dressed provocatively, too much really, desperately seeking to arouse desire and fill the piggy bank.

Saigon is, in that respect, a young but cheeky Bangkok. Every night since my arrival I had been offered women several times. Sometimes a motorcycle with two beautiful girls, sometimes a *lady–boy*, stopped next to me: "Lady, Massage, Boom–Boom" was the advertising message. "Very cheap, very cheap: $30." And, definitely, it was cheap. At other times, it was the motorbike driver: "Do you want lady tonight? Very young, very cheap: $30." Which must include his fee. One afternoon I was having coffee at a table by the cafe window when my eyes accidentally met those of a woman walking by, who then, assuming a nonexistent interest, leaned against the glass, saying, "You and me boom–boom." On another occasion, as I was arriving at my hotel, a girl next to a street vendor asked me where I was going; when I said to my hotel, pointing toward the entry, she shouted, "I can come with you?" As in Bangkok, there were many old Western men with beautiful young Vietnamese dining or having a drink in an arrangement as common as it is old. However, I didn't fall into the daily temptation; the Thai experience had been enough.

The semicolon key on my laptop had been stuck for several days. I removed it to see if there was anything underneath it, but didn't see anything unusual. The problem was getting worse, and sometimes I could not type the password to log in, so I went to the local Asus office to make use of their global guarantee. The office, located on the eighth floor of an office building, looked more like a trendy bar than a repair shop. Behind the counter two attractive young ladies cared for clients. As I sat down I was offered a bottle of cold water. At first, I was asked if I could leave the notebook for a couple of days, and at my refusal they asked me to wait. A few minutes later, my notebook was returned with a new keyboard. Sign here, please, sir. Fantastic service, totally unexpected in a communist country.

On the way there I had seen a cafe with a terrace and a Wi–Fi sign on the window, very common in most Vietnamese cafes. I sat down, ordered a black coffee with ice, and turned on the laptop, now that I could use it without difficulty. The waitress, tall and skinny, with long hair tied in a ponytail and a white miniskirt over long legs and a slightly transparent black shirt, apologized, saying they had a technical problem and the Wi–Fi didn't work. I was the only customer on the terrace, and soon she sat down next to me to practice her English with a pronunciation somewhat difficult to follow. Her name was Phuong, she was twenty–two, from the Mekong Delta, and, in addition to working as a waitress every day until 3 p.m., was a teacher of Korean. She also spoke some Japanese and was learning English. She was so nice and determined to learn languages that I invited her for coffee that afternoon to practice. She immediately accepted, asked for my hotel's address, and said she would pick me up at 6 p.m.

She came on a motorcycle escorted by a young man. At first I thought he had just brought her, but it turned out he was her cousin, her chaperon for our meeting. It wasn't surprising that a girl her age was cautious about meeting up with a foreign stranger. Her cousin did not speak any English, so as she and I chatted, he remained like a soldier invisible in a sentry box. Phuong brought her English dictionary and a notebook to write in case our pronunciations couldn't be reconciled. When asked if she had a boyfriend, she said she didn't want one because she didn't have much free time, and in her spare time she just wanted to study English. I invited both of them to dinner. They took me to a restaurant set up inside the owner's home, with a few tables on the sidewalk outside and several in the family's living room, with photos of grandparents on the walls. We had boiled rice with beef and vegetables, a small bowl of vegetable soup, and iced tea for 70,000 *dongs* (less than four dollars). Phuong gave me her phone number, and I thought about calling her if my stay in Saigon was prolonged due to my health.

I noticed a little swelling in the upper end of the scar that worried me, though I thought it might be normal. When I went back to the hospital, the doctor examined the area, gently removed the stitches, explored the swelling, and concluded I must take antibiotics again and come back in four days, since the incision seemed to be infected. What a frustration! It was only four days, and in the meantime I could go to the beach—but the bus journey of over four hours there and back didn't attract me at all, so I remained in Saigon, enjoying its cafes and restaurants, writing, and going out for a drink in the evenings.

Many evenings I walked the park along Pham Ngu Lao Street. At that time of the day, the park welcomes exercisers out for a brisk walk, badminton players in the park's courts, and dozens of women attending the daily aerobics class. The park also has several small kiosks where classes for different dance styles take place. On my first afternoon visiting the park I stopped by one of them, where several couples were dancing to a tango song sung in Vietnamese. Also young students looking for tourists to practice their English on come to the park. One afternoon two girls invited me to sit with them to speak in English; one was a student of economics, the other studied accounting. I agreed willingly. I love the dynamic attitude toward learning that some young Asians show, the initiative they take to alleviate their lack of resources, and I chatted with them about my travels, my country, and me for half an hour. Finally, when night settles over the park, physical activity turns to the emotional, and the park welcomes loving couples to its benches. When the benches are occupied, many couples simply embrace on their motorbikes, loving on wheeled benches.

I took advantage of my break in Saigon to visit the dentist. I found online a clinic with good references, asked about their rates, and made an appointment. The young dentist diligently cleaned every one of my still full set of teeth for only $40. Health tourism is booming. Asian and Latin American countries are becoming regular destinations for Western patients requiring procedures that are relatively cheap there but expensive in their own countries. Globalization has no respite, and outsourcing and offshoring will continue to grow until the cost differential is reduced sufficiently to make them inefficient. Unless the drastic implementation of protective measures is imposed, difficult to adopt in such an integrated world, the standard of living in developed countries is doomed to decline. The costs of both labor and public services are too high to be maintained, and labor arbitration is very attractive, not only to the multinational giants, but also to medium and small businesses. Design, programming, accounting, information processing, and many other services can be hired and executed efficiently anywhere in the world. The technological revolution is having a major impact on a world that is moving towards greater integration and lower inequality between the average incomes of the world's richest and poorest countries

On their last day in Vietnam David and Lisa wanted to go shopping. I met them at one of the entries to Ben Thanh Market, the central market of Saigon. We said goodbye after having lunch and talked about seeing each other again in Europe after I returned from my trip. Despite both David's and my being Spanish, we had never seen each other in our own country, which we always commented on with a smile. We had been together in London, Paris, the French Alps, New York, Stockholm, and now Saigon. Someday we'd have to break the habit by meeting in Madrid or San Sebastian. I was glad to have enjoyed a few days in Saigon with them and thanked them for visiting me in hospital on their first vacation day.

My doctor asked me to continue with the antibiotics and return in another four days. The visa would expire in ten days, so I'd have to extend it if I wanted to continue with my trip to the north of the country. In an agency I paid $35 for a one-month extension that would take a week to process. Meanwhile I continued with my life in Saigon. One of my favorite places for dinner was one of the restaurants that sprout every evening on either side of Ben Thanh Market. All of them extremely popular among locals and tourists, they offer a variety of dishes at reasonable prices, from rice and noodles to grilled seafood. The restaurant waiters wear shirts of the same color but different from those of their neighbors, like teams ready to compete in attracting customers, which they actively do, menu in hand. During one dinner, the manager, a woman, asked me where I was from. She was dressed in a strapless short black dress, the top of her back and her chest bare, more appropriate for the bar of the Sheraton than for a street restaurant. She had two plasters symmetrically placed on her cheeks. I asked if she was okay, and she said she'd had surgery to have dimples added to her cheeks, and with them a more attractive smile. She told me she wanted to whiten her gray teeth, the result of a reaction to a drug, but the high price of the procedure prevented her, for now, from getting the perfect smile she had longed for since she was a child. I returned a few evenings later to see the success of the procedure: her smile was flanked by two perfect dimples.

There are beautiful women in Southeast Asia. In Saigon I loved women of fine complexion, dark and slanted eyes, high cheekbones, and wide white smiles outlined by thick lips. Those who walked with elegant grace proved irresistible. Furthermore, there were some who wore beautiful dresses or tight trousers and shirts extolling their slim figures. On motorbikes, the shorter ones have to sit on the front end of the seat to reach the handlebars; some even have difficulty reaching the asphalt with their feet when stopping at a traffic light. Many were fully covered despite the sweltering heat. To protect themselves from the sun, pollution, and dirt, they wear stockings even with sandals, put on a jacket, or cover their arms and hands with sleeves, their mouth and nose with a mask, and eyes with sunglasses, with the obligatory helmet over their heads. Others, however, just wear pants or skirts as short as they are provocative, showing off those sexy slender legs. With their knees touching and their backs straight, they are the city's emblems. Those in skirts traveling on motorcycles as passengers sit on the side, cross—legged, as on a moving cafe. It's an addictive visual feast. On several occasions I noticed the looks that Western women gave their Asian counterparts. Women are usually very observant, absorbing details about clothes, shoes, and bags, but also looking at other women's bodies comparatively. I thought some, especially those with larger bodies, might suffer a little when traveling through Southeast Asia.

One Friday night I went for a drink at Vasco's, a bar hidden in an alley that has a lounge with live music and a bar with a seating area for people wanting to talk. I ordered a beer while listening to a rock band. The place was packed, and the air conditioning could not maintain a comfortable temperature. In short, I had to leave for a moment to sit at a table next to an open window in a quiet part of the bar. A young Vietnamese guy in perfect English asked me, "Are you alone?"

"Yes," I replied.

"I need your help. We are three friends with a group of four girls; could you give us a hand?"

"Are they all attractive, or are you going to leave me the ugly one?" I asked him.

"The four of them are gorgeous."

"Will I be able to choose?"

"Well, that's still to be clarified. Come and I'll introduce you to the group."

He had a good sense of humor, so I returned to the musical sauna to meet his friends and the girls. The girls were very attractive but too young for me, except one who was Taiwanese. The young man then explained to me that he liked the one in white, his friend to my right the Taiwanese, the one to my left the one in yellow, which left me, to my surprise, the one in a pink dress, who I had considered the most attractive of the four. But I soon realized that the strategy had not been well defined, and the one who in theory liked the one in yellow began to attack the one in pink. What are you going to do! Youthful indecision. I danced with them before they took me on their motorbikes to Apocalypse Now to end the night with one last beer.

On the following day I called Phuong, and she came to the hotel to pick me up. She arrived on a motorcycle, this time without chaperon. I borrowed a helmet from the hotel, and she took me to the west of the city, through the narrow streets of District 3, with balconies full of laundry hanging, green plants, towering antennas in search of an optimal signal, and many electricity and telephone cables running parallel to the buildings. We stopped for lunch at a small restaurant where we had boiled rice with squid curry and soup. She paid before I could reach for my pocket, and we went for coffee. Every Vietnamese city is full of cafes, a vestige of French culture and a result of the excellent coffee Vietnam produces. It's served the local style: a glass with a bit of condensed milk and a container that rests on the rim of the glass with ground coffee in freshly boiled water. The fine holes in the bottom of the container act as a colander allowing only the black liquid to drip into the sweet milk. This time Thuong didn't bring her dictionary but a booklet of English basic grammar, including irregular verb conjugations. She had left her job at the cafe and moved from the city center to the periphery of Saigon to devote herself to studying English. I was pleasantly surprised by her attitude. She later took me back to the hotel because she wanted to return home to continue studying. I was going to give her the novel *Catfish & Mandala*, which I'd already finished, but she didn't understand me and disappeared on her bike before I could stop her.

When I wanted to drink a beer and enjoy the warm evening, I would go to one of the small bars open to the street, with their typical low tables and chairs occupying the sidewalk. They were much cheaper than a regular bar, and the street entertainment was unique. For 15,000 *dongs* (a little more than 50 cents) I got a cold Saigon beer that I could take with some peanuts purchased from one of the many street vendors who walk the streets in the evenings. Much better than anything on television, the street activity provided an extremely interesting entertainment: Motorcycles passing, some carrying a whole family, a child in front, another, even two, between father and mother, the kids training for what would be their vehicle in a few years. Dried fish vendors using a bicycle pushed on foot while they approach bars, with a battery-powered fluorescent bar illuminating the merchandise. Women, some dressed in pajamas and ready for bed, carrying a basket at the hip with different snacks. People carrying fruit, sweets, and other foods in two trays hanging from a wooden stick rested on their shoulders in the traditional Vietnamese style, usually with a conical hat still on their heads, even in the dark. Girls selling flowers, tissues, chewing gum, and tobacco in wide wooden boxes with all kinds of cigarettes and lighters. There were also women selling books, carrying them in a tall column, one book above the other tied with ribbons, up to fifty books on one hip, jutting out like a narrow shelf. The itinerant shoe shiners lent you a pair of sandals as they polished your shoes with dedication. Young men offering massages shook a rattle to attract attention. Others sold hacked DVDs of the latest

Hollywood blockbusters or porn movies and CDs sounding through the speakers of their bike–trucks. Beggars also took advantage of the street crowds to try to fund their existence.

Several of these bars employ young, attractive girls who camp out on the sidewalks, calling at every tourist who passes by. Normally dressed in skimpy clothes, they sit in groups outside the bar and are both waitresses and companions. The bar I frequented employed two young girls who weren't as exhibitionistic as most. I always saw them wearing jeans, never those tiny miniskirts or shorts some dare to wear. The bar owners, an old couple, were usually present, so the bar didn't have the same character as that of their neighbors, hence many Vietnamese stopped there for a drink. After I had gone a few times, one of the waitresses, as the good sellers they were, recognized me and sat beside me to chat. Linh was her name; she was twenty and also from the Mekong Delta. She had been working there for just a few months, and her shift was 7 p.m. to 7 a.m. daily. This kind of bar doesn't sleep. Early morning coffee and breakfast are served, drinks in the evenings, and a bit of everything during the day. (Despite having no kitchen, the bar kept at hand the menu of a restaurant across the street in case a customer wanted something to eat.) Linh had long black hair, round eyes, and a protruding smile; her lips had difficulty concealing her teeth. Both she and the other young waitress were of Cambodian descent, quite common in southern Vietnam, since at the time of the Khmer Empire, southern Vietnam belonged to it. Her life was fully dedicated to the bar. She shared a room with her colleague; their lives were in perfect synchronization. She had learned her broken English from foreign customers at the bar. I invited her for a drink; she poured a Red Bull to keep her awake during the night. She earned 1,500,000 *dongs* per month (about $100) and lived in a small room shared with her colleague, for which they paid 450,000 *dongs* each. The room had no cooking facilities, and the bathroom was outside, common to several rooms.

Communism no longer exists in Vietnam. The fact that the country has no political choices other than the Communist Party doesn't make it communist. In the center of Saigon the wealth that a small part of the population has accumulated could be seen everywhere. In any of its modern cafes and restaurants, iPhones, Macs, and other expensive gadgets could be seen on any table. I even found a couple of iPads, Apple's latest innovation that had just launched a few days before in the United States. Mercedes–Benzes, BMWs, and Audis were more shown–off, flaunted, than driven on the motorcycle–packed streets. The latest models of Vespa shone in the crowds of motorbikes. Women with authentic Louis Vuitton handbags, gorgeous dresses, and high heels exited taxis and entered shops and cafes with catwalk steps. All this was the result of economic liberalization, *Doi Moi* (Renovation), adopted by the Vietnamese communist leadership in 1986 following the Chinese model, which culminated with the entry of Vietnam as a member of the World Trade Organization in 2007. Vietnam is a developing capitalist country with a closed political system dominated by the Communist Party. It seems utter nonsense, an immense contradiction, perhaps, that a country is ruled by one political party of communist ideology while its population lives in a capitalist economy. The hypocrisy of their leaders is unparalleled. Their only interest is to stay in power, and therefore they succumbed to the need for economic liberalization, thereby alleviating the wishes of democracy in a population that today is more concerned with economic growth than with political maturation.

Nevertheless, the political stability that one–party rule brings should not be ignored. While in democracies the election cycle gives citizens the possibility of change or punishes political parties that are ineffective or corrupt, it also encourages governments to choose short–term policies to ensure re–election, and to avoid taking decisions necessary for the medium and long term even when they might be negative in the short term. The recent financial crisis is a case in point: while everything seemed to be going well, despite some alarms, no country took any action to deter the housing bubble. Moreover, in countries like the U.S. the funding of political parties has a direct impact on what decisions are taken by the government. In the West we criticize the lack of democracy in countries like Vietnam too easily, without reflecting deeply on our own systems. In Spain, as in much of Europe, the leaders of political parties choose the candidates the party then puts up for election without open, internal elections within the party; this gives a few party members total control of their parties, and while they boast of their country's democracy, they ignore democracy within their organizations in order to maintain party control. Of course, I am not defending the current regime in Vietnam. I just want to point out how we easily we criticize other countries without looking a little more closely in the mirror.

I met Phuong again before leaving Saigon. She picked me up one morning and took me to Dam Sen, an old but charming amusement park. There was hardly anyone at that hour. She wanted to go to the Enchanted Castle, so we changed the day's brightness for the supposedly terrifying darkness of the castle. It really was not that scary, designed more for children than adults. We left the park to return to my hotel area and pick up my passport with my visa extension before going to a nearby cafe for a final farewell drink. When I announced to her that I was leaving for Mui Ne the following day, she was saddened because she'd hoped to see me the day of her twenty–third birthday, just two days away. I congratulated her ahead of time and gave her the book *Catfish & Mandala*, as I had wanted to do the last time I saw her.

I dedicated the next morning to scanning all of the documents related to the treatment of the cyst and claiming the related medical expenses from my travel insurance. The small infection had disappeared; the only related task ahead was to protect the scar from the sun. I went to the post office to mail to my New York address a detailed prospectus of the temples of Angkor, another of Tuol Sleng prison, and the documents related to my hospitalization in Saigon. In a secondhand bookstore I bought a copy of *The Catcher in the Rye*. I had read Salinger's novel many years ago, but I wanted to read it again. Finally, it was time to leave Saigon and continue my journey through Vietnam.

★ ★ ★

I arrived in Mui Ne at sunset and got a bungalow by the beach. The wind blew strongly, which makes Mui Ne one of the world's most popular places to practice kite surfing. I went to a terrace to have a beer and admire the skill of the surfers on the choppy sea. Some of them made some impressive leaps over the waves. For dinner I went to an old wooden house converted into a friendly local restaurant with terrace. The manager wore a white *ao dai*, the traditional Vietnamese female attire composed of trousers tight at the hip but wide at the foot, with a top also tight around the shoulders and chest, opening and widening around the pelvis. I think it's one of the most sensual and elegant clothing designs for women.

The young waitress who took my order told me she was exhausted. She had gotten up at 6 a.m. to clean her house, wash clothes, and go to market to buy food before going to work in the restaurant at 2 p.m., and she would end her shift around 11 p.m. I mentioned this to the manager, who said she was a great kid, a good student who had to leave school at fourteen to work and help her poor family. After dinner, I asked about her in more detail. Her name was Thuy; she had a baby face, although she was nineteen, with round features and shortish thick, black hair. She looked more Cambodian than Vietnamese, which was nothing unusual in southern Vietnam, and lived with her parents and four younger siblings, two boys and two girls, the youngest being nine. She said she felt extremely sad for not being able to continue her studies; her eyes vividly transmitted her sadness as soon as she shared with me her frustration. She, as the eldest, had to help financially because all her brothers were still too young to work. I asked her what she'd have liked to study; she said accounting. I told her she was still young, and perhaps she could continue her studies in the near future. She said maybe, but it looked rather difficult. Then she went to serve another table. The manager told me she gave all her wages to her mother.

I began to mourn, my invisible tears quickly reaching my

heart. Listening to her sadness, her frustration at being the eldest in a poor family, and also a good student and avid learner, who had had to assume an imposed responsibility, was extremely painful for me. Few of us know what it means to be a firstborn in a poor family in countries like Vietnam. There is scientific evidence that firstborns are the most responsible among siblings, while the youngest are the most adventurous. Perhaps the wisdom of nature is willing to risk the latter, but not the firstborns, whose responsibility in the care of parents and siblings can be vital for their family's subsistence. My mother, as the eldest, had had to sacrifice part of her primary education when my grandmother couldn't take care of my mother's younger brothers during periods of intensive work in the fields. She was the one who had encouraged my brother and me to get a good education and pursue our studies in college, sometimes having to fight against my father's working-class mentality. Perhaps that was the reason Thuy's story affected me, surprisingly, with such intensity. I am also the firstborn, but I was fortunate to have been born in a place and time where my biggest burden was having to fight my parents' old-fashioned attitudes. I exchanged email addresses with Thuy and her manager in case I was able to find a way to help the young waitress, since that had been the first thing I had thought of while listening to her; I had to find a way for her return to school.

I said goodbye to them and went to Sankara, a modern and luxurious cocktail lounge on the beach. Upon entering, I saw an indoor bar on the left with a few tables. At the other end, the lounge opened out to its most beautiful and busy part, with a long, narrow pool with more tables along each side and a section furnished with small, round love-seats with curtains for privacy. A square-shaped bar illuminated in orange was the center of attention. On one side was a small dance floor with a position for a DJ, and tables fronting the sea. After my conversation with Thuy, I felt really strange in that place. A super energetic guy, pretty drunk (he probably had something more than alcohol in his veins) danced stupidly. Some people responded to his invitations, others drank tequila shots. A middle-aged couple sat to my left. The woman wore a necklace with the word "Poison" over her chest. How appropriate, I thought! Thuy's sad face was still with me. Then the DJ played a mix of *Everybody is Free (to feel good)* by Rozalla, and I thought: Yeah, right, let Thuy know that. It was the last straw.

I thought there had to be a way to get a scholarship for her or to contact an NGO about her case (I even considered creating a fund and asking for help from friends and acquaintances). The humility and honesty of Thuy contrasted strongly with the pretentiousness and artificiality of the bar patrons. I also imagined what Holden Caulfield, the protagonist of *The Catcher in the Rye*, would say right now: "It kills me to see people pretending to be so happy, dancing to a stupid song, simply following a drunk."

I went to the hotel to try to sleep, which was not easy, Thuy's sadness still present to me, her memory constant and fresh like a bad catchy song that won't leave your mind and whose melody is repeated endlessly.

With only three hours of sleep, I got on the minibus to Da Lat, a city located at an altitude of 4,900 feet surrounded by hills with pine trees—a popular local tourist destination for its climate, an ideal place to escape the intense heat that settled in the lowlands of the country in April. I managed to get some sleep during the journey. In Da Lat, an Easy Rider took me to the Peace Hotel. Easy Riders are a group of experienced motor bikers who offer tours around Vietnam's Highlands. At the hotel my driver offered the services of the group, ranging from day tours around Da Lat to several days to Nha Trang, Hoi An, and Saigon. The prices were high, but the experience of traveling by motorcycle in the Vietnamese countryside and visiting the less touristy areas was very attractive. That night I went for a walk in Da Lat, and the cool mountain temperature, delicious after the oppressive heat of the last few months, forced me to wear my thin fleece for the first time since leaving Nepal.

The next day, I hired a guide to hike to Lang Biang, a mountain of 7,100 feet, the highest in Southern Vietnam, and to visit a village of the Lat ethnic group. The climb had some very steep sections, and the altitude forced us to slow our pace. The lower part of the climb was through pine forests, the upper part through a jungle. It took almost two hours to reach the top, where the view was extensive; were it not for the clouds, we would have sighted the sea. We had lunch on the mountain's top, sitting on a plastic sheet, and I took advantage of the respite to ask my guide about Vietnam. First, I asked about Buddhism, which he said really only 15 percent of the population practiced regularly. According to him, two—thirds of the Vietnamese don't follow any religion at all, although (somewhat contradictorily) most Vietnamese believe in Buddha and even go to a Buddhist temple once a year, usually at the beginning of the new year (mid—April). When I asked him about the communist government, whether the Vietnamese were pleased with it and with their political system, he replied that people just didn't talk about it. After the war, with unification achieved, the Vietnamese just wanted peace. Political conflict was not on their agenda. No wonder pragmatism was so prevalent after long periods under Chinese, French, and American control.

The clouds began to darken, and halfway through our descent we were caught in a torrential downpour. The rainy season was approaching. We covered ourselves with the plastic sheet on which we had eaten lunch, but we arrived at the bottom of the mountain fully soaked. As it seemed the rain wouldn't stop for several hours we decided to return to Da Lat without visiting the village. My guide lent me a thin transparent orange plastic cover to wear as a poncho, and we ventured to fight the storm on the motorbike. The journey back to Da Lat was amazing. The storm intensified. Thunder burst within seconds of each lightning bolt. I feared lightning would strike the bike or, worse, my helmet. I protected my face against the heavy rain with the guide's body, but couldn't understand how he was able to guide the bike wearing an open—face helmet, his face constantly slapped by the violent rain. Within a few minutes the road had become a river, and driving was extremely difficult, particularly through the huge puddles. After arriving safely at the hotel, but dripping wet, I showered with the background sound of the rain pounding against my room's window and balcony door. When I left the bathroom, I saw the water was getting in underneath the balcony door and through the window. Hotel workers rushed to inspect the rooms facing the front, where the wind and rain were especially strong, and mop up the water that had gotten in. In the evening calm, after the storm had passed through, I started searching the Internet for NGOs that provided financial assistance for people like Thuy. I found five and contacted them by email.

My prolonged stay in Saigon had been more expensive than expected, so I rejected the idea of an adventure with an Easy Rider, and traveled by bus to Nha Trang, reminiscent of Benidorm, the high–rise down–market tourist magnet of Spain's Costa Blanca. I arrived on Thursday, April 29, a day before Liberation Day, Vietnam's national holiday, the reason the weekend was one of the busiest in Nha Trang. I had no trouble finding a room for Thursday, but the weekend was almost full, and the few rooms available were offered at double the usual price. I paid for a night at the first hotel I visited, since I wanted to take a nap immediately, and found another hotel for Friday and Saturday. For dinner I had a tasty grilled squid on a low outdoor table, then went for a massage to ease my muscle soreness from the climb up Lang Biang. On the way to the hotel I remembered reading in my guide that evenings usually ended at Nha Trang's Sailing Club, not far from my hotel. On the way there, it didn't take long for two attractive ladies on a motorbike to stop by me, offering their "massage" services.

At the Sailing Club, while enjoying a beer at the bar, I met a Vietnamese woman who was there with a group of friends. She'd just opened a beauty salon, and also offered me her services immediately: "Why don't you come tomorrow for a head massage or a manicure?" One of her friends was a gay man who had spent six weeks in Vitoria with his Basque boyfriend. Another was a young Australian who had been working as an English teacher for a few months in Nha Trang. He complained about Vietnamese women, many hungry for foreigners' money. "The problem here is you don't know which one is a whore," he said.

When I told him that during my trip I hadn't been

interested in any Western woman, he replied that I would soon be so. One of the girls in the group was really attractive, with black slanted eyes and a feline smile too sexy to be ignored. I looked repeatedly at her to see if she'd answer back, which she did. I introduced myself and asked her name; Hien, she replied. After telling her where I was from, she left, cutting the flow of the conversation. Didn't she like my nationality? She went to dance with another friend but I didn't follow her; I wanted to be sure of her interest before investing sweat on her.

Later, as my eyes continued to be fixed on her attractive face, she started to look back at me more often.

"Why don't you dance?" she asked.

"It's too hot," I replied, and she invited me to follow her, which I did promptly.

In the middle of the dance floor, dancing face to face, staring at each other, we surrendered to the music. I got closer to her, she turned, giving me her back, I grabbed her by the waist, our bodies moved together in unison. Her tank top showed off her glowing skin because of her sweat. Her proximity excited me intensely. We continued dancing for a while. She stopped a few times to catch her breath, saying the temperature was high. I noticed the many male gazes falling on her from all around the dance floor. We returned to the bar, but she, for the second time, left me there. I did not know if she was shy because of her limited English, if she just wanted to flirt and have fun dancing, or if she wanted to make it difficult for me.

Hien soon came back, I grabbed her, extolling her beauty, and asked her if she'd like to spend the night with me. After thanking my compliment, she asked if I was going to pay her. The Australian was a good connoisseur of Nha Trang women. I replied negatively. "If you lived here it'd be different, but I'm not going to have sex with you without getting something in return," she pointed out. It was clear that sexual liberation of some Vietnamese woman was a monetary issue. I told her the transaction didn't interest me and that ended the conversation. She continued to look at me from time to time, perhaps hoping my inseminating instinct would beat my common sense, while I was hoping she'd lose her feminine materialist position in favor of lust. In the end, no one gave in and we ended in a stalemate, between my common sense and her mercantilism.

I arrived in Buon Ma Thuot (BMT), the main town in the Highlands, late in the evening. I had a quick dinner at a restaurant next to the hotel that specialized in fresh spring rolls because I wanted to take some pictures around 10 p.m., with the intention of sending one to *The New York Times* Global Mosaic project, consisting of photos from around the world taken at that precise time. In Vietnam that time was quite late, but the worst was the rain that had begun an hour earlier, sweeping BMT's citizens off the streets. Despite the rain, I managed to take a few interesting images of street food stalls. I chose one of a woman cooking in a street kitchen while another served customers, to send by email, hoping it'd be chosen for the project. The photo was published along with thousands sent from around the world.

The next day I went by local bus to Lake Lak. A woman in her canoe took me to the opposite shore of the lake where there was a village of the Mnong tribe, a village of long houses, some of 80 feet, built off the ground, on pilings, with two or three windows on each side, and sloping roofs so water can run off easily during the rainy season. Each of the houses had a log with steps carved into it that was used to climb to the main entrance. The oldest houses still had thatched roofs. I took pictures of the houses and captured the smiles of a group of children who jostled in their struggle to get to the fore. Again the rural children captivated me with their honest smiles and playful attitude.

I went by local bus to Kon Tum. My Lonely Planet did not show a map of the city, so when I got off the bus at noon, under a searing sun, I decided to take one of the motorcycle taxis waiting for customers at the stop. We negotiated the price, I put my backpack between the driver's legs, and rode behind him. The bike went forward, turned right after about 300 feet, turned right again after another stretch of similar length, to turn right a third time before stopping at the door of my hotel. I picked up my bag and paid the motorcyclist, and then realized that three consecutive right turns after stretches of similar length drew a square. It was at that moment that, my taxi driver quickly driving off, I turned around and saw the bus stop where I had got off a couple of minutes before: my hotel had been right across the street. I laughed at myself and smiled at the dishonest driver. In Kon Tum, a charming town, I booked a one–day tour to visit some ethnic minority villages. I went with the guide on his motorbike: a young Hungarian followed us on his bike, an old motorcycle he'd bought in Hanoi for $300. The guide described me as a handsome man, claiming that Vietnamese women would find me very sexy thanks to my stubble. According to him, local women consider men with facial hair very masculine and good in bed, a view that hadn't resulted in any pickups in Vietnam until then. I regretted that Vietnamese women's opinion was not more popular in the world.

We visited the village Plei Weh, a beautiful village belonging to the Jarai tribe. The land surrounding it was deep red, very fertile, and therefore used for one of Vietnam's star crops, coffee. At the center of the village stood a very peculiar building; a community building called a *jong*, used for communal meetings. Its main feature, visible hundreds of yards away, was its tall, sharply pointed roof, maybe sixty feet high. The interior is a single room accessible by the typical staircase carved into a log. Once inside, we admired the complex series of beams that hold up such a huge structure. There was also a Catholic church in the village since most of the tribes in the area are Catholic as a result of the French occupation. We visited the school, through whose window we discreetly observed the teacher and her large group of students, and the cemetery. The tombs were tiny houses, each with a roof and surrounded by a protective fence. Inside the tombs there were flowers and also water and other beverages, animal bones, and various personal items (there was even a bicycle in one of them). It seemed the dead were buried with everything they might need in their new life.

One woman yelled to us to come inside her home, where, despite its being just past 10 in the morning, a celebration was taking place. A large family, several couples and their children, sat on the wooden floor, males at one end, females at the other, and they all appeared to be happily drunk. They were celebrating the completion of the house. Men played cards while drinking rice wine; women chatted and drank another liquor, made from wheat. The females' liquor was in several earthen jars, where it had been diluted with water. To drink it, they sucked through fine bamboo straws. They invited us to sit and drink with them and refused to accept our first negative response to such an early spree. We sucked the bamboo straws to drink a liquor that was as strong as it was tasteless.

In the afternoon, we went to visit a beautiful Montagnard Church, built entirely of wood. At the back of the church there is an orphanage with more than two hundred children. We talked to the English teacher, a sixty—year—old from Kon Tum, an orphan himself. He had worked as an interpreter and translator for the U.S. Army during the war. After the Americans were defeated, he had to pay for each year of serving the Americans with one of "re—education": three years in prison doing hard labor—the forgotten part of the war museum in Saigon. When asked about the current situation in Vietnam, if he could see any improvement, he said yes, especially for Communist Party members. We also learned about one of the most barbaric customs I've ever heard. In the villages of the ethnic minorities, when a mother died who had a baby less than a year old, given the difficulty of care and lack of breast milk, the custom was to bury the baby alive with the mother. To facilitate the cruel task, the baby was made to drink alcohol to soothe him before placing him still alive in the coffin with the mother. In the orphanage there were three children who had been saved from this terrible fate by neighbors who had literally ripped them from the jaws of death.

The journey from Kon Tum to Hoi An took almost six hours through the beautiful mountains of the Highlands. In Hoi An I stayed along the Thu Bon River at the Hoang Huy hotel. My room had a bathtub, the first since I started my trip, so I quickly filled it up and enjoyed a relaxing bath. It's when we lack basic things that we realize their true value; nothing like shedding possessions and comforts for a while to begin, in perspective, to value them. I felt like a Roman emperor for half an hour.

Hoi An became an important port in the seventeenth century. When the draft of its natural harbor wasn't deep enough for the large new ships, the port moved to nearby Da Nang, and Hoi An became what it is now: a charming relic of the past, with its cute houses and temples of Chinese influence. Many of the old buildings have been converted into cafes, restaurants, and gift shops, showing the great attraction of the old town of Hoi An, one of the most beautiful cities I visited during my trip. Hoi An is the kind of place where you miss not having arrived with a woman. Its beauty, its tranquility, its nice cafes and restaurants, are ideal for a few days of romance with a woman around a tasty dinner with a good red wine.

From Hoi An I went to Hue, a city that under the Nguyen Dynasty was the country's capital from 1802 to 1945, the year when Emperor Bao Dai abdicated and the communist government moved the capital to Hanoi. On the north bank of the Perfume River stands the Citadel, which houses the former residence of the emperor and his government. I left the hotel on foot to go to the Citadel. When I was halfway there, a man sitting on a motorcycle and reading a newspaper called out to me and asked where I was going, at the same time assuring me he wasn't going to try to sell me anything or offer his services as driver. He was a teacher and killing time until his children arrived from Saigon for a family celebration. When he heard I lived in New York his eyes widened, and he asked if I had some time to have a drink with him. I agreed, got on his bike, and he took me to a restaurant a couple of blocks away where we ordered two beers. He said he was from Saigon but had been stationed in Hue for the last three years, where he taught Vietnamese. He lived with his wife, a music teacher and granddaughter of Bao Dai, the last emperor of Vietnam. When the war ended, much of his family left the country, mainly for France, though he also had family in Bilbao and Barcelona. We talked about my family, my work, and my life in New York as well as my travels. He was sixty, and it was extremely nice to chat with him. I asked for something to eat (he had already eaten before leaving home) and ordered two more beers.

Upon leaving, he insisted on paying. I refused, to which he replied that I could buy him a bottle of wine to take to the temple that night for a family celebration performed every five years to remember their ancestors. I accepted the deal. He paid for my food and the beers, and we rode the bike toward the Citadel, stopping at a store to buy the wine. The shopkeeper asked me about the quality of wine I wanted to buy, I asked for the best and got a nice bottle in a box and paid for it. The man smiled happily, warmly thanking me for the gift, promising to pour a glassful of wine in the temple to pray for my good fortune during my travels. We said goodbye and I walked towards the Citadel. Once alone, I started to think about the price of the bottle, and then realized I'd paid 700,000 *dongs* for it (about $45). I don't know if it was the two beers or the charm of the man that made me part so thoughtlessly with my money, which rarely happens. I had wanted to be generous with the gift, but that was far beyond what I had initially intended. That money was the equivalent of a three nights' stay at a hotel in Hue. I began to wonder if I had been the victim of a clever scam perpetrated by an expert street artist. I immediately discarded the idea. If I had been, the man, for his genius, certainly deserved his reward. I wished he'd really enjoy the bottle with his family.

To get to Hanoi from Hue I went by train; although somewhat slower and more expensive than the bus, I preferred it because it's much more relaxed. In Hanoi, I stayed at a budget hotel in one of the narrow alleyways next to Saint Joseph's Cathedral. I went out for dinner and walked around Hoan Kiem Lake at the center of the city, always with great activity around its perimeter. Posters throughout the capital announced the celebration of its first millennium after the official foundation by Emperor Ly Thai Tho in October 1010.

The following day I visited the Museum of the

Revolution, where what attracted me the most were the very interesting photos of the celebrations in Hanoi after the conquest of Saigon in 1975. I also went to the Ho Chi Minh Mausoleum, where access is gained after passing through a tight security system. The rest of Hanoi, including the beautiful Temple of Literature, founded in 1070, I knew already from my first visit in October 2002. At that time, the tour I was with went from Hanoi to Ha Long Bay and Sapa in the north, where we did a six-day trek, meeting some of the ethnic groups that live in that remote part of the country, near China. This time I overlooked Sapa despite its great natural beauty, but could not resist a second visit to Ha Long Bay, a World Heritage Site since 1994; it's a large marine area that contains about two thousand limestone islands. I booked a two-day tour by boat with the intention of, as I had enjoyed eight years before, spending a night in that magnificent setting. I shared the boat with a French couple, two young Englishmen, and an Australian woman. Despite the cloudy weather that deprived Ha Long Bay of the splendor I experienced in 2002, we enjoyed sailing through the islands, visiting the caves, swimming, and rowing on a kayak. The last day was spent in Cat Ba, the main town in the area.

The busiest border crossings between Vietnam and Laos are in Central Vietnam. But I was going to enter Laos through the northernmost passage, near the town of Dien Bien Phu, famous for the battle that took place there in 1954 between French and Vietnamese troops. After the severe French defeat and the Geneva Accords of the same year, French troops withdrew from Indochina permanently, leaving Vietnam divided into two halves along the 17th parallel. The French defeat marked the first substantial step in the achievement of an independent and united Vietnam.

By then I had received replies from the five NGOs I had contacted with details of Thuy's situation. Two of them told me that the case was not within their reach; the other three asked me, since Thuy was an adult, if she would contact their organizations directly in order to properly evaluate her case. I sent to Thuy (with a copy to her manager) all the information

I had gotten and the steps to follow in each case, with the hope of getting her the financial assistance that would allow her to resume her studies without her family having to suffer from it. I felt very good, and hopeful.

VALLEYS, RELAXATION & FONDLING

"Wandering re-establishes the original harmony which once existed between man and the universe." —Anatole France

"Not all those who wander are lost." —J.R.R. Tolkien

The bus departed from Dien Bien Phu at 5:30 a.m. as daylight dawned on the horizon. Vietnam shares the same time zone as Laos, Cambodia, and Thailand, but since it's the easternmost of the four countries, the sun visits it first. At 6 a.m. farmers were already working in the rice fields, taking advantage of the cool morning. The valley around Dien Bien Phu is beautiful, surrounded by mountains on all sides. After less than an hour's drive, we stopped at a small roadside restaurant for the driver to have breakfast, a fact that irritated me slightly; couldn't he have had it before leaving and delayed our departure for half an hour? While he "recharged his batteries" for the long haul, I watched the women of an ethnic group I didn't know. They wore huge buns on top of their heads, pyramids of black hair. Some of the women were wearing the Vietnamese conical hat, which seemed ridiculous, and others a motorcycle helmet absurdly protecting the bun more than the skull.

We soon moved into steep terrain and began the ascent to the border with Laos, which is only twenty−one miles from Dien Bien Phu. We arrived at the Vietnamese border station, where we got off to get our passports stamped. The Laotian station was two miles away on a road under construction. We had to walk because a large mound of earth blocked the way of our bus. After processing our visas in Laos (this included taking our temperatures in case we were carrying swine flu, which was still present in parts of Vietnam,) we waited until the bus could get through, which did not happen until after 10 a.m. It'd been four hours and a half already, and we had hardly covered twenty−seven miles. From there to Muang Khua, our destination, the distance was only fifty miles, but that road also was under construction. A couple of times we had to stop when a truck couldn't climb one of the ramps because its wheels skidded in the loose soil. We arrived in Muang Khua at 2:30 p.m., after nine hours for a journey of less than eighty miles. However, the torture of the delay was severely lightened by the wonderful landscape of rugged mountains that welcomed us into Laos. It was the most beautiful border crossing I had ever done.

I decided to spend the night in Muang Khua and go by boat to Muang Ngoi Neua the next morning. It was a four-hour descent down the Nam Ou River, a beautiful river that cuts through the dramatically steep mountains. We encountered several rapids. The waves hit the boat and splashed us. I was the only one who got out in Muang Ngoi Neua; the rest went to Nong Khiaw.

Muang Ngoi Neua is a small riverside paradise that has become quite popular with tourists in recent times. Only accessible by river, it's an oasis of tranquility. Many guesthouses line the riverbank and offer spectacular views of it and the surrounding mountains. The village itself is just one long street at both ends of which stand two Buddhist temples, one inhabited by monks. From Muang Ngoi Neua it is possible to walk into the valley and visit several villages of ethnic minority tribes, even spend the night in them. Because it was the low season, there were hardly any tourists, and I got a bungalow with a hammock on the balcony overlooking the river for only 30,000 *kips* ($4). Never has the enjoyment of paradise been so cheap.

There's almost no electricity in Muang Ngoi Neua; a generator provides it for a few hours after dark, so there's no TV or music during the day, only the sounds of nature interrupted infrequently by that of a boat engine. That evening for dinner I had one of Laos's typical dishes, *laab,* a noodle dish with chicken sauteed with peanuts and vegetables seasoned with lime sauce, all accompanied by sticky rice and a Lao beer. I tried to meditate in my room, but the alcohol made me feel a little sleepy. I stayed in Muang Ngoi Neua for three nights, soaking up the serenity of such an incredible place. In the afternoons I lay in a hammock and read or slept, or went for a drink at one of the balcony bars, watching the river come alive before sunset; then the villagers come to the river to bathe and wash their clothes. Naked children played among the adults in the river, teenagers playfully fought among themselves, splashing each other, women came carrying small plastic baskets that held soap, combs, and hairpins besides the clean clothes. I carefully watched a woman following her daily routine. She was already in the water, her sarong covering her body from armpits to knees. She had just finished washing herself. She climbed to one of the boats stranded on the shore where she had deposited her basket and her clean clothes. She wrapped herself in a blue towel, which covered her entire wet sarong. Then she pulled her sarong under the towel and took one that was clean, to wear as a skirt. She then put her panties on with care not to lift the towel and show her thighs, pulling them up through the fabric. She took her bra and put it over the towel, then an orange tank top and a second one with long sleeves over the tank. Once she was fully dressed, it was time to let go of the towel, pulling it under her skirt. Finally clean and dressed, she washed the dirty sarong in the river, combed back her long black hair, gathered her belongings, and got out of the boat to go home. The ceremony was performed without haste and with accuracy and care. For Westerners, it's unusual to see a woman washing in public; so, something normal in Asia was, for me, a ritual appealing to follow.

The next day I went for a long walk to visit two beautiful villages a couple of hours away. During the walk I spotted buffalos, some pink, grazing and bathing in the river, and fishermen trying to catch something to eat. I ate in a restaurant in one of the villages before a woman guided me to a nearby waterfall. I took the solitude of the place to undress under the showering water and freshen up naturally. What a feeling of freedom and freshness to be naked under a waterfall! Part of my walk along the river was accompanied by hundreds of butterflies flying, some in my direction, others against it, so close to me they seemed to be engaged in combat with my solitude. I'd never seen so many butterflies. Some were bright white, others intense orange, some tiny, almost imperceptible, others huge and velvety. On the banks of the river they rested in what looked like military formation, waiting for the order to attack with their beauty. Some flew in line, with their typical slightly chaotic flight coming towards me and almost crashing into my face, altering their flight at the last moment. It was a sublime walk, one of the most beautiful I can remember.

Due to the nature of my father's job, for him vacations were synonymous with relaxation and rest; what he longed for was to move as little as possible. Every summer he enjoyed a full month of rest, dividing his vacation time between his village and my mom's. We'd get an early start, driving from San Sebastian, my dad so keen to arrive that he always tried to make the journey without stopping (my mother had to insist on stops to let her go to the bathroom). My mother liked to visit places and sometimes managed to convince my father to stop in Burgos, Segovia, or Madrid for some sightseeing. His vacation days were spent with the family, but also helping my grandparents in the fields. I thought my father would have loved a place like Muang Ngoi Neua.

It wasn't easy to leave Muang Ngoi Neua, as difficult as saying goodbye to a summer love. Under a thin but intense rain I got on a boat to go to Nong Khiaw, one hour downstream. Although beautiful in itself, the city has a tall, ugly bridge between the river banks that, along with the noise of crossing vehicles, makes it much less enjoyable than its upstream neighbor. I spent one night in Nong Khiaw before taking a van to reach Luang Prabang, the stunning ancient capital of the kingdom of the same name and later the capital of Laos until the seizure of power by the Communists in 1975. It is located at the confluence of the Mekong and Nam Khan Rivers, on a beautiful peninsula with a hill in the center overlooking both rivers. Numerous Buddhist temples and monasteries stand in a not very extensive old area full of hotels and restaurants converted from neighborhood houses because of the city's recent popularity. After finding an accommodation, I spent the afternoon strolling in quite a beautiful, if somewhat touristic city, and visiting the museum in the former Royal Palace. At dusk a market full of souvenir stalls is set up on Luang Prabang's main street. I bought a black shirt with a red five—pointed star that I couldn't find in Vietnam, and a long, checkered cloth used by Laotian women to carry their babies on their backs that I would use as a scarf or sun protector.

Luang Prabang reminded me of Hoi An, both old cities that because of their beauty have become museums attracting thousands of tourists each season in an economic invasion that has the local population serving the invaders. Luang Prabang's old houses have been converted into hotels, restaurants, cafes, and gift shops, forcing part of its people to become refugees in their own city. I wonder if there is a Luang Prabang somewhere on the planet that has deliberately refused to exist for the exclusive enjoyment of rich visitors. Of course, the spending by tourists in these towns is significant, and the local population enjoys a clear economic benefit. Nevertheless, it can't be easy for the locals to accept wealthy foreigners taking over their city every day.

Two days in a row I got up before dawn to witness and photograph the local Buddhist monks in orange robes receiving food at 6 a.m., a ceremony that takes place every morning and that every tourist in Luang Prabang should experience. Many Thai visitors come and kneel while offering alms to the monks. Vendors of sticky rice sell it to tourists so they can also participate in the ritual donation. While the Burmese monks' robes are maroon and Thais' are yellow or mustard, in Cambodia and Laos they are bright orange; by the end of the two mornings I had taken a trove of pictures of the colorful ceremony, the intense orange of the robes illuminating the dim morning light, every monk an errant flame of human head and limbs. I had never seen so many monks since my days in Myanmar, which was, by far, the country in which Buddhism was most prevalent during my journey. There, as in Cambodia and Laos, I had been told that very poor kids, some orphans, entered Buddhist monasteries to ensure food and shelter for themselves. I imagine that, as has been happening in rich countries with Catholic populations, the number of Buddhist monks in

Southeast Asia will probably diminish with the economic development of their countries.

I traveled by bus to Vientiane, the present capital of Laos. The change in landscape was remarkable; the mountains gave way to the plain. Although it is usual to find plenty of activity in the streets in any capital of a country, Vientiane was as quiet as a small provincial town. Traffic was light and almost silent; the inhabitants looked scared to walk the streets. Moving from Vietnam to Laos was like leaving a nightclub in the rush of evening hours to go to an empty cafe about to close. Vietnam is dense and very active, cafes and restaurants usually packed, its streets and roads infested with motorcycles, their engines roaring relentlessly. If walking the Vietnamese streets is a constant stimulus to the senses, in Laos the senses can relax and enjoy the reigning quiet. Despite their proximity, the differences between Laos and Vietnam are greater than the similarities, particularly between their respective populations. The Laotians have darker skin, a more rounded face, and less angular features. Many have small slanted eyes that seem almost closed. Those women, with their elongated faces, look like Modigliani's models, while other faces seem Andean, bringing to mind the Asian origin of American Indians. I visited some of Vientiane's Buddhist temples, which were stunning, and the National Museum, and went to the Thai embassy to apply for a month–long visa, since the Thai government had cut the visa a visitor gets when entering the country by land to fifteen days (in contrast to the thirty days allowed those who enter by air). In the evening there was no shortage of offers of women from *tuk–tuk* drivers and from some street prostitutes, including a *lady–boy*.

In the mid–nineteenth century Laos didn't exist as such, its current territory occupied by a number of small states. It was French colonization beginning in 1893 that led to the formation of the current Laos as a result of the colonial rivalry between Britain and France. The French had no special interest in Laos other than to serve as a barrier between Vietnam, the French colonial jewel in Asia, and a possible British expansionist thrust from Burma. Laos won brief independence after the end of the Japanese occupation in 1945, but France regained control of Laos until its independence in 1954. A civil war broke out soon afterwards that resulted, after more than two decades, in the seizure of power in 1975 by the Pathet Lao communist movement. Two of the country's provinces, Xiangkhouang and Houaphanh, were occupied by the communists at the beginning of the Vietnam War, their territory used to transport supplies to South Vietnam. Therefore B–52s bombed Laos without respite, without the knowledge of the U.S. Congress, beginning in 1964. It is estimated the U.S. military dropped more bombs on Laos than during the entire Second World War, a bomb every eight minutes twenty–four hours a day, every day between 1964 and 1973, which makes Laos the most bombed country per capita in history. Some 260 million bombs rained down on its territory; 80 million of them failed to explode, leaving a deadly legacy.

My extended stay in Vietnam forced me to cut my stay in Laos to three weeks, and I had, unfortunately, to overlook its southern half. I wanted to visit the north of Thailand and some of its southern islands during the soccer World Cup to be held in South Africa and broadcast worldwide (so I could watch it at a local Thai bar), and to arrive in Malaysia a few days before the start of a vipassana meditation course I wanted to take in late July. In Laos I followed the news about riots that were taking place in neighboring Thailand, resulting from a political conflict that had led thousands of supporters of former Prime Minister Thaksin Shinawatra, the "red shirts," to occupy the streets of Bangkok. I wished the waters to calm down before entering Thailand. It had been several days since my email to Thuy with the information from the NGOs that could help her, but I hadn't received any response; so, even though she had been addressed in the original email, I sent a follow–up email to her manager, thinking that Thuy might not have seen it yet, and probably connected to the Internet very sparingly.

From Vientiane I turned back north, stopping in Vang Vieng, a town ensconced in a beautiful riverside location. It took only five minutes to regret my stop there. Vang Vieng attracts a high number of young tourists in search of "tubing," an activity that involves descending the river sitting in a truck tire, making occasional stops for a drink, usually alcohol. Thus, the town has a stupid college party atmosphere, utterly unattractive to me. Rounding out the nightmare, most restaurants and bars had the television constantly on, showing chapter after chapter of the American television series *Friends*. What torture. During the night, I had to use my disposable earplugs because the music from a nearby bar entered my room with impudence. I wasn't able to meditate that evening even though, since I had entered Laos, its quiet calm had helped me to meditate almost daily. My only positive experience in that town was that I finally found a copy of *The Sorrow of War*, a novel written by Bao Ninh and set in the Vietnam War that had eluded me in recent weeks. It's a wonderful novel, a subtle love and despair story set during that disastrous era. I ran away from Vang Vieng by bus at noon in the direction of Udomxai. We arrived in Luang Prabang at 8 p.m. and dined at the bus station before restarting the long haul. I got to Udomxai at 3 a.m., about the worst time you can get anywhere. I was not alone; there were people sleeping on the station floor, others on chairs, waiting for the next bus. In Udomxai I intended to rent a bike to explore the surrounding villages, but the rainy season had arrived and it rained regularly every day, so I only made a couple of short walks once the rain eased in the afternoons.

The bus to Luang Nam Tha parted at noon from the bus station where two days before I'd arrived at night. It was a minibus of around twenty seats. My backpack, due to the lack of room inside, had to be carried on the bus roof. I made sure the young man on the roof tied it well. I sat behind an attractive young Laotian woman carrying a huge, fluffy orange teddy on the only pair of free seats. After leaving the station, the minibus stopped several times to pick up more passengers. On one of those stops a mother and son got on, and when I realized they couldn't sit together, I moved to the seat in front of me, beside the attractive young woman, leaving two seats for them. The mother thanked me with a smile. I looked at my seat companion in more detail, and appreciated the beauty of her profile, the subtlety of her toasted skin. Looking down, I noticed a more revealing neckline than usual in Laos, the blue edges of her bra surfacing above her round breasts. She hugged the orange teddy, an orangutan, to keep its long hair from touching the dirty floor and dusty window edge. I wondered if the teddy was hers, or maybe a gift for a younger sister or even a daughter. At another stop, a man got on with several chickens in a cage and had to sit on the steps of the exit door in the middle of the minibus. It began to rain. My neighbor handed me the orangutan to close the window. We stopped halfway along at a small market to stretch our legs, visit the bathroom, and buy a drink.

Back in the bus, she boldly leaned her head on my shoulder. Not that she had fallen asleep; she simply seemed to wish to rest her head on a foreign shoulder. I crossed my arms to provide her better support. She adjusted her position, looking for a perfect fitting. After that, she picked up one of the orangutan legs and put her arm, hidden by the orange hair, on my left thigh. I could not believe her attitude. What seemed like an innocent rest was becoming a playful approach. I wanted to know for sure what her intentions were, and I thought my crossed arms gave me the opportunity to caress her bare arm without anyone being able to notice. Her response to my touch would show the reason for her previous movements. When I touched her arm, she not only didn't separate from me but got even closer. I became intensely excited. I glanced to my right, to the young man sitting across the narrow aisle of that bus too tiny to hide in, and thought he was looking at me: he might have noticed the woman's arm on my thigh. The excitement continued and, given the response of the young woman, I didn't hesitate to stretch my arm so my fingers could reach her right breast. I glanced back to make sure the mother and child behind me weren't able to see my movements. With my hand grabbing her breast, the woman again got closer and adjusted the protecting orangutan.

I could not believe what was happening in broad daylight. Two complete strangers unable to communicate verbally, with no problem doing so physically, the rest of the passengers oblivious to it all. I walked my fingers to the edge of her top, where the blue bra appeared, and slid them down to her pointy nipple. She continued with her head on my shoulder, her body pressed against mine, her arm on my thigh, the orangutan hiding the carnal communication. Then I noticed her left hand stroking my arm, stopping to feel my abundant Latin hair, certainly a novelty to that young Laotian woman. Her right arm moved slightly, as if wishing to get closer to my crotch. I wanted her right hand to slide onto my sex, but the orangutan's leg didn't reach up that far, and the young man to my right would have witnessed such a brazen approach. I continued, extremely excited. I uncrossed my arms and slid down my left hand, hidden by the orangutan, down to her thigh and onto her pubis. I lamented the fact she was wearing jeans and not a skirt. She opened up her legs slightly while the teddy shielded her.

The bus turned right and entered a bus station. We had arrived at our destination even though the town of Luang Nam Tha was a few miles away. The groping stopped abruptly, her head stood upright, our bodies separated. We stepped off the bus. She got into a *tuk–tuk*, hugging the teddy. The *tuk–tuk* filled up and left while I waited for my bag to come down from the roof. I regretted not being able to share the *tuk–tuk* to Luang Nam Tha and seeing where that bold and playful woman was going. The *tuk–tuk* pulled away, the orange orangutan still visible over a long distance. I wanted to see her again, so once we got in Luang Nam Tha, I carefully watched street after street, waiting for the orange teddy to take me to the cheeky young woman. I also thought it'd be much easier for her to find me if she wanted to. I didn't see her again. On the way to the hotel, I could not stop smiling at the surprising encounter. Unexpectedly, I'd satisfied, although not completely, one of my sexual fantasies. In my London days I fantasized being in one of the back seats of the train that took me home after work, with an attractive woman next to me, and without a word between us, we'd begin to touch each other under our winter clothes and end up at her home, or mine, making love passionately. This time

I masturbated under the shower.

Luang Nam Tha is not very beautiful in itself, but its location, close to the mountains bordering China, is certainly gorgeous. Much of the nearby forest had been felled and the timber exported to China, a country so thirsty for raw materials that it apparently financed the construction of the excellent road that now connects the two countries. I read that in recent years the Laotian government was actively pursuing and combating illegal logging, and I sincerely wished it was effective in its fight, because places such as northern Laos, peeled of trees, would sadden anyone who visited it. All of northern Laos is a beautiful area ideal for rural and adventure tourism, and if the authorities are smart about resource management, Laos could turn into one of the stars of tourism in Southeast Asia. I rented a mountain bike for a couple of days to explore the surroundings of Luang Nam Tha and visit several ethnic villages. The rain continued to make an appearance, but this time it didn't stop me in my plans. In fact, one afternoon on the bike, in shorts and with my raincoat protecting me, I intensely enjoyed the feeling of the light rain falling on my body, refreshing my skin.

On my last day in Laos, I got an email from Thuy's manager in which she first apologized for the delay in her response, and then informed me that Thuy had quit a few weeks ago to get married. I felt deeply saddened by the news. Maybe she found a good husband to take her out of the pit she was in; marriage, for better or worse, remains an escape for many young women around the world. I was reminded again of my mother, who left her village in the province of Avila to go to Madrid to work as a maid for a wealthy family of three unmarried sisters and a brother. After six months in Madrid's district of Salamanca, during a trip to San Sebastian one of the sisters became ill and the doctor advised her to reside in a humid climate. The coastal city of San Sebastian, where the family had an apartment overlooking the city's main boulevard, became the permanent residence of the four siblings, who invited my mother to stay with them. She, pleased with her bosses, accepted the move from Madrid. My father, meanwhile, had left his village in Burgos to do voluntary military service in Madrid. During the twenty months of service he got his truck—driving license and subsequently became the driver for a colonel. Once his military service was over, he went to Barcelona, where his sister, my aunt Carmen, lived, to work in the kitchen of a hotel. After living in the Catalan city, he decided to change the Mediterranean for the Atlantic and settled in an aunt's house in the old part of San Sebastian. My parents met in 1966 in one of its streets, where they lived not much more than a five minutes' walk from each other. They held a three—day wedding in my mother's village two years later, and I was born ten months after the wedding. That's life, a continuous flow of circumstances, of crossroads, and wonderful people we met along the way.

CHAMPIONS & SAILING

*"To awaken quite alone in a strange town is one of the pleasantest
sensations in the world." —Freya Stark*

"Half the fun of the travel is the aesthetic of lostness." —Ray Bradbury

The soccer World Cup, beginning in South Africa, was the reason I had crossed the Mekong River, the natural border between Laos and Thailand, thinking it would be much easier to get a room with television that showed the matches in Thailand than in Laos. The crossing was the easiest and most relaxing of my entire trip. For my departure from Laos, I had my passport stamped in a small outpost east of the Mekong, in Huay Xai, and then took a boat with an Irishman and an Australian couple to reach Chiang Khong, on the opposite bank, where another small post welcomed us to Thailand. From there I traveled by bus to Chiang Rai, where I spent a night. After enjoying a fantastic Thai massage, I saw the match between Japan and Cameroon at a bar where the Asian patrons and staff cheered the Japanese victory goal. As emerging continents in the world of soccer, both Africa and Asia show support for the countries representing them, a nonexistent sentiment among Europeans.

I woke up, unaware of where I was, a feeling that had visited me several times over the last months, especially during periods of constant travel, and that I would continue to experience from time to time during the rest of my Asian tour. When it happened, while I was still in bed, it usually took me several seconds to become aware of my location on the globe. Typically it was the memory of the last leg of my journey or something I had done the previous day that gave me enough clarity to place myself exactly. It was a feeling I loved waking up to; a sense of possibility, of movement, of abandonment, impossible in a sedentary existence; an awakening that brought awareness of how lucky my nomadic situation was.

I went to Chiang Mai, where I would spend two weeks before flying to Phuket and going to Koh Phangan and Koh Tao, where I'd booked a six–day sailing course. That was the plan during the World Cup. I felt sorry somehow that it was taking place during my adventure, but it would also give me the opportunity to enjoy it as much as I wished to. The last one, as well as Spain's victory in the European Championship two years earlier, I had followed with difficulty from New York because of the time difference. Now, despite it, I could stay up late watching any game that interested me without the obligation of daily work.

Chiang Mai is what I call a village city. Its historic center, surrounded by the remains of a wall and a moat protecting it, is full of cafes, restaurants, and guesthouses, many with cute terraces and gardens and well integrated with the residential areas and city's numerous Buddhist temples. I immediately appreciated its healthy balance, more so after visiting cities in effect colonized by tourists, such as Hoi An and Luang Prabang. I stayed at Rendezvous, a central guesthouse with spacious rooms with television, refrigerator, and Wi–Fi. My days in Chiang Mai were spent visiting many of its Buddhist temples, reading and writing in cafes, eating the delicious Thai food, getting Thai massages, and watching soccer in the evenings (the last game of each day began at 1:30 a.m., local time). Spain, having won the European Championship two years before, was one of the favorites, but they lost their first match, against Switzerland, a defeat that caused the typical regrets for Spain's mental fragility and lack of forcefulness.

During most of my early years, I played soccer as a right midfielder. I was a mixture of David Beckham (good at pass, cross, and shoot) and Frank Lampard (good at arrival from deep field, shoot, and scoring), but not good enough to make a living as a professional player. I started playing on La Concha Beach with my school team before playing for my neighborhood club, Sporting de Herrera, where I can claim to have played for several years with Bittor Alkiza, later a Real Sociedad player. My idol as a child was Zamora, the talented creative midfielder of Real Sociedad's great team in the '80s that won the only two league titles the team holds.

Years later, already in college, I qualified as a youth coach and began coaching one of the kids' teams of my former club. A couple of years later I took over one of the two under–eighteen teams in the club. I have great memories of that period, especially of the afternoon practices with kids, who were so excited about learning.

In Chiang Mai, I took a Thai cooking course one day in a house garden with an open kitchen fully equipped for group classes. We were eight Westerners that morning. We first visited the garden where they grew herbs and vegetables, before going to the local market to learn the different varieties of rice, vegetables, and fruit. Then, with everyone in an apron and at a prep table, we chose six dishes to prepare. I chose papaya salad, chicken soup, two sauteed chicken dishes, a green curry, and sticky rice with mango. The spicy papaya salad also included tomatoes, garlic, soy, peanuts, and chilies, and was dressed with sugar, fish sauce, and lime juice. The soup had chicken, lemongrass, kaffir leaves, galangal, chilies, shallots, and mushrooms. One of the sauteed chicken dishes included rice noodles and oyster sauce, the other boiled rice and basil. The green curry had green chilies, garlic, lemongrass, coriander, ginseng, galangal, and kaffir lime leaves. The dessert was prepared by mixing boiled rice with coconut cream, sugar, and salt, with fresh mango on the side. We enjoyed a huge feast, as everything we cooked we ate on the long wooden table strategically placed next to the kitchen.

It was already June, and the breather I took in Chiang Mai was a good time to take a look back after the resumption of my trip in early January. No doubt, I had enjoyed my time intensely. The four weeks in Myanmar, the short stay in Bangkok and eastern Thailand, the month in Cambodia, the two months in Vietnam (despite the stagnant period in Saigon when I was undergoing medical treatment), and the three weeks in Laos were full of memorable moments. I love Southeast Asia; it's a wonderful region in which to get lost in its natural beauty, to wander around its cities, explore its gastronomy, and discover its culture. Its people are noble, humble, sincere, and direct. They don't show much tension on their faces, in stark contrast with the attitude of a large part of the Western population, so stressed about anything. I think a couple of weeks living in a village in northern Laos would have greater success in lightening the over–loaded Western mind than pills and therapy. During those months news from family and friends had also arrived; although it seemed that life had taken a long hiatus, it never stops but continues unabated. Facebook had become my main connecting point with them. Thanks to technology, I could know what was happening in their lives, as they were able to follow my adventures and, through my photos, know where I was. My friend Johnny had bought an apartment in Brooklyn with his wife, my friend David and his girlfriend Eleanor were engaged and would marry in July in New York, my friends Marc and Ivy were expecting their second child in Hong Kong, my London friends were arranging for a friends meeting in October in France and for a vacation together in Bali during Easter 2011, my cousin Ana was pregnant for the second time, my mother would travel to India in September, and my brother had already been more than five months with his girlfriend and he looked happy.

It was after my cousin Ana's wedding in October 2003 that the arrhythmia returned to my heart with ferocity. The ceremony was during the evening, and after dinner we went out until dawn. I had a great time and drank more than usual, plenty of wine at dinner and several whiskeys after the cava. The next day I had lunch with my college friends before I was to take the flight from Biarritz to London. After lunch, as I was coming to my mom's, my heart rate shot up as if something evil had triggered a hidden switch. I couldn't believe it. I could clearly notice the crazy tachycardia, my heart totally unbridled, galloping when it wasn't necessary. I chose to take a walk instead of waiting for the arrival of my uncle and aunt, who were taking me to the airport. I walked calmly, sometimes quickening my pace, desperately wanting the switch to go back to the off position. Upon arriving home, I announced to my mother, my uncle, and my aunt that the destination was not the airport but the hospital.

Upon entering the emergency room, I recounted to the

physician the episode I'd suffered in London year and a half earlier. He immediately did an EKG and took me to the operating room for my second encounter with electric shock, my second toss of a coin. A couple of hours later I was out of the hospital and on my way home. I asked for a copy of the electrocardiogram to carry to my cardiologist in London, where I flew two days later. The blow was terrible. This time it hadn't been the result of intense exercise after a soccer game, but as I was getting out of my brother's van on my way home. Immediately, I thought about the previous night's drinking, knowing that alcohol can disrupt the heart's rhythm. But what was the real cause of this sudden attack? Was I doomed to live with the constant threat of the capricious switch on my heart? Or was there any treatment, current or coming, that would fix the switch? I felt very heavy, deeply concerned and saddened to be thirty–four years old and possessing a defective motor that could stop working prematurely.

It was four days before my flight to Phuket when, after I had returned from a visit to one of Chiang Mai's temples, a man called out to me from a travel agency I was passing. I turned to face him, and although I almost ignored what I thought would be a tour offer, stopped to chat with him. In addition to his travel agency, he organized promotional events and even beauty contests for women, men, and lady–boys. He hastened to show me some pictures, and I noticed the latest Miss Lady–Boy was more beautiful (or handsome, should I write) than the latest Miss Chiang Mai. I had noticed right away that the man talking to me was gay, and he quickly inquired about my sexual orientation. I could see he was disappointed with my response, and I was about to say goodbye when he offered to get me a Thai girlfriend. Thanks to the events he organized, he knew many local women who were interested in *farang* men (originally the Thai word for "French" that is today applied to all white Westerners). I suspected it was another prostitute offer like the many I'd received throughout Southeast Asia; however, he assured me it was far from it. He suggested I come back that evening; by then he'd have made some calls to see if any girl would like to come for a drink with us. I remembered the experience in Battambang in Cambodia; I had nothing to lose and everything to gain.

I returned that evening, and he told me his research had paid off. A tall woman with slender and firm legs and tanned skin arrived on her motorbike and sat down for a beer with us. Her name was Khae, thirty-six years old, twice divorced, both from Americans, with whom she'd had a son and a daughter respectively. She'd just come back to Chiang Mai to look for work after spending some time in her village with her children and her mother. We drank a couple of beers before heading out. I rode on her bike, my hands on her hips, and went to Chiang Mai Night Bazaar, with the cool night air caressing our unprotected heads. She took me to a disco bar where there was live music. We had a couple of beers. I sat on a high stool; she danced, sometimes between my legs. From there we went to another bar, more beers, same position, but now she danced sitting on one of my thighs. We spent the night together, and the next morning, and the remaining days I spent in Chiang Mai, days that became what I thought was the ideal life for the common man: morning sex, eating, relaxing afternoon, soccer, dinner, beer, soccer, pool, soccer, sex, sleep, and start again. How easy it can be to satisfy a man, at least temporarily! The last night in Chiang Mai, as we made love, Khae asked me not go to Phuket, and in the morning, before leaving for the airport, I noticed her briefly mourning in bed; she didn't say why.

I had thought of Phuket merely as an area full of vacation resorts, but thanks to Lonely Planet, I was pleased to learn the town also has an important history. During the seventeenth century Dutch, British, and French traders settled on the island to trade tin, which led to the arrival of thousands of Chinese immigrants to work in the mines. The old part of Phuket is an example of Sino-Portuguese architecture, houses that combine Lusitanian design with Chinese: two-story buildings entered through a large door of Chinese design, with a courtyard garden inside, and a second floor with a balcony overlooking the street.

Spain was able to straighten out their awful start in the

World Cup when, after the defeat against Switzerland, they won the next two games, against Honduras and Chile. Portugal would be the next opponent in the first knockout round. Besides soccer, I continued reading. Specifically, I immensely enjoyed the book *Among Insurgents: Walking Through Burma*, by Shelby Tucker, an American professor at Oxford who decided in 1988 to cross Burma, in the company of a young Swede, through the jungle in the north, from the Chinese border to India, defying the Burmese military conflict with the tribes of the area. It was thanks to Kachin guerrillas that Tucker and his companion managed to reach India after more than three months of journeying through the thick and dangerous Burmese jungle. An awesome adventure.

It was the rainy season. The monsoon lashed the west coast intensely and it rained daily in Phuket, a fact that forced me to ignore its paradisiacal islands and go to the Gulf of Thailand, where it hardly rains at that time of year. I traveled by bus from Phuket to Don Sak pier, and there took the ferry to Koh Phangan, where I stayed for almost a week, enjoying several beaches on its west coast. After our victory over Portugal, I stayed in Koh Phangan to see the quarterfinal match against Paraguay, very intense, and the semifinal against Germany. Finally, Spain had reached the final of a World Cup! Many Thais following the championship were glad about it; many said they had bet money on Spain.

Koh Tao, Turtle Island, is a small island, perhaps too small, famous for its excellent diving. However, I was more interested in sailing than browsing the seabed. I was the only student of the sailing course; the recent violence in the streets of Bangkok had drastically reduced the number of visitors to Thailand. The instructor was a German from East Berlin, who gave sailing lessons on his 36–foot sloop. The boat was anchored in a small cove on the east side of the island. I stayed in a simple log cabin in front of it, a peaceful, quiet, and beautiful place. I'm a sea lover. I love its smell, its air, its extent, its strength, its calm, its colors, its touch; so sailing has always attracted me. I never did any sailing in my city, San Sebastian, where at the time soccer was my passion. However, I was fortunate that both my grammar school and high school faced the beach, and so, on many a day, I went down to the beach with friends either to play or watch the rough waves at high tide. One becomes addicted to the sea, to its presence and smell. And I missed it a lot in London. On a couple of occasions I had enjoyed a week's vacation on a boat in the Mediterranean, in Greece and Turkey, which got me to dreaming of owning a sailboat. The six–day course on Turtle Island was made up of morning lectures followed by four hours of sailing in the afternoon. Despite a light wind, I got to learn the basics of sailing and greatly enjoyed being on the sea, with no sound other than the wind and the waves.

The day of the final against the Netherlands arrived. I walked from my isolated cabin to the west of the island, where the social life of Koh Tao happens. I'd been told of a spacious beachside bar that had a giant screen on the sand, but when I got there the bar was flooded with the Dutch orange, so I decided to go looking for the red fury of Spain. However, there was no trace of it on the island. It seemed impossible that the colors of a small country like the Netherlands would be more apparent in the bare streets of an island in the Gulf of Thailand than those of a much larger country like Spain. I opted for an English pub to find a more neutral environment. The final was tense, but Iniesta's goal will remain forever in the memory of all Spanish soccer fans. At last we were World Champions.

SENSATIONS & IMPERMANENCE

"One's destination is never a place, but a new way of seeing things."
—Henry Miller

"Remember that happiness is a way of travel, not a destination."
—Roy M. Goodman

Thanks to AirAsia's low prices, I opted to use them to travel from Phuket to Kuala Lumpur. I would be in Malaysia only a short time, most of it at the meditation course, before continuing on to Indonesia. So when I arrived in Kuala Lumpur, I requested a sixty–day visa at the Indonesian embassy, because the one obtained on arrival is only for thirty days, insufficient to explore such a vast country. Later I went to the historic city center and to Chinatown. What struck me the most during my first walk around Kuala Lumpur was not the contrast between the old and the modern, spectacular as it is, but the contrast between the Malay women, Muslim and modestly dressed, their hair always covered by a hijab, and the ethnic Chinese women, who just cover the bare minimum, usually wearing very short pants, tight tops, many sleeveless, with deep necklines, most of their fair skin exposed. I have never experienced such a discrepancy in a dress code. Looking more closely at how Malay Muslim women dressed, I could notice differences amongst them. Many of the young women covered their hair but wore tight jeans that marked their hips and bottoms without shame, and although the hijab is designed to cover not only the hair but also the breasts, some carried the hijab short, above the top line of their breasts. I found it totally absurd to see so many young Malaysian women with their hair concealed, but showing the contours of their breasts, hips, and bottoms. I don't know of any man who is sexually aroused by the exclusive vision of a woman's hair, but many whose testosterone levels soar hopelessly at the sight of the curves of a woman's breasts and buttocks and hips.

Kuala Lumpur, with its modern shopping centers, attracts

a large number of Arab consumers, easily detectable by their women, who dress in the black niqab that in some cases covers even their faces, with slits their eyes' only window to the outside world. At least the long, wide black robes successfully hide the females' bodies; if the objective is not to ignite males' passions, long black robes are clearly more suitable for the task, although they also surely excite males' imagination besides adding a sense of mystery and inaccessibility. Modesty, however, did not extend to the accessories that many of the women carried. Gucci sunglasses, LVMH handbags, and ostentatious jewelry shone with great intensity against the niqab's black background. The discrepancy between the male and female dress of these Arabs visitors bordered on silliness. I saw a couple in which she wore a black robe with her face uncovered, D&G sunglasses, and an LVMH handbag, while he wore shorts, sneakers, and an AC Milan soccer team T—shirt.

It was Saturday evening, and I went to dinner at a Thai restaurant in Changkat Bukit Bintang, Kuala Lumpur's latest nightlife street, which was parallel to the guesthouse where I was staying. It's a very popular street with a section devoted exclusively to restaurants and bars. After dinner, the street was full of people drinking and walking from one bar to another. I found an outdoor table where I could have a beer and be entertained by the activity of the evening. On my way there I'd seen a very pretty woman on the terrace next door; fortunately I could see her from my table. She noticed my gaze and began to look back from time to time. She was sitting with a man and another woman; the first two were involved in a conversation while the woman seemed left apart. I had an idea that, although her eyes kept returning to mine, the man she was with was her partner. Minutes later the man, a blond Westerner of around forty—five, left for the bar—I figured to go to the washroom—so I took the opportunity to fix my gaze on the beautiful woman with more intensity. She responded with a greeting, raising her beer glass. Then she put a hand to her ear with the typical telephone gesture, a gesture that confused me. If she wanted to give me her phone number, it didn't seem the best time while being accompanied by the blonde guy, who quickly returned. I thought it'd be easier if her female friend came to my table as an intermediary, which didn't happen. She continued conversing with the man; I figured she might have been just flirting, with no other interest. Although I considered it, I didn't dare approach their table. Minutes later I watched them all leave the bar together.

The next day I went for lunch to an Italian restaurant down the street, and to my surprise, one of the waitresses was the female friend ignored by the couple the previous night. I decided to talk to her when I finished my lunch, but she approached me before I had a chance to, saying she'd recognized me. She told me the attractive woman was her sister; the blonde man was her sister's ex-boyfriend. Apparently, they had bumped into him and had a drink together. I told her I'd like to have a drink with her beautiful sister. She suggested I come to the bar across the street at 9 p.m., the same where I had seen them last night; she would make sure her sister came to the appointment.

I had dinner beforehand, and as it was still a bit early, I decided to go to one of the second-floor balcony bars common in Changkat. A little before 9 p.m., to my despair, I saw the ex-boyfriend and two friends sit at a table on the terrace of the bar where we were to meet. Immediately I wished I had suggested a different bar. My date, however, didn't turn up. I waited half an hour before I saw her coming down the street, going to her sister's restaurant, talking to her, and without even peering into the bar where her ex-boyfriend was, start walking back the way she had come. I was about to go down to meet her when she looked up. I smiled at her from the balcony and made her a gesture inviting her to come up.

Her name was Lani, a beautiful, petite Filipina with a sensually curved body. While we drank a couple of beers on the balcony, she told me she'd broken up with her boyfriend three months before after a four-year relationship. I felt she was still affected by it. The conversation didn't flow as I expected; she seemed somewhat shy or aloof. After the breakup she went to the Philippines and had just returned to visit her sister. We changed bars, ordered another drink, and gradually began to be more relaxed, more participatory—not (I hoped) because I had told her I lived in New York and had been almost a year traveling, details that can drastically alter the interest of some women in that part of the world. She suggested going to a bar where there was live music. It was late and the place was almost empty. As a young woman, she had been married, in the Philippines, to an Englishman, who became violent with alcohol. She divorced him, and years later she immigrated to Kuala Lumpur, where she worked as a cosmetologist. She told me that her features and skin color made her appear to be Malay in Malaysia. However, she dressed more like women of Chinese origin, with shorts, miniskirts, and sleeveless tops, which usually made her receive critical looks from Malay men and women. She was surprised, even incredulous, at my celibacy, or rather over the fact that I'd never married or had children. She asked me if I were bisexual. I was surprised by the question, but later I learned the reason for the breakup with her boyfriend had been that she'd caught him with a lady–boy. We had a couple of whiskeys and kissed with the background sound of loud rock.

Back in Changkat, where she was staying with her sister in an apartment shared with other Filipino waitresses, I invited her to spend the night with me. She declined unconvincingly, before accepting, though warning me that nothing would happen between us. My room had a single bed, too narrow to accommodate two people comfortably, but perfect to force our bodies to be in full contact. Her "warning" had little effect that night or the next morning. However, to my surprise and frustration, it did over the following two nights. Although I changed to a double–bed room, due to her caution and determination not to suffer after her recent breakup, she refused to have sex with me but not to sleep beside me. If Sokun in Battambang represented the good woman and Khae in Chiang Mai the fun one, Lani had a bit of both. I liked her quite a lot, although not enough for a long–term relationship. However, had I lived in Kuala Lumpur, I would probably have liked to go out with her for a while.

After the three days in Lani's company, it was time for one of my trip's most anticipated experiences: my meditation course at Dhamma Malaya. The bus from Kuala Lumpur went east and stopped three hours later in front of the University of Malaysia Pahang, near the road to the meditation center Dhamma Malaya. I got off with a young, freckled, blonde woman who was also going to the vipassana course I was taking. She was English and admitted being a bit nervous ahead of the course. We walked along a path flanked by oil palm trees to the meditation center. Malaysia is, after Indonesia, the second largest producer of palm oil. In both countries large parts of their forests have been cleared for its cultivation. At the meditation center, several posters directed us to the registration area, one for men and another for women. As I'd done in Nepal, I read once again the discipline code of the course, filled out a form with personal information, and deposited my books, writing materials, cell phone, computer, money, and other valuable possessions. Each dormitory building had eight very basic, single, functional rooms, each with a mattress on a tiled platform, a fan in the ceiling, and a separate bathroom. There was no closet; just a rope with some clips for hanging clothes. I was assigned room 5 in building Q and took a bed sheet, a pillow cover, and a thin blanket to settle in.

I returned to the registration area, where students were arriving. The majority were ethnic Chinese Malaysians (the course was taught in Mandarin and English). A young man spoke to me in Spanish: "You are Spanish, aren't you? I heard you say it while you registered." His name was David, and he was there with his girlfriend Maria, whom I didn't meet until the end of the course, as the women had already been separated from the men. Both from Santillana del Mar, just a couple of hours west of San Sebastian, they'd been traveling through Europe, Africa, the Middle East, and now Asia for the past three and half years. Months ago they met a couple who told them about the vipassana course, they found it interesting, and there they were, without knowing much about it but willing to experience it.

After dinner there was a talk about the course rules, a

position in the meditation hall was assigned to each student (mine was E2), and we headed into the hall for our first meditation session. Everything was exactly as I had experienced in Lumbini eight months ago. In fact, all of the Goenka meditation courses follow the same rules and routine worldwide. In the meditation room not one but two teachers, male for the men, female for the women, waited for us. The large room had a high pyramidal roof with fourteen fans hanging from it (several more were attached to the walls). We began by focusing on our breath, feeling the air coming in and out of our nostrils. This was the prelude to the next three and a half days of anapana, the practice necessary before facing vipassana meditation. The course had begun, and with it, a vow of silence not to be broken until the morning of the tenth day as a prelude to the return to the outside world. I was happy to be there after the long wait, this time without any physical problems, for what I expected to be a unique and unforgettable experience. We retired to our rooms at 9 p.m.

The bell rang punctually at 4 a.m., struck (actually, it was a recording that sounded from the center's speakers) repeatedly to ensure that even the deepest sleep would be interrupted. I got up and did some stretching exercises for my legs, back, and neck; the Lumbini experience had taught me how stiff my body was immediately after waking up. The first session of each day lasted two hours, and was perhaps my favorite. Still dark out, with my body fully rested, it was not too difficult to meditate for two hours. Being an evening person, I find the darkness of the night calms me down, and my mind felt totally disconnected from the world outside. I sat down, crossed my legs, and concentrated on the air coming in and out of my nostrils. Within minutes my legs were already complaining about the discomfort imposed. I shifted numerous times, alternating the leg closest to the body, kneeling with the cushion as a seat, even bending both legs in the same direction. In every position I took, my knees or calves soon screamed with pain. When my legs didn't, my back did. My strong and muscular soccer player legs didn't have the necessary flexibility to sit on the floor crossed, something I had known for a long time, and that, I feared, would be my main obstacle during the course.

The first day of the course is dedicated to disconnecting from the outside world. Each student comes with recent personal experiences and thoughts that continually interrupt his or her concentration on breathing. It's a constant mental battle. To my mind came my days spent with Lani and my latest conversations, mainly the long talk I had had with David about our travels. But my recent anapana practice slowly helped me get these intrusive thoughts increasingly sparingly. However, the fight with my legs went on, and became more distracting than my thoughts. I took two more cushions to raise my sitting position and a third one to support one of my legs. I looked like an invalid in need of scaffolding to sit.

The second day, once there was notable progress in disconnecting, was dedicated to paying attention to the breath in more detail, noting if it came through the right nostril or the left, maybe both, if it was a deep breath or a shallow one, without altering or influencing it in any way. The mission was to observe and return to our breathing as soon as we were aware that our mind had gone astray again. When this happened, it was necessary not to show any frustration or anger, but to remain calm and to focus on our breath, to observe it as a scientist observes natural reality. Focusing on our breath, we were forced to live in the present, which is all we can really experience; the past is gone, the future is not yet here. The only way to get the feeling of mindfulness is to be present with full attention; otherwise, we live somewhat numb and mentally contaminated. During the second day, the thoughts that haunted me the most were those of several women whom I had liked in recent years. Their names and faces came into my memory, as if a mental review were taking place.

My daily routine was soon defined: stretching after waking up before the 4:30 to 6:30 a.m. session, followed by breakfast, a walk, and a shower, two meditation sessions between 8 a.m and 11 a.m, then lunch followed by a siesta, three sessions between 1 p.m. and 5 p.m., a walk and shower after the 5 p.m. tea, a one—hour session at 6 p.m. followed by a recorded discourse by Professor S. N. Goenka of more than an hour, and a final short session at 8:30 p.m., then filling my water bottle before going to bed around 9:30. Between sessions, there were leg and back stretches interspersed with short walks to relieve my body of its stiffness after the long meditation stints. The walking area was located behind the bedrooms, near the intensely green jungle, where from time to time I could distinguish a tropical bird. My walk was slow and relaxed, my attention focused on nature, the humid heat, and the warm breeze.

On the third day, we focused on the sensations in the triangular area formed by our nose and upper lip. With our minds calm, and with the concentration necessary to notice our breath in detail, it was the turn to feel the different sensations continuously present in that area of our body but that our mind does not grasp due to lack of training. It might be a slight stinging or slight tingling sensation, some tension, for example of air touching our skin, some heat, maybe sweat; sometimes I felt something I couldn't explain. It wasn't necessary to do anything else; just to concentrate and observe the sensations when they appeared or, when there were none, to feel our breath. It was an exercise I liked because it required more effort than simply observing my breathing; the concentration was easier for me, and my mind didn't wander as often. On this day, when my mind did wander, it was to think about my friends, with the feeling of how really lucky I was to have so many good friends scattered around the world. Despite continuing difficulties with my physical position, which I often changed, trying not to disturb my colleagues, that day I felt energetic during breaks; I even walked fast, or at least faster than my classmates, who usually walked with short, slow, relaxed steps.

Finally the fourth day arrived. It was on the fourth day of the course in Lumbini when I had to leave to go to the hospital in Kathmandu. I remembered the light feeling I'd had in the taxi to the airport that afternoon. Today, the morning was dedicated to noticing sensations, but now only in the upper lip. By reducing the area of concentration, the mind becomes more acute, able to notice sensations in increasingly smaller areas. My mind had reached great calm and concentration, broken that morning only by a few memories of my family. In the afternoon the novelty of the course began for me; all of the above I had experienced eight months earlier. The vipassana class started at 3 p.m. (the prior practice had been anapana), with the following instructions: try to notice sensations on the top of the head, to continue with the face, neck, one arm, then the other, chest, abdomen, back, buttocks, pubis, one leg, and then the other. The order could be altered, but it was important to follow it, once chosen, and not to miss any part of the body. The task was to note any physical sensation without reacting to it, whether wanting it to disappear (an unpleasant sensation, such as pain or muscle tension) or wishing it to continue (a feeling of lightness, a pleasant tingling or sense of relaxation). The goal was to remain with a feeling of equanimity toward our physical sensations, whatever their characteristics.

We were learning that our body is composed of matter that is constantly changing, of chemical reactions beyond our control that occur relentlessly. We only control a small part of ourselves. We can move most of our muscles, but with limitations; we can influence our body through nutrition and exercise, but our genes come from nature. By meditating we realize that we don't even control our thoughts because these often spring independently; they come and go, uncontrolled by our supposedly powerful ego (the "monkey mind," as Buddhists call it, always jumping from branch to branch). Sensations also come and go. This experience helps us to understand that everything that happens in the world and to us is impermanent, including pleasing sensations and painful ones, which helps to dilute our ego and our attachment to our body, our feelings, and our thoughts. We were experiencing the three characteristics of existence, according to Buddhist philosophy: the first is dissatisfaction or suffering, duhkha; the second is the transience of all life, of all experience (anitya in Sanskrit); which leads us to the third, the non-self, the lack of ego (anatman). When you understand that everything in nature is constantly changing and that much of yourself is out of your control, when you experience that your physical body, your feelings, and your thoughts don't fully depend on you, you start to see reality with a less self–centered view. "*Anitya, anitya, anitya,*" the teacher Goenka kept repeating in his instructions during the course. If you understand that everything is impermanent, then your desires and fears won't take root in your ego and will eventually vanish.

When he died, my father, for almost two years previously, had been suffering from a mild depression that made him feel down and have trouble sleeping. He did not work for a long time and took sleeping pills (it bothered him tremendously not being able to enjoy a full night's sleep), but neither the psychologist who treated him or we considered the depression as very troubling or a symptom of a serious condition. We blamed it on his arrival at his sixties and his slight apprehension and doubts whether to retire early or continue to work stoically until he was sixty–five. The cancer that took him away at sixty–one, much too soon, was of the pancreas, one of the most difficult to detect, very little studied and with a high mortality rate. During my desperate research online, I discovered that a high percentage of its victims suffer from depression, and medicine still doesn't know what the relationship between the two is: if depression might have something to do with the development of this form of cancer, or if the cancer is a trigger of this form of mental distress. In any case, it was very frustrating for me to accept that my father had been treated for mild depression when inside him a tumor was literally devouring him. How important it should have been for the psychologist to be aware of this study, and in her attempt to heal my father, ask for a detailed analysis of his physical condition (something we should also have considered immediately). Mind and body are totally and intrinsically connected.

During the long vipassana class, I began to worry about how hard it would be to concentrate on the task of scanning my entire body with my constant changing of position. When the target area was only the nose and upper lip, I could alter the position of my legs without seriously disrupting my concentration, but now that the whole body became the object of exploration, any substantial movement broke my concentration. At the end of the day I recognized the impossibility of combining vipassana meditation with the instability of my position on the floor, and opted to ask for a chair to sit on and at least be able to go into deeper meditation without being constantly worried about the pain in my legs and back.

The next day, as I sat comfortably in a low chair with a cushion on the seat and another on the back to force my back to remain straight, the practice became much easier. My level of concentration multiplied, and I began to feel sensations in all my body as I scanned it down from head to toe. The blind areas were my left arm and leg, where I had to linger for a couple of minutes to be able to feel anything.

From that day on, there were also three daily one–hour sessions during which we tried to remain motionless, an exercise in determination (*addhitana* in Sanskrit). During one of these sessions, I experienced something really strange. I tended to rest the fingers of my right hand on the left, with both hands on my lap, a position that relaxed my arms and shoulders completely. First I started to feel my left hand twisting out until it turned completely and the two backs of my hands were in full contact. After that, the hands, still touching, began to travel to the left, diagonally upward, to a point above my left ear, and remained there for several minutes without any discomfort whatsoever. In fact, the whole feeling was very pleasant. Several minutes later, my hands began, at a slow speed, to return to their original position, and upon reaching it, the fingers of both hands were stuck together by an incredible force, as if the strongest glue had been applied to them. The intensity was maintained until the session ended. I opened my eyes and looked directly at my hands, which were in precisely the same position as at the beginning of the session. The movements obviously hadn't been more than an illusion of my mind, but I couldn't release my fingers, so intense was the force that held them together. Therefore, I chose to close my eyes, skipped the five–minute break, and continued meditating.

After about twenty minutes—after almost an hour and a half, all told, without my having moved more than to open my eyes—my right leg started to fall asleep because of the pressure on my buttock. I started to move slightly to release the pressure and in doing so, gradually, the strength in my fingers began to fade and disappear completely. At the end of the day, during the question period, I asked the teacher about my experience. The teacher replied that, as when something unexpected happens in life, these extraordinary sensory experiences serve to train us to remain equanimous at all times, regardless of the degree of strangeness. I realized that vipassana is a practical exercise of consciousness that allows us to understand the close relationship between body and mind. All emotions produce a physical sensation. We were preparing to notice how mechanically we react to different situations in our lives, to notice the physical sensations produced in us by them, and be able to stop in time to evaluate our reactions and, if we decided to, to rectify them in time. It's a struggle against the psychological automatism that we all are subject to; we are prisoners of inherited and acquired mental habits that can impede full and healthy action in our lives.

After the shock that caused my tachycardia, I began to listen to my heart more closely; not only in a figurative sense, but also physically. The fear of a second attack made me pay attention to it, so much that I noticed when my heart skipped a beat (something common, but most are not aware of it). The times I heard my heart the clearest was when I lay in bed to sleep on my left side, when the pressure of my weight on the mattress enhanced my sensitivity to my heart. In that position, I often couldn't sleep, as I felt the beating so clearly I had to turn to my right side or sleep face down. In a way, I thought this had been a limited vipassana meditation, with my mind totally focused on the sensations produced daily by my engine muscle.

The fifth day I can call a transition day. The sessions were enjoyable and serene, but a certain tedium began to blossom due to the accumulated hours of meditation. During breaks, my mind began to wander, perhaps seeking some external stimulus to be entertained with. I started giving nicknames to my colleagues. I called one of them The Buddha from the second day, because of his completely shaved head and his serene face. He was the inspiration for the rest. Baby Buddha was a short young guy with a baby face; Naughty Buddha had a roguish face; there was Skinny Buddha and his opposite, Belly Buddha; Daddy Buddha, for his appearance of being a good father; Girly Buddha, because of his feminine face and demeanor; Pinky Buddha, due to the color of his loose trousers; Samurai Buddha, a man with a Japanese face and clothes; Professor Buddha, for his glasses and intellectual looks; Smart Buddha, a young fellow who looked like he knew everything; Brutus Buddha, for the opposite; Hooligan Buddha, an Englishman who seemed to have taken the wrong turn on his way to the soccer stadium; and Playboy Buddha, a man in his fifties dressed in disco attire and always on a visual hunt of the women meditators. Had they known my Spanish origin, perhaps my nickname would have been Bullfighter Buddha or Matador Buddha, although I would have chosen Nomad Buddha.

The next day, the sixth, as I carried on my meditation, some questions began to surface: could I be imagining or causing my sensations? How fast should I move from head to toe? In large areas, such as the thigh or the back, how should I make the exploration? Could I visualize parts of the body where I had difficulties? I wrote down my name on the list for the daily interviews after lunch. The teacher cleared all my doubts. Given the possibility of autosuggestion, he invited me to provoke a cold sensation or any other feeling. There wasn't an ideal speed; everything depended on the level of sensations experienced, but ten minutes to go down from head to toe and another ten to climb up was a good time to take. In large areas of the body, it was best to go in patches of three to four inches in diameter, and then move forward as soon as a sensation appeared. If nothing was felt, it was advised to enlarge the area, then reduce it progressively, as our mind sharpened its ability to detect sensations. Visualization of any object, including of our own body, was a distraction to the task of feeling sensations.

That afternoon, an experience of intensity returned, this time a strong sensation of heat on my head, all around the scalp. And with that sensation, it seemed as if sweat was streaming down to my neck and behind my ears to my back. The feeling was so intense I was sure I'd leave a puddle of sweat under my chair. It was a sensation that could qualify as very unpleasant. At the end of the session I opened my eyes and saw no puddle of sweat under my seat. My back was a little wet and the cushion a little soaked, but much less than expected. I realized then that, given the high sensitivity achieved during intense meditation, every drop of sweat felt like a stream running down the steep mountain of my head.

That night I woke up at half past eleven and had trouble falling asleep again. Though I didn't look at the clock, I know I spent hours awake that night; when I finally fell asleep, it was so late that the 4 a.m. bell was about to ring. When it did, I chose to stay asleep until breakfast even if it meant missing my favorite session. I wanted to face the long day with enough rest. The day was extremely pleasant and fluid. I was glad I'd stayed in bed until 6:30. The heat again made the afternoon sessions somewhat uncomfortable. My head sweated again, but this time less intensely. In the daily speech he made each evening, Professor Goenka spoke of a technique for those sleepless nights (a shame it arrived a day late, I thought). He suggested staying quietly in bed, with eyes closed, concentrating on breathing and feeling the sensations of the body, as if we were meditating lying down. And so I did that night, to fall asleep quickly, and woke up feeling really rested. During one of the next day's sessions, I felt, literally, each fiber of my chest muscles expand one by one, slowly, as if my pectoral muscles were uncontracting, relaxing so much that my shoulders seemed to moved backward, regaining their natural posture after so many years of sitting work had resulted in them being slightly forward. That day my whole body, especially my legs, my neck and shoulders felt fully released of any tension, and I walked is if my body could float, my arms free as pendulums. Even the best massage couldn't have achieved such a feeling of lightness. It was clear that a retreat like the one I was enjoying also brought a substantial physical improvement, resulting from the lack of alcohol, the vegetarian food proportional to our physical inactivity, and especially the release of the accumulated stress.

The dawn of the eighth day was beautiful. When I began my daily walk after breakfast, I looked toward the east as a soft, warm, orange light illuminated the morning. The sun, about to appear, painted the high clouds. After observing the dawn with admiration, I turned to walk back and was surprised to see in the sky a perfect, crisp rainbow. I tried to remember, without success, the last time I had seen a rainbow of that size and clarity. For the afternoon sessions I decided to move my chair from the corner to the middle of the back wall, next to a window that at least would let me feel some cool air. The improvement wasn't as much as I expected but was still welcome. However, upon returning after the break for the start of the next session, I noticed my chair had been returned to its original position, "punished" back in the corner. One of the volunteers had moved it because the teacher considered it too close to the women, having slightly crossed the imaginary gender boundary dividing the meditation hall. I almost exploded at the ridiculousness of the argument, and looked angrily to both the volunteer and the teacher. However, once seated, I decided to calm down quickly and concentrate on the meditation, on the present, without letting myself become so upset by an insignificant event. It seemed that vipassana was paying off. I was sure that, in other circumstances, the effects of anger would have remained in my mind much longer.

During the evening I experienced another strange sensation. In this case my left arm, from the elbow to the fingertips, tightened to the limit. It seemed to want to push my other arm up, without succeeding, though not because the right arm offered any resistance. My left arm remained strongly contracted until the end of the session. In the dining room, while having tea with fruit, I felt several of my left fingers trembling slightly as a result of the previous tension. That night, once again, my sleep was unstable. I was not upset or worried; I just seemed not in need of sleep. I concentrated on my breathing while remaining calm. I fell asleep at midnight and got up at 4 a.m. without difficulty.

The penultimate day was difficult. Doubts came back, especially on how meditation could help dissolve our minds' bad habits. Also, I felt tired, more mentally than physically, and I was sure my sleeping problems worsened it. Meditation was uneasy, anything but smooth, interrupted constantly by my thoughts. I began to wonder if bodily discomfort were a necessary tool, to help the meditator learn to ignore negative sensations; those who were very flexible or those who, like me, meditated in relative comfort on a chair, wouldn't be as successful since they wouldn't be as challenged. If discomfort is part of the process, as the professor said when I asked him about continuing to meditate on the chair, might it be necessary to impose a minimum of discomfort on those with very flexible joints (though not to the point where the discomfort made meditating impossible)? Finally, I was disappointed with the lack of comment on the characteristics of the thoughts that surfaced during meditation, cluttering our concentration. What kind of meditation was it that completely ignored our spontaneous thoughts? The day came to an end, and after the last meditation session, I approached the professor to ask about thoughts. "Why are they ignored?" I asked curiously. And he calmly explained: "Thoughts are like the body's sensations; they come and go, and therefore should be treated as such, without further attention to them." His answer didn't satisfy me at the time, but on the way to fill my water bottle before going to sleep, it became clear to me: thoughts are indeed sensations. I felt too tired to delve deeply into the idea at the time, so I put it off for the next day.

With the arrival of the tenth day a certain excitement was noticeable during breakfast. The vow of silence would end after the 8 a.m. session. The dining room was to be the meeting point and had been prepared with several panels displaying information about the center in Malaysia and other centers around the world. There were also books and articles about vipassana. The barrier between men and women collapsed, and the first thing many divided partners did was meet and talk after almost two weeks of forced separation. I talked to David and met his girlfriend, Maria. All three of us had had trouble sleeping, David from the second day on, Maria and I especially during the second half of the course. After lunch, I took a short nap before going to watch a video about the center in the outskirts of Mumbai (Dhamma Hill, the world's largest, where there's a research center on vipassana meditation), followed by videos about programs with children and prisoners in India. To end the course we were taught *metta* meditation, which is a practice of a few minutes before finishing each session, with the focus on projecting love and compassion to everyone as we feel the vibrations move through our bodies.

That evening we ended the day almost an hour ahead of schedule, so I walked for a while under the bright stars, pondering more deeply the idea of thoughts as sensations. I focused on the thoughts that arise in our minds when we are idle, not the productive thoughts when we work or plan something specific, and I realized that what we seek with these ramblings of the mind are not the thoughts themselves but the sensations they bring to us. If, for example, we think of some positive event to happen in the future, what we really seek is the feeling of success, satisfaction, and achievement. Then I realized why vipassana meditation focuses on sensations rather than thoughts. Physical sensations are paramount in our observation of our body. Thinking is characteristic of our mind, but given that every thought produces a physical sensation in our bodies, sensations are the key to understanding our mental reactions and our emotions. That night, in bed, my mind was still very active, and sleeping was almost impossible.

The eleventh day began with a speech by our teacher at 4:30 a.m. followed by a short *metta* meditation before breakfast and the course closure. We cleaned our rooms and the center, and I gave a donation (all S. N. Goenka courses are free, and the teachers and meditation center workers are volunteers) before we all left. David and Maria went to Kuantan in the car of one of the students. I had considered spending the day there too but was offered a car ride to take me to Kuala Lumpur, so I opted for that. In the car we were two Malaysians of Chinese origin, a young man from Singapore, also ethnic Chinese, a Japanese, and me. I was so sleep–deprived that I fell asleep for half the trip. When I woke up, the Japanese told us he had left his country on a merchant ship heading for China, and from there he was traveling through the Buddhist countries of Southeast Asia with the intention of ending his trip in India (which had been my intended itinerary backwards). He just carried a backpack with a few belongings and had no fixed plans in each country; he simply walked in any direction, and when tired of walking, hitchhiked wherever the driver who picked him up was going. Unless he was invited to sleep indoors, he slept rough. His adventure was based on discovering by wandering, wandering aimlessly in whatever direction life took him. He certainly deserved the nickname Nomad Buddha.

VOLCANOES, RAMADAN & TRIBE

"Travel is fatal to prejudice, bigotry, and narrow-mindedness."
—Mark Twain

"Do not tell me how educated you are, tell me how much you traveled."
—Muhammad

At 9:45 p.m., my flight took off from Kuala Lumpur to Medan, a city in the north of the huge island of Sumatra, the world's sixth largest. I sat in the aisle seat; my two companions were an Indonesian man and a woman returning to Medan from a business trip. I told them where I was from and what my plans were in their country. As I was filling out my Indonesia landing card, a woman across the aisle (she was around fifty, with her hair hidden under a hijab) asked me, with gestures, to lend her my pen. After returning it, she asked the man to my right for my nationality and then asked me if I could be her private English teacher before adding that I was very attractive. I'd have never expected a Muslim woman would make such a compliment to a Western man in the middle of a plane. There's nothing like someone shredding your prejudices by their actions. How wonderful the world is and especially many of its people!

I had dinner at the hotel and went to bed early with the idea of sightseeing a bit of Medan in the morning and leaving for Berastagi in the early hours of the afternoon. My first visit of the day was to the city's main mosque, Mesjid Raya.

"*Salam alaykum,*" a young guy said to me at the entry. "*Alaykum salam,*" I responded to his cordial greeting. Considered the Arabic hello, it literally means "peace be with you." My stay in Malaysia had been short; other than the meditation course, I really only visited Kuala Lumpur, so my two months in Indonesia would be by far my longest period in a Muslim country. Although I'm extremely tolerant of religious beliefs, I confess I don't agree with the extreme differences that exist between men and women in many Muslim countries. I'm a firm believer in equality and individual freedom, and therefore it makes me uncomfortable to witness societies where both are applied selectively.

In the afternoon I arrived at Berastagi, a pleasant inland town with a name that sounded Basque despite the distance, which lies near two active volcanoes: Sibayak (7,257 ft) and Sinabung (8,071 ft). I chose to climb the first one the next morning, a day trip for which my alarm clock was the call to prayer from the local mosque when it was still dark. The smell of sulfur at the top of Mount Sibayak was intense, almost toxic. I had to distance myself from the natural streams to eat my lunch while sitting on a rock overlooking the valley. In one of the valley's skirts you can bathe in thermal waters that spring from the bowels of the earth. It's a simple, open-air, rustic hot spring that, when I came up, was being used by only one person, a Dutch woman I had met on my way up the volcano. A few minutes later a large local family (an old couple, their two daughters, and their grandchildren) turned up. The children were quick to jump into the water while their mothers and grandparents spread a cloth and served the food. The Dutch blond attracted their attention, especially of the young man who must have just entered puberty, who asked his sister to photograph him next to the blonde (he even asked her to kiss him on the cheek). I also attracted the local attention. One of the mothers, brazen and daring, flirted with me regardless of the proximity of her parents and children. She called me handsome repeatedly, asked for my address, pleaded that she was in love with me, and followed the tactics of her son to get photographed in my arms and with my lips kissing her cheek, to the delight of the entire family. Everyone had a great sense of humor, and both the Dutch woman and I had a great time with them.

The Dutch arrived in Indonesia as merchants. Initially, they simply took control of the main ports of Java and other Indonesian islands active in the spice trade. In 1602 they established the Dutch East India Company, which became both a land power and a trading company, and exercised almost complete control of the island of Java in the mid-eighteenth century. Areas of Sumatra, particularly Aceh, fiercely opposed the Dutch occupation, leading to decades of fighting. Something similar happened in Bali the following century, hence it wasn't until the early twentieth century that Holland got an iron grip on the area from Sumatra to New Guinea, with the exception of the Portuguese colony in East Timor.

The next stop was Lake Toba, the largest volcanic lake in the world (sixty–two miles long by nineteen wide). In the lake lies an island the size of Singapore, called Samosir. Approximately 70,000 years ago an eruption took place there of such intensity and scope that it caused a brief period of climate change across the planet. In the '90s Lake Toba was an attractive place of pilgrimage for tourists in Southeast Asia, but Thailand had stolen Toba's fame in the last decade. I was grateful for this because, although it had a feeling of abandonment (given the state of many of its hotels), I always prefer enjoying a beautiful landscape in tranquility. I got a room with a balcony overlooking the lake for only five dollars a night. In addition to a daily swim, I rented a bicycle to visit some of the towns on the island. People in the region are Protestant Christians and belong to the ethnic Batak. While exploring a village of traditional houses, I met three Spaniards, one from Cadiz and two Basques, with whom I had a few beers that evening.

After a long, uncomfortable, overnight bus journey to Bukittinggi, I hired a motorist to explore the beautiful surroundings, whose main attraction is the traditional houses of the ethnic Minangkabau, with roofs shaped like buffalo horns. My arrival in Bukittinggi coincided with the beginning of Ramadan. As long as the sun illuminated the town, the local restaurants were closed, with the exception of a couple that had signs on the door saying "Open to Tourists." It wasn't until sunset that the terraces of the restaurants were peopled and the city gained some street life. At one point, three young female cousins came up to greet me and asked me if they could sit and talk in English with me. "Of course," I said, and invited them to sit at my table. Two of them were in college; the third was still in high school. The first two covered their hair with a scarf; not so the youngest, who when asked why, said her family didn't impose it and she hadn't yet decided whether to wear one or not; however, I was told that Sumatra's educational authorities required female students to wear a headscarf in schools and universities. They inquired about my religion, and when I mentioned I was an atheist, they asked for my reasons and were quite open and curiously listened to my arguments, although I sensed some discomfort in their faces. I enjoyed chatting with them as much as I was surprised that three Muslim young girls would come to speak openly on the terrace of a restaurant with a Western man, an example that Indonesia is a more tolerant Islamic country than many others.

Once in Padang, a young motor biker took me down a road with beautiful views over the sea to the Bungus port terminal, where the Ambu Ambu ferry departed to the distant Mentawai archipelago. After buying a business class ticket (a reclining seat in an air–conditioned room), I went to one of the stalls to eat something and drink tea until the time of departure, 8 p.m. Several men approached me in the small stall and insisted on talking Indonesian with me even though I didn't understand a thing. One of them kept saying Puyol, Puyol, referring to Carles Puyol, Barcelona's defender. Another, to show off his soccer knowledge, would add Torres and Villa. Since the World Cup victory in South Africa, I was surrounded by congratulators as soon as I said I was Spanish.

When boarding, a man approached me, asking for my intentions in Mentawai. I told him I wanted to do a trek in the jungle. He said he was a guide and could show me photos and a map of possible routes he had at his home. The Ambu Ambu ferry is a big ship with space for vehicles and cargo, a lounge with a seating area on the upper deck and a business lounge at the front with room for fifty people. I settled in the lounge and chatted with a couple of Australians who were going to Mentawai to surf, the main attraction of that remote archipelago, regarded by many as the best place in the world for surfing because of its thirteen– to twenty–foot waves that break at a distance from the shore. Shortly after, I leaned back and tried to sleep during the night journey.

We arrived in Palau Siberut, Mentawai's main island, at 7

a.m., and a motorcycle took me to the guide's house, located in the marshes near the main village. To get to his house, because of the high tide, I had to take off my shoes and walk barefoot through fifty feet of shallow water. He showed me some photos of recent trips to the jungle and a map indicating the places to visit. I asked the price for a three–day trek, and he said $275. Too expensive, I said. I had read that Mentawai was not cheap, because of its remoteness and the small number of tourists who visit, but the high price surprised me. Then I realized I had come a bit short of cash, and the only bank on the island still had no ATM. I managed to get the price down by 20 percent. Still, I think I paid too much, but I wanted to start the trek as soon as possible and get back to Padang on Tuesday's ferry (there were only two ferries a week) and not lose a day wandering around looking for a cheaper option.

While Mas, my guide, bought the supplies, I went for a walk around the village. I ran into an Englishman living in Australia who had been four days anchored there waiting for the ferry to Padang because he hadn't brought enough cash to pay the exorbitant prices demanded to go to other islands.

After loading the wooden boat with food, Mas and I left at 11 a.m. under a light rain that in a few minutes became torrential. Under the roof that partially covered the food and me, the rain was so intense I had to bail water without respite, using a small plastic bucket. We stopped for half an hour to pick up our cook, the guide's niece. We continued along the river for about an hour and a half before reaching our destination in the Rorogot area. We landed under a heavy rain, and with my boots in hand I walked barefoot through the flooded jungle to the house where the first family of our visit lived. The lady of the house, protected by a black umbrella, came out to greet us. "*Aloita*," she said in the native language, and headed for the boat to help carry our supplies into the house. The house was made of wood with a roof of dried sago (which, I later learned, was the most important tree for traditional life in the jungle) and was raised off the ground by a little more than three feet. To get inside, a log with steps carved into it functioned as a ladder. There was a hall with exposed beams and a bench on one side and a swing on the other, followed by an open area with a kitchen on the left side and a sitting area on the right. Beyond these lay the first big room of the house, with space for sleeping in the corners, followed by a second room with another kitchen to the right, kitchenware to the left, and sleeping areas in the remaining corners.

The man of the house came from the inside darkness (the windows were small and usually closed) with his hand outstretched and a well-pronounced welcome. He wore only the traditional local loincloth, his hair in a small bun, a cigarette as thick as a hand-rolled cigar in his mouth, his body decorated with the blue tattoos common among these jungle people, in an image as unforgettable as it was shocking. His name was Amandirit. He wasn't very tall, but his muscles were well sculpted. Bairiri, his wife, was wearing knee pants and a shirt; it was long ago that women had abandoned the traditional skirt, and now they covered their breasts. Four children completed the family. Later I learned that Bairiri was Amandirit's second wife. With the first one, now deceased, he had four children, and continued his practice of fertility with six more with Bairiri. Only the four youngest children still lived with them. Sotriana was ten, a gorgeous girl, always obedient to the commands of her parents, at all times helping cleaning the house, washing clothes, feeding the pigs and chickens, and taking care of her younger brothers when necessary. Shamba was six years old, a shy girl with a shaven head to treat an infection of the scalp, which her sister Garatai also suffered from; she was the baby of the house, who barely crawled and cried as soon as her mother moved a few feet away from her. Among the children was Tagiyaibu, the naughty boy, four years old, a whirlwind of energy who would not stop mimicking his father, following him whatever he did.

Our cook began to prepare lunch in the kitchen near the entrance. Amandirit, Mas, and I sat on the balcony. Mosquitoes soon came. Amandirit lit a small fire under the house so the smoke would leak between the floorboards and chase away the pesky insects. On the walls of the front room many skulls of monkeys and wild boar hunted by Amandirit adorned the shelves with numerous bows and arrows, basic items for survival in the jungle. He showed me a couple of pieces of wood that are struck to communicate in the jungle, since each family lives in an isolated house and the nearest neighbors are more than a half hour away. Apart from the pigs and chickens they breed, they live on what they collect in the forest, hence, it's necessary for every family to have exclusive use of a jungle area sufficient to ensure their survival.

The rain flooded the jungle. The mud was deep and made you think twice about going for a walk. The original plan had been to visit three different houses while hiking in the jungle, but the persistent rain convinced us to settle there for the duration. All the houses were similar, as were their inhabitants, and the jungle wouldn't vary much from that surrounding the house, so I wasn't irritated by the change of plans. On the contrary, I thought three full days there would give me an opportunity to know the family a bit better and establish at least a simple relationship with them.

One of the attractions was learning their traditional ways of life. First, they showed me the tools with which they draw their tattoos, called *titi*. The ink is juice from sugar cane, which, with the help of a punch and a small hammer, is injected beneath the skin, decorating it with a pale blue. The tattoos were like necklaces adorning legs, arms, and chest; long blue lines broken with little circles every few inches. Amandirit also showed me how to make the poison they apply to arrows to hunt in the jungle, an activity no longer in use because there are hardly any monkeys and wild boar left to chase these days, the reason why they currently raise chickens and pigs. First he stripped a leaf of a plant locally called *dagi*, then a piece of stem of *uratuba*, to which he added a piece of ginger and a few small chilies. Once everything was chopped and well mixed, he put a handful of the mixture into a small circular wicker ring that he squeezed with large wooden pliers to extract a deadly juice, which he collected in a shell. With the help of a brush, he painted the tips of his arrows with the poison and then dried them by the fire, a process he repeated three times. A monkey would take about three minutes to die, a wild boar five, after being hit by one of those arrows that were sufficiently poisonous to kill a man.

The next morning was the turn of Bairiri, who showed me river fishing. To that end, rather than going to the main river, too mighty for this lesson and for me to follow her closely, we took a canoe upriver to a shallow stream, which rose about halfway up my thighs. Bairiri took her orange shirt off to show her pointy tattooed breasts. With her machete at her waist, a bamboo tube at her back where to gather the fish caught, and a conical net in hand, she began walking upstream, tracing the riverbanks with the net with the help of her free hand, sometimes with her feet. Into the net she pushed sand and leaves from the stream bank, with the hope that some small fish would fall prisoner. A few did, and even a shrimp, as I followed Bairiri with my camera, a fishnet of moments.

The last activity was procuring the traditional dress, the *kabit*, the loincloth that every man in Mentawai wears in the jungle. We crossed the river in the canoe. Amandirit sought a straight trunk tree, not very wide, maybe eight inches in diameter, called *baeko* in the local language, which he chopped down with his machete in a few seconds. With the trunk now on the jungle floor, he made two long parallel cuts and pulled a long strip away from the bark. Then he deftly removed the outer bark to just keep a strip of fiber that would become the loincloth. He struck the strip along its entire length with a wooden mallet against a smooth trunk to widen and flatten the strip. Then, after washing it in the river, he hung it up to dry, after which it would be ready to wear. Back home, he invited me to try one on, pret−a−porter. I undressed fully, and he showed me how to tie such a revealing garment around my waist. The guide took a picture of the two of us dressed only in the *kabit* which, when I put it up days later on Facebook, became an event among my friends.

To shower, I was told to go to a hidden area behind some trees about 150 feet from the house, where there was a small pit dug in the ground filled with rainwater, a wooden plank across it, and next to it a rope to hang clothes. I undressed, got on the plank, and with the help of a small bucket, showered outdoors. The sensation of being naked in the jungle, feeling the cool water running down my skin, was fabulous. I think there are physical sensations that unconsciously lead us to the past, thousands of years ago, when, as there in the jungle, humans lived in nature. Our current lifestyle is so recent, so new from an evolutionary point of view that we still are, unknowingly, psychologically, tied to past feelings and experiences, many of which we haven't even experienced in our lives but that our brains have inherited from our ancestors. Something similar has happened when I have walked barefoot in the forest: atrophied by urban life, the soles of my feet regained sensitivity. Our brains are still attached to that primitive life, so that it's not just these basic sensations, or our phobias regarding spiders and snakes, for example, that hinder a full and happy life, but also our fears of the unknown, the strange, and the future, fears that should no longer have the weight of the past but that continue to emerge unconsciously. For a large part of humanity, life has never been safer. We have nothing to fear, but ourselves.

The children didn't go to school, so, like their parents, they couldn't read or write, and only spoke Mentawai, being completely ignorant of Bahasa, the official language of Indonesia. With no close neighbors, their friends were few; family life was the only social reality. Apart from the natural stimuli the jungle offers and the daily tasks necessary for survival, the children didn't have any other activities to develop their intellectual capacities. With no visible toys or games to entertain themselves or learn different skills, they spent the day playing with anything they could find, following their parents in their activities, or simply looking at the strange intruder staying with them for a few days. I asked about marriage, specifically what would happen to Sotriana. I was told that when she reached fifteen years of age, she would be "sold" to a young male chosen by her parents. He'd have to pay for her with animals and tools. I thought at least women were valued in Mentawai; in many parts of the world, it is the brides' families who have to pay to get them married.

Since they didn't grow anything and feeding the chickens and pigs didn't entail more work than cutting a log of sago, picking some coconuts, and grating and mixing both, they didn't really work much. The day was spent quietly with not much to do, rolling and smoking a cigarette being the most common daily activity (tobacco is one of the few things which they, using money they get partly from hosting visitors like myself, purchase at the main village where they go by boat to obtain it). A view as painful as it was natural was to see Bairiri breastfeeding Garatai, holding her with one arm while the other was busy with a cigarette between her fingers. Smoking helps pass the time, and there in the jungle, time was their most abundant property, indigenous people's wealth. When Amandirit smoked, he often stared into the intense green wild jungle, and I wondered what he might be thinking, what occupied his mind during his frequent downtime, what psychology dwells in a person whose existence is limited to a few square miles of lush jungle, totally oblivious of technological advances, international news, economic crises. I also wondered if he had dreams, aspirations, or if the most basic survival, his and that of his family, was the sole purpose of his existence.

The last afternoon, while we let the hours pass just sitting on the railing, Amandirit appeared from the jungle carrying a black piglet, with its legs tied together and growling shrilly. Shamba and Tagiyaibu simultaneously got on their feet and ran to their father, who left the piglet by the kitchen, found a long knife suitable for the killing, brought a plastic bucket to collect the fresh and warm blood that would spout in a moment from the animal's neck, grabbed the snout with one hand, and firmly stabbed the piglet's neck with the knife. The piglet was soon silenced. Shamba and Tagiyaibu, squatting by their father, watched the spectacle of death from the front row while I captured it with my Nikon. Drained of blood, the pig had its guts opened, its organs removed, its blackish hair burned in a bonfire of leaves improvised in an instant, and its skin washed with water before the carcass was cut up for cooking. Amandirit gave Tagiyaibu and Shamba two pieces of raw meat (I think it was the brains), which they devoured with satisfaction. The suckling pig was not as tasty as one from Segovia; I think its poor nutrition made the meat quite insipid. I also tried sago, all carbohydrate and the main source of nutrition in the jungle. After being grated, it is placed in sago leaves and heated for a few minutes on the fire. The starch becomes dry and hard, and it's pretty bland, so I slathered the sago "flute" in chili sauce brought by the cook. What I did enjoy eating was cocoa pulp (this was the first time I'd tasted it) and a white, round fruit called *sabui*, which we found during a walk through the forest and that tastes like a delicious citrus fruit.

On my last day Amandirit asked me for a present: my raincoat. I gave it to him despite not wanting to imagine him walking through the jungle with his machete being protected from the warm rain by the navy–blue nylon. He gave me a ring and a bracelet hand–made from rattan. *Masurabagata* ("thanks" in Mentawai), we said to each other. In a moment when the guide wasn't close by, Amandirit confessed that he didn't like him; he just wanted money ("Money, money, money," he said). I didn't know how much the family received for my three–day stay, but I was afraid not much and that Mas would be the biggest beneficiary. Later I regretted not having asked Amandirit about it. I liked Amandirit. It's amazing how little it takes to find out if you like someone. Not even to speak the same language; just to spend some time together and watch how he treated his family were enough. My father would have liked him too, and would have been fascinated to spend a few days in the jungle living so simply and close to nature. But now it was time to leave the jungle, to say goodbye. We did it following the local tradition: "*Meikai*," said those who left; "*Oo*," answered those who stayed behind.

When we got back to Mas's home, his wife was praying, facing Mecca. I went for a walk through the village to one of the beaches for a swim. On the way back, I saw the vast esplanade of Palau Siberut being prepared for the celebrations that would take place the following day, August 17, Indonesia's Independence Day. The national motto is Unity in Diversity, entirely appropriate for a nation made up of over 17,500 islands, 230 million people, about 300 ethnic groups who speak 742 languages and dialects, and that, despite having the largest number of Muslims in the world (87 percent of its population) also officially recognizes Catholicism, Protestantism, Buddhism, Hinduism, and Confucianism.

Before leaving for the jungle, I'd asked Mas to buy me a ticket for the ferry because the boat leaving on Tuesday wasn't a very large one and I didn't want to risk its being full. I had given him the money, and he'd told me his son would be responsible for buying it. The night of my departure I asked for the ticket, and he said it was waiting, in my name, at the ticket office on the pier. I remembered the words of Amandirit about Mas—"money, money, money"—and began to suspect he hadn't bought the ticket and had kept the money. That afternoon he left for the southern islands of the archipelago with a group of Brazilian surfers who had arrived on the morning ferry. His son didn't show up, and a family friend took me in his battered car to the pier. When I arrived, as I feared, there was no ticket in my name.

★ ★ ★

The overnight trip to Padang was going to take at last ten hours on a wooden boat in not very good condition. Onboard I met two Spanish couples on their honeymoon in Indonesia. Their guide shared peanut cookies with everyone. Later, we went down to our cabins. I had to change mine, which was flooded because of water leaks, for a dry one shared with three other travelers. The heat inside the cabin was stifling, and soon I felt dizzy and had to rush on deck to throw up the cookies. I stayed there a while, breathing in the fresh sea breeze that I love so much to calm me down before going back to the cabin and trying to sleep. We moored in Padang after 7 a.m., and I went to a travel agency and bought a flight ticket to Jakarta for 400,000 rupees ($45), a great price. I still had time to eat something before taking a motorbike to the airport. I had lunch at a Chinese restaurant, which was open despite Ramadan, with the diners concealed behind a curtain.

The flight of an hour and a half arrived on time, my bag came up in the baggage carousel almost first, and the stop for the bus to the center of Jakarta was right out the domestic arrivals' exit—one of the most efficient arrivals at an airport I'd ever had. The bus left immediately, but the perfection of the trip evaporated within a few miles when Jakarta's dense traffic broke sharply my idyllic journey. It took two hours to travel twenty–two miles when ninety minutes had sufficed to complete the distance from Padang to Jakarta (568 miles), both examples of the best and worst in transportation. Traffic jams must be one of the stupidest punishments many human beings impose on themselves, and are proof of the inability of society to find solutions to a problem that shouldn't be that difficult to solve. Looking out the bus window at the tremendous congestion, I started thinking about Amandirit. I imagined him sitting on the railing of his house, of course smoking, maybe rolling his next cigarette, staring at the jungle, or sitting on the swing at the entrance to the house with little Garatai in his arms. What would he think if he were sitting next to me? No doubt, to him it would seem extremely foolish to be caught in a tangle of metal and iron for hours moving little faster than walking. Usually, we are unable to reconsider what we do automatically. Our inherited customs become as automatic as the everyday sun, though they have no real necessity. We are such slaves of routine, of task repetition, of existential inertia, that we accept situations that would be incomprehensible to someone who had never experienced them. Traffic jams are one of these, but so are most of our religious and social rituals and many of our societies' customs. I also began to ponder how we measure our quality of life and our happiness. Is a wealthy New York banker happier than Amandirit? It's clear that Amandirit would repudiate life in Manhattan as the banker would an indigenous existence. What both have in common, and all of us, is their survival instinct, the most important reason behind our existence. The only difference is what is required to survive in each of the environments that each lives in. If in Amandirit's case, this included his skills in hunting, fishing, and the exploitation of the natural resources available in the jungle; in the banker's case it included his ability to function in his particular jungle, which requires its own set of specialized skills and attitudes toward his environment, different from those needed by Amandirit.

In Jakarta there's really not much to see. As the capital of the country, it would be expected to have the typical rosary of interesting historical buildings. Nothing further from reality. To go to Kota, the old part of Jakarta, which the Dutch christened Batavia, I boarded a commuter train, spacious and comfortable, whose carriages reminded me of New York's subway. Kota is an untapped area, somewhat ugly and forgotten; at least, the fabulous Cafe Batavia is noted for its colonial splendor. I ate at the restaurant, on the second floor, which is decorated with pictures of celebrities, and went down to the bar for coffee. In a few hours I had passed from a remote jungle where indigenous people live how they have done for thousands of years to the modern steel and concrete jungle, where human density is extreme and breathing the air disgusting. The global population is increasingly urban, and Asian cities are experiencing such extreme growth recently that they are unable to adequately accommodate their population. Jakarta, for example, had less than five million people in 1970 but nearly ten million (twenty million in the metropolitan area) in 2010.

In the train back to the hotel, I got into a carriage containing only women. Soon one of them warned me it was exclusively for females (to avoid rush hour groping by males) and I had to move to the next one. I hesitated whether to stay a couple of days in Jakarta (it was a weekend) or leave for Yogyakarta, in central Java, which is considered a much nicer city than the capital and near which the Hindu temple of Prambanan and Buddhist temple of Borobudur can be found. I had read that Jakarta's nightlife is one of the best in Southeast Asia, but, being by myself and since the city lacked a European–style city center, exploring Jakarta's nightlife didn't seem very attractive. In addition, some bars closed early during Ramadan, some even by force due to the pressure of Islamic fundamentalists. After researching on the Internet, I read about a vodka bar called Red Square, located in the south of the city, in Plaza Senayan Mall, featuring good music and where young local women interested in Western men went without asking for money.

I arrived at Red Square by taxi at 11 p.m. to find a place not very big, with a DJ at the front, a high, long table taking up most of the space, and an elevated bar to the right. I liked the place, but it was still nearly empty. I feared Ramadan would deprive the weekend of its normal energy, but in half an hour I realized this wasn't the case, and little by little Red Square filled up with young Indonesian women and men, plus a few Westerners. On the Internet I had read that one of the reasons for the success of the bar was the absence of prostitutes, which I honestly wished to be true. The cover included a drink. I ordered a whiskey and Coke and began to enjoy the music from the bar balcony. A group of young Indonesian women stood around me. I greeted one with a smile; she approached and introduced me to her friends, all very nice and some pretty attractive. I invited two of them to a drink, and we danced, overlooking the bar from the balcony. It was 1 a.m., and Red Square, which during Ramadan closed at 2 a.m. instead of its usual time of 4 a.m., was at its peak, with a couple of girls dancing on the top of the bar, and the long table converted into a dance floor with several women on it enjoying the rhythm of the music. Amanda was the name of the girl I liked. She almost looked more Spanish than Indonesian, her eyes and other facial features more Mediterranean than Asian. She was funny and accessible, without the pretentiousness many attractive women show in this type of bar. I flirted with her; she playfully threw her hand to mine or to my hip.

When Red Square closed at 2 a.m. she suggested going to Musro, a hotel disco that remained open until 5 a.m. We jumped into a cab with two of her friends (the rest went in another with two Dutch guys). Musro was almost empty, and only those who arrived from Red Square endowed it with some life. At a high table, I sat on a stool while Amanda danced with her back to me, her ass between my legs. I remembered the night I met Khae in Chiang Mai. Soon we were kissing. She came to the hotel with me where she stayed until midmorning. Before leaving, she gave me her phone number, asking me to call her to go out on Saturday evening. It'd been so easy to pull a woman in Red Square, I decided not to, even though the night and morning with her had been really great, and to check how easy it'd be to pull another woman. I'd never been very successful with women in bars and nightclubs, but in Asia I was a novelty, I was exotic. My long and slightly aquiline nose, my graying stubble, and my body hair, as well as my skin tone certainly made me more attractive to some Asian women than to most Western ones.

I spent Saturday afternoon writing at a cafe in Plaza Indonesia Mall. There, Ramadan didn't seem to exist: restaurants served food, and cafes were full of wealthy clientele of fairer skin than average. There are over a hundred malls in Jakarta, many of them occupied by luxury shops. The air conditioning makes them the perfect place to shop and spend an afternoon. Throughout Asia, from Bangkok to Jakarta and Kuala Lumpur, malls have become cities' central squares, meeting places in the vast and hot Asian cities. In the evening I went back to Red Square, this time later than on Friday. The place was more active than the night before and the number of Western men much higher. Greater competition. I went to the bar, sat on a stool, and ordered a whiskey and Coke while exploring the place like a beast looking for his prey. I have never been a sexual predator, but I have to confess that's how I felt that evening while sipping my drink at the bar. Two young attractive girls I'd seen the previous night arrived. One wore a tight black dress, the other a red one, both very short. The one in black had danced on the top of the bar Friday evening, and the one in red had climbed on top of a speaker in Musro. They came to the bar and stood next to me. It was so crowded that the one in red stood between my legs for a while. I introduced myself; Liana, she replied elusively. Once the stool on my right became free, she sat down but remained aloof from what was happening in the bar. A friend of theirs I hadn't seen on Friday arrived and introduced herself. She tried, unsuccessfully, to encourage Liana to dance with me. I invited her for a drink. Still hungover from the night before, she ordered an orange juice.

The evening went on. I decided to stay there, without playing any other card, my bet fully on the red. The lights came on and the room began to empty slowly. I looked at Liana.

"What are your plans?" she asked.

"I have none."

"Musro is still open, do you want to come with me?" she suggested.

"Of course," I said, feeling like a winner. We departed together without her friends. Leaving Red Square, she offered me to take her hand on the way to the taxi. Once in the cab, she changed her mind and suggested going to another place in Kota. Upon arriving, we found it was already closed because of Ramadan, but a neighboring bar was still open. It was a huge place as wide as a theater with a stage and a dance floor, two terraces, and tables on the balconies. We sat down to have a beer. The music was very loud. Almost impossible to speak, I decided to flirt with Liana dancing with my eyes fixed on hers, sometimes looking down her red dress to her thighs. She responded by moving her left hand to her neck and down toward the channel between her flat breasts, later reaching her abdomen. Then she approached me, and we kissed. I took advantage of the darkness to slip my left hand boldly between her legs, and she responded saying she was coming to spend the night with me.

We sought a taxi. We had to walk to a main street to find one from a respectable company (in Jakarta it is not recommended to take just any taxi at night). Halfway there, Liana stopped, pulled her low shoes out, and put her high heels away in her handbag. In the hotel she was reluctant to be stripped of the red dress and asked me to lower the light intensity. Once the dress was removed, I noticed she had many marks on her abdomen, lots of grooves in various directions. I thought they might have been caused by a burn, and looked away so she didn't feel observed, because I realized she had a problem with those marks. She slept clutching a pillow covering her front. Upon awaking, her face downright angelic, she stroked my chest before going down towards my waist. To make love she rested her belly on the bed, hiding again her only part that was without beauty. She left after asking me for money for a taxi, giving me a kiss, and thanking me for the night with her natural sweetness.

Upon checking out, I went by taxi to Gambir train station, where airport buses also depart. I had decided to fly to Yogyakarta (a.k.a. Yogya) because the fare was only slightly more expensive than the train and the air journey was about an hour as against eight by land. Also, being Sunday, traffic to the airport would be light. The flight, however, was delayed long enough to prevent my catching the bus from Yogya to Borobudur, since my plan had been to enjoy the temple the next morning and celebrate my 41st birthday in the beauty and tranquility of the Buddhist temple (I'd had the "party" in Jakarta). I chose to stay in Yogya and spend my birthday there. I visited the Sultan's Palace, which was quite disappointing, and the old part of the city, including the Water Castle, in reconstruction after its collapse during the violent earthquake of May 2006. One man told me that two days earlier a strong earthquake had been felt during the night and woken the whole population, forcing them out of their homes in terror. Fortunately, the earthquake was not as scary as in 2006 and produced no significant damage. In the afternoon, I decided to gift myself with a massage, but the spa was closed during Ramadan.

The next day, I got up early to go to Prambanan, the largest Hindu temple in Indonesia and one of the most beautiful in Southeast Asia. It is dedicated to Trimurti, the three Hindu deities: Brahma, the creator of the universe; Vishnu, the preserver; and Shiva, the destroyer. Its main building is 154 feet high. Damaged by the earthquake in 2006, it was being repaired. In Borobudur I found a nice guesthouse with a rear balcony overlooking rice fields, where

I read during the afternoon until dinnertime. I got up when it was still dark, to reach the temple at 6 a.m., its opening time. The morning was cool and foggy, the temple, shaped like a low pyramid with a broad base, barely visible as I approached it down the long promenade. I climbed to the summit of the temple, the central dome surrounded by fog, and because of the low visibility chose to descend to the first level of the pyramid, to its western side opposite the entrance, and meditated in the morning silence for three—quarters of an hour. Opening my eyes, I saw the fog begin to clear and the blue sky to flourish. With the fog fully gone, I could really appreciate the dimensions of the temple. The base of the pyramid is a square of 390 feet long, and its total height 116 feet. Built from about two million rocks, its total weight is approximately 3.5 million tons, making Borobudur the largest Buddhist temple in the world. I started to climb the temple for the second time, this time exploring the wonderful stone reliefs observable around each of the first six, square, levels. There are 1,460 scenic reliefs and 1,212 decorative reliefs, which, together with 504 statues of Buddha, give an idea of the magnificence of Borobudur. On the last three levels, which are circular, stand 72 stupas, each containing a sculpture of Buddha.

Seen from above, Borobudur forms a mandala, a cosmological symbolic diagram used in both Hinduism and Buddhism. In the case of Borobudur, the first level represents the world of desire, home to beings still attached to their feelings; the second, the world of shapes, where beings are aware of shapes but have no attachment whatsoever to them; the third, the shapeless world, nirvana, where forms are diluted and only reality is experienced. The temple's name comes from the words *boro*, "temple," and *budur*, "over the hill." Some believe volcanic eruptions in the area forced the move of Java's capital to the east; others that the spread of Islam in the fifteenth century was the cause of the temple's total abandonment. The temple was re—discovered in 1814 by Sir Thomas Stamford Raffles, the governor of Java while it was under British control between 1811 and 1816. Until then, the Dutch never knew of the existence of such a majestic building.

I said goodbye to Yogya and the imposing volcano Merapi (9,737 ft) that has custody of it, to travel by train to Surabaya, the largest city in East Java. After spending a night there, I traveled by bus to the village of Cemoro Lawang, where I stayed in a simple guesthouse with a good restaurant with two women from Madrid I had met on the trip. One of them, Monica, had taken several vipassana courses, and despite recognizing that meditation had been helpful, she said that, after last year's retreat a few months before, she had stopped meditating. While we dined in the hotel restaurant, Miguel, the talkative guy from Cadiz I'd met at Lake Toba, walked in. What a coincidence.

We woke up at 3:30 a.m. to go by jeep to Mount Penanjakan (9,088 ft), from which to enjoy the sunrise over Mount Bromo (7,641 ft) and the Tengger caldera, over six miles in diameter, with a view of the imposing volcano Semeru (12,060 ft) in the distance. After photographing the stunning sunrise over the caldera, we descended to the foot of Mount Bromo and proceeded to walk up to its steaming crater. After breakfast back at the guesthouse, Toni, Monica, and Miguel left for Yogyakarta; I took a bus to Ketapang, where I took the ferry to Bali.

When I arrived on the west coast of the island, it was too late to go to Lovina, in the north; I had to take a bus to Denpasar and from there a motorbike to Kuta, where it'd be easier to find accommodation, as well as a place to dine, at such a late hour. I stayed one more night in Kuta, a kind of Torremolinos in Bali, full of tourists, gift shops, and stalls in every street, bars and restaurants with a TV on at all times showing all kinds of sports, Australian football being quite popular because of the large number of Aussies who visit Kuta.

In order to get away from Kuta, I got on a *bemo*, the local minibus, to take me to Denpasar. There I had to take another *bemo* to the city's northern bus terminal, where yet another *bemo* transported me to Singaraja on the north coast of Bali and only six miles east of Lovina, my final destination. In Singaraja, having crossed the entire island of Bali along its central axis, I had to take a *bemo* to the west end of the town, from there jumping on the last *bemo* to Lovina. More than an integrated transport system, *bemos* seemed like an organized racket designed to finance the highest number of drivers possible. To make the experience as unpleasant as possible, most of the drivers tried to scam tourists, asking exorbitant prices for each ride. From Mount Bromo to Bali, in sharp contrast to Sumatra, transportation had become a nightmare; by far my worst experience during my trip in Asia.

Northern Bali, much less developed than the south, is a quiet beach area ideal for a few days of rest from my hectic recent travels. One day I rented a motorbike to go to some hot springs in a beautiful setting amidst the lush tropical vegetation. After the long trip from Bromo to Bali, as well as the five *bemos* I had had to take to get to Lovina, and the difficulty of getting from there to Padanbai to take the ferry to Lombok, I decided to spend at least one night in Ubud, a cute town located near the center of Bali. I loved it so much when I got there, and was so tired of the constant back and forth, spending so many hours traveling and changing means of transport, planning the next trip, the next connection, that I thought of staying there for a few days. The place I spent my first night was somewhat expensive despite its charm, so I searched for a cheaper option to stay maybe a week. I found one at an affordable price, but it was full for the next two weeks, until September 15, showing how popular the place was, hidden at the end of a long narrow alley and overlooking a beautiful rice paddy field. Each room had a small balcony with chairs for sitting. It seemed perfect for a few days of writing.

I had twenty—three days left before my flight to New York. My ambitious plans for Indonesia included the possibility of reaching Flores, Sulawesi, and Kalimantan. Obviously, it was going to be impossible to get to all of these, but I thought I had enough time to reach two of them after Lombok. However, east of Bali travel becomes more complicated, with longer trips, and flights between the islands scarce. In addition, at the end of Ramadan, millions of

Indonesians travel to celebrate Eid with their families, so most flights were full and more expensive. I felt lacking in energy to spend the next twenty days jumping from place to place, from island to island, from beach to beach, from volcano to volcano. I wanted to regain a little of a daily routine and concentrate on my script to try to finish it. I decided to forget the rest of Indonesia, go to Lombok as planned, then return to Ubud on September 15 to stay in the charming Ubud guesthouse until the day of my flight to New York. One of my original plans to end the trip was to find a quiet place for a few days to devote myself to writing, and although I'd thought of a waterfront place, Ubud, with its beautiful and cute cafes, restaurants, and temples, seemed ideal. Besides, it also offered the possibility of daily yoga classes.

The ferry trip from Bali to Lombok meant five quiet hours admiring the blue sea from the deck. In Lombok I booked a trek to climb Mount Rinjani, a volcano of 12,224 feet, the second highest in Indonesia. These were three days and two nights shared with an American couple honeymooning and two French friends, as well as the guide and the porters carrying our food and tents. The first day we climbed up to 8,530 feet, to the edge of the main crater, under a heavy and intermittent rain. We went to bed early to tackle the climb to the summit before sunrise, which meant waking up at 2:30 a.m., having breakfast at the wrong time, and climbing for three hours on a steep terrain of volcanic sand and small stones that made us lose two steps for every four we took. The climb was intensely painful, my left knee the part of my body that suffered the most, but the sunrise seen from the mountaintop, above the clouds, with the view of Mount Agung (10,308 ft) in Bali and the Rinjani crater with its blue lake and a second crater inside the first, made us forget the terrible beating we had just taken. The descent was a snap; the sand and the volcanic rocks allowed us to almost slip down the slope.

We had a second breakfast before going down to the lake, walking on rocks. The pain in my knee increased with each step. At last we were able to relax a little with a dip in the hot springs by the lake. Under a drizzling rain our muscles thanked the watery heat rising from the bowels of the earth. In the afternoon, we climbed back to the crater rim, this time on the north side, where we spent the second night, completely exhausted and sore. The day had been brutal, arguably the toughest trek I'd done. The next day, after a last look at the fabulous view of the crater and its blue lake, we descended to the village of Senaru, where I stayed a couple of nights to recover from my knee pain and a couple of blisters that had erupted on my feet. After the unforgettable experience of the ascent of Rinjani, I decided to ignore the touristy Gili Islands. I found a great place to stay a week in Senggigi. I got a bamboo bungalow with sea views, a porch with a hammock, and some cushions on the floor, to sit and drink tea that was always available in a thermos.

I flew back to Bali and enjoyed a fortnight of yoga, meditation, and writing in Ubud, Bali's cultural capital. Apart from its numerous temples and art galleries, there are small towns that specialize in producing wooden reliefs, jewelry, and paintings. I thought about renting a motorbike to explore the surroundings and even do some hiking, but the unseasonable heavy rain that visited Ubud daily made me give up that idea. Every morning, on my way to the Yoga Barn for my yoga class, I watched the Balinese open their shops and proceed with the daily offering to their gods. In a small square tray made of a palm leaf, they laid flowers, rice grains, and incense, sprinkling it all with a few drops of water. The trays are placed on the sidewalk in front of a store's entrance, and there remain all day, although occasionally distracted tourists accidentally kick them. The day of Saraswati, the Hindu goddess of knowledge, music, art, and science, is one of the most important festivals in Bali, and all the Balinese dress up in ceremonial clothing to go to the temple to make their offerings. In Bali, I saw many women carrying on their heads trays crammed with fruit in tall pyramids that defied gravity.

Ubud is where Elizabeth Gilbert, author of *Eat, Pray, Love*, found her love. Due to the popularity of her story, the number of Western women in Ubud, especially from the U.S., was very high. The Yoga Barn as well as the cool fashion stores and cozy cafes were crowded with love hunters who dreamed of finding their exotic prince.

BUREAUCRACY & ROOTS

"The whole object of travel is not to set foot on foreign land; it is at last to set foot on one's own country as a foreign land." —G. K. Chesterton

"I travel a lot; I hate having my life disrupted by routine." —Caskie Stinnett

One of the rules for keeping a U.S. green card is not to remain abroad for more than twelve consecutive months, a rule that, against my desire to continue my Asian journey, forced me to return to New York. I flew with AirAsia from Bali to London via Kuala Lumpur, an airport where I spent a sleepless night. I landed at London's Stansted Airport and by train got to Liverpool station, from which I walked to my friend Gerry's office.

That walk, which I, with all my backpacking gear, made through the City of London at the end of a working day, was truly special. I walked at a leisurely pace, relaxed after my long Asian tour, everyone around me hastening to take the train or the subway, phones at their ears, most dressed in black or gray to match the almost permanent cloud cover. It seemed impossible I'd lived in that city for more than eight years, had walked at that stressful pace, had dressed in such dull clothes, and had survived so repetitive a routine.

Gerry left his office, and we walked to the garage where he parked his convertible Porsche, a luxury rickshaw, to go to his apartment in Chelsea. That night I had dinner at a restaurant in Covent Garden with Gerry, Dave, Steph, Ed, and Mari Carmen, who exulted over my lost weight, better color, and happy air. Once again I enjoyed their company as much as I regretted the brevity of the encounter. I landed at JFK the next day, 364 days after taking off for Kathmandu.

"How long have you been away?" the immigration officer asked.

"About 11 months," I replied.

"What day did you leave?"

"September 29th, I think."

"That's almost a year; you know you are close to the limit."

"Yes, I know."

"What did you do during this time?" he carried on.

"I was traveling through Asia."

"How did you finance your trip?" I guess he suspected I'd been working abroad.

"With my savings."

"So, you don't have a job?"

"No, but I'm writing a book about my travels that I hope to sell."

"But the U.S. is your home, where you plan to stay, right?" he insisted.

"Of course, New York is where I live and have everything."

"It's fine, but be careful and don't abuse it."

"Sure. Thanks."

The conversation was tense, but I remained calm, relieved once it was concluded, and I went to pick up my backpack.

In New York I stayed in the apartment of my Peruvian friend Maria on the Upper East Side, and the three weeks I spent in there went by quickly. On the one hand, I was glad to be back in New York, particularly to see my friends, but also I felt a stranger in a city where the density of pretentious people is far too high, with their insufferable self–marketing, their tireless self–promotion, and a too common superficiality. The contrast with the people I'd met in Asia was significant. The people there hadn't pretended to be anything they were not. They were sincere in their views and direct in their questions. They didn't distrust my motives because they themselves didn't hide what they were. There I didn't perceive the psychological tension rampant in Western minds.

People in the West are often caught in a competitive mindset, are so obsessed at times with what others might think of them, how the rest of the world perceives them. One of the aspects of New York that I despise is how many times you can notice that your interlocutor is, as you talk to them, evaluating how you can benefit them, what they can get from you, either professionally or personally, and how your value as a person is determined—or "priced," I should write—based on that evaluation. I read once about an encounter the Swiss psychiatrist Carl Jung had with a Native American chief in New Mexico in the 1930s. Jung later wrote about it, particularly the chief's remark that white people are always seeking something, always uneasy and restless, thinking with their minds more than with their hearts. I could then well understand the chief's opinion, as I had just spent a year working with my brain's right half, the one that mostly deals with emotions, instead of the one I had predominantly used before then, the left side, mainly focused on the logical processing of information and tasks, with all the categorizing and judgments this constantly brings.

My passport didn't expire until October 2011, but since many countries require a passport that is valid for six months from the date of arrival, mine would be useful only until April. I also wanted to eliminate the cursed stamp that the Indian consulate in New York had put on it. So I went to the Spanish consulate in New York to try to renew it. I was told that Madrid would deny renewing a passport a year in advance, but when they learned I was going to Spain soon, I was assured I wouldn't have any trouble renewing it there. Bureaucracy remained an obstacle for the nomad.

The script I had been writing seemed to be finished, but every time I sat down for a final review I found things to change: the order of some scenes, the information revealed here and there, some of the dialogue. It was clear more work was still needed. The distractions brought by the Big Apple made me stop meditating. It was as if I felt unable to concentrate, to have the quiet time necessary for it. As my stay was going to be short, I allowed myself to be carried away by New York's social life.

After three weeks in New York I returned to London and after a couple of days left by car with Will, a friend and former French colleague, to visit Normandy, where we rented a country house to enjoy a long weekend with a great group of friends I had met in London, although some, like me, no longer lived in the British capital. The only absentees would be David and Lisa. Besides Will and me, a number of others arrived from London: Dave and Steph with their two kids, Tony and Maria, Gerry with his new girlfriend Lucy, and Marc and Ivy, now living in Hong Kong but due to an incredible coincidence in London for work. From Paris came Emmanuelle, Mathieu, and their daughter. The last time we had gathered all together was at Marc and Ivy's wedding in the south of France in July 2008. It was a fantastic weekend. From Paris I traveled by fast train to Spain.

My mother was at my father's village, Quintanarraya, a tiny village in the province of Burgos. It was All Saints Day and time for my mom's annual visit to the grave where my father is buried. My cousin Ana, about to give birth, lent me her car to go there. It was eight years since the last time I had visited my dad's village, where we have a house inherited from my grandparents. It only has around a hundred inhabitants, although these multiply during the summer. I have great memories of the August vacations we used to spend there with my family. As a child I loved going with my grandfather to water the fields and pick plums, tomatoes, potatoes, and alfalfa to feed the rabbits. I was not very fond of them being skinned before dinner, nor watching my grandfather kill a chicken. With adolescence came summer loves, usually with Catalan girls. The first one I fell in love with was Montse, her smile as bright as her green eyes. Then came Silvia, so beautiful I still remember the first time I saw her in a pink dress on her red BH bike, with her wavy, long brown hair, her big green eyes, and her gorgeous smile. Silvia was followed by Olga, another Catalan but much more voluptuous than the other two, and also more fun and engaging. With the first two I had no luck; the third time I got lucky.

There were summers I didn't do more than party; Castilla is so full of villages that vacations were party time. During the morning we slept, woke up for lunch, went to the pool at a neighboring village (Quintanarraya is so small it doesn't even have one), played a soccer game before sunset, and showered before dinner to get ready for the daily evening out. I have great memories of those years. One felt so free, living in the countryside. It's where my father is buried. He loved his village, where he spent most of his vacation days. His absence also brought me summer memories of him roasting lamb chops for the whole family, winning bets on the traditional game of *tuta* because of his fabulous aim, setting the pace at the *brisca* cards game, playing with my cousins, who adored him, and working on remodeling the old house inherited from his parents.

Back in San Sebastian, I made an appointment to renew my passport. My ID card had expired in May; I renewed the latter without any problems, but the official in charge of passports told me that, because I was a New York resident, the Spanish consulate in that city would have to renew my passport. I explained I had tried there, that I was about to travel to India, China, and Japan, among other countries, and that my passport would be useless to enter those countries from April onwards. She asked me to renew it wherever I was then, that's what Spanish consulates and embassies were for. I insisted on my request, arguing that to seek a Spanish consulate in India or China would not be very convenient. At my insistence, she took my passport and went to ask a superior about my situation. She came back with a negative response: passports are only renewed in the place of residence; temporary passports are issued elsewhere only in emergencies. I thought the word *funcionario* meant someone who helps the country run smoothly, but it seemed that the only thing that mattered was their own operations and not the citizens they serve.

Luckily, when I commented on my bureaucratic odyssey with a friend, he said he knew someone with a good contact in the police office in charge of these arrangements. A few days later I went back and asked for the commissioner whose name I'd been given by my friend; I explained to him my situation, and he called an officer to help me; the officer led me to another colleague, both somewhat ignorant of what to do but willing to meet their superior's request; they then escorted me to talk to the same officer who had been so "helpful" the previous week, and she found a special code for the computer system to allow the issuance of a new passport. That's the way Spain works, I thought. I often think that so-called economic development is leading us to neglect our freedoms, and that in many cases laws, rules, and procedures are more important than the results obtained, complicating our lives unnecessarily, with the survival of officials, their systems, and their hierarchy prevailing over the quality of service they provide.

Curiosity about my trip was lower among my Spanish family and friends than among Americans. This didn't surprise me because I had experienced it many times since I left Spain, when I got very few questions about England and London. I think the attitude of "If I don't know something, it doesn't make me question my life" is too widespread in Spain. Despite the general lack of interest, whenever I did talk about things that worked better in England than in Spain, I would be criticized for being critical of my own country. About the trip, the star question was: What is the country you liked the most? Much more interesting would have been: What impacted you the most? Absolutely nobody asked me a question close to that one. The rankings of countries were more interesting than how people live in them, their culture, or their religion. Curiosity was at its lowest.

If traveling to remote, unknown areas is an adventure that satisfies my curiosity for the exotic, returning to San Sebastian and Quintanarraya is a journey to my roots, to the known, to my home, which usually arouses mixed feelings of familiarity and strangeness in each visit. When I lived in San Sebastian, a stunning city, I believed I was living in the best place possible. San Sebastian was my only world, and I shared with my neighbors that local pride. Now, however, I see it as a beautiful town, but too provincial, conservative, with something stupid in its arrogance, boring in its daily placidity, an ideal place to spend a weekend, but where a few months could be endless. There's nothing like leaving home, like living in another city or another country, to have a broader perspective of our cultures and ourselves. Distance provides relativity, and with it comes a more accurate assessment of our existence.

It was mid–November already when I sent my passport by courier to the Indian embassy in Madrid. It would take a week to get it back, and, due to the high prices of flights to India during December, and above all, to the fact that I hadn't spent a Christmas with family since 2004, I decided to postpone my trip to India until January. Days later I received, with great joy, my passport with the Indian visa on it. Finally I'd be able to visit India.

A week before Christmas we received the sad news of my aunt Petra's death in Barcelona. My mother and I went to her funeral, a trip that gave us the opportunity to see the numerous family we have in Barcelona. Just a few weeks before my aunt's death, Lorea was born (my cousin Ana's second child). Life goes on, nothing is permanent: *anitya, anitya, anitya.*

GODS, COLORS & DESERT

"Travel and change of place impart new vigor to the mind." —Seneca

"If you reject the food, ignore the costumes, fear the religion and avoid the people, you might better stay at home." —James Michener

Finally, India. A year later than planned, I landed in Delhi happy to be in the country I'd wanted to visit for so long, and also to be a nomad again. However, I didn't arrive in the best condition: I had contracted a flu in San Sebastian three days before leaving, which made me feel weak and lacking the excitement I expected on my first day in India. I had flown to London and from there to New Delhi the next day on an overnight flight, thanks to my accumulated miles with Virgin Atlantic. During the twenty—eight hours I had in London, I saw my friends Gerry, Steph, Dave, Mari Carmen, and Ed. I had dinner on Saturday with Gerry and stayed at his apartment, and we celebrated the news of his new job, which was going to take him from London to Monaco. The next day, a beautiful, sunny winter Sunday, the six of us, plus the children of the two couples, had lunch in a Greek restaurant in Primrose Hill; it's always great to see them all.

I hardly slept on the flight to Delhi. During dinner I enjoyed the movie *The Social Network*; after that I watched *Wall Street: Money Never Sleeps*, which, although I'd read it didn't have the quality of Oliver Stone's earlier *Wall Street*. I was interested in as it deals with the financial crisis, as my script did.

India had introduced new rules for its visas a few months before. These limited to ninety consecutive days the maximum period of stay for many nationalities, who then had to remain outside the country for sixty days before being allowed to return, either with their original six—month visa or with a new one. My plan to see much of India in three months was downright ambitious. I'd have to take advantage of overnight trips by train and to spend only the time necessary in places that didn't seem to deserve a longer stay. My route would take me to the northwest, specifically to Punjab and the southern foothills of the Himalayas (going further north was too cold in January), then to go down to Agra, explore the states of Rajasthan and Gujarat, then cross the country from west to east at its widest part to reach Kolkata. From there I'd fly to Mumbai, and continue south, stopping briefly in Goa before visiting the states of Karnataka, Tamil Nadu, and Kerala.

I landed in New Delhi on a cold day, and went by taxi to the hotel I had booked; it was near the train station that was ideal for going to Amritsar, the Punjabi city I would visit after the capital. I ordered something to eat and took a nap that, although planned for two hours, ended up lasting nearly seven. I wanted to use that afternoon to rest and try to beat the flu. I had dinner in my room before planning the first day of sightseeing in Delhi. The next morning I felt better. The rest had been fruitful. As the morning was quite cold, I decided to start my exploration of Delhi at the National Museum, great in its collection of reliefs and statuary, not in the quality of the building. After the museum, I walked through the majestic Rajpath to India Gate, which pays homage to the Indian soldiers who fought in the First World War, and from there rode an auto-rickshaw to the tomb of Humayun, the second Mughal emperor. It is a beautiful example of sixteenth-century Persian architecture, made from Indian marble, and considered the forerunner of the famous Taj Mahal.

Humayun was the son of the first Mughal emperor, Babur, who entered India in 1526 after settling his capital in Kabul in 1504. Although Muslim forces had already entered India in the eleventh century, the Mughal Empire marks the cusp of the Islamic presence in India, which reached its apogee in the late seventeenth and early eighteenth centuries. Thereafter, the Mughal Empire went into a severe decline until its formal extinction in 1857. I ate at a restaurant near Lodi Gardens before walking to Connaught Place, the commercial hub of the British section of Delhi, an area more chaotic than expected. To continue with my recovery, I went to my hotel early and had dinner in my room.

The next day I visited the Red Fort with its impressive high gate and walls, but the interior was somewhat disappointing, as the original buildings had been destroyed during the British incursion of 1857. After the fort, I went to Old Delhi and to Jama Mosque, a beautiful building overlooking the ancient city of narrow, dirty, and smelly streets filled with shops of all kinds. In the mosque, I climbed the steep stairs leading to the top of one of the minarets to observe, without much visibility due to fog or pollution, the spread of the Indian capital. Delhi was not an easy city to enjoy, something I had already expected. Occupied by heavy traffic, unavoidably noisy, dirty, and neglected, it was hostile to the pedestrian, like many other large Asian cities I had visited. However, I had imagined it even worse. I thought it would be a form of torture, with poor urban children chasing every tourist, demanding a few rupees, stinks emanating from every corner, with peace impossible to find in the capital of the second most populous country on the globe. New Delhi, the city created by the British, consisted of broad tree−lined avenues on which traffic flowed with relative ease, an area that reminded me of some parts of Yangon. Perhaps it was the cold winter days that had watered down the odors, but I couldn't believe the low temperatures had frozen out the beggars. In my two days of walking several miles through the city, I got just a couple of monetary requests, both without any pressure. The most emblematic and visited places in Delhi (the Red Fort, Jama Mosque, and tomb of Humayun) were true oases of peace, beautiful places to stop and admire their architectural beauty without distraction. Outside them, it was common to see people living on the streets, trying to survive a colder winter than usual. Blankets were used as winter coats, and especially in the morning and after sunset, most Indians walked about wrapped in one.

On one hand, I was glad to be in India, traveling again, but at the same time, either because of the flu or the long period stationed in San Sebastian, I felt lacking in the energy needed to meet the basic daily routines of a nomad, such as negotiating the price for an auto−rickshaw or finding a place to eat. I feared that my adventurous energy had vanished. Perhaps after having spent two and a half months with my mother, I'd become addicted to the presence of a loved one, and my previous existential lonely fortress had cracked. Having someone who as a mother cares for you every day was a situation I was not used to, a very rewarding situation that might have resulted in my feeling lonelier than usual during my first days in India. I even thought this was enough of my solitary adventure (including my last years of bachelorhood), and it might be time to seriously consider settling down in one place, creating a home and a family. Perhaps I just needed to show some improvements in my energy, both physical and mental. A few days would be sufficient to get the answer.

I got a train ticket to Amritsar, Sikhism's holy city where my goal was its famous Golden Temple, for the next morning. The train left the New Delhi station on time at 7:20 in the morning. I had a window seat in a full carriage. The early departure from Delhi was marked by one of the most common views of all who travel by train in India: the daily visit of many citizens to their outdoor toilet. The proximity to the city's slums of the train tracks make them latrines where slum inhabitants go to evacuate their digestive spoils, all in sight of the travelers. Men squatting and relieving their guts enlivened our departure from Delhi, a sight as bizarre as it was unforgettable.

We arrived quite late at Amritsar due to the thick fog that blocked both our progress and our views of the landscape. Instead of arriving at 1:15 p.m., we made it at 4 p.m. I took a rickshaw from the station to the old part of Amritsar, to make my stay as close as possible to the Golden Temple. The entrance to the temple is free, and I had read it's best to visit at different times of the day to enjoy the different light. The hotel was, like Delhi, somewhat pricey for what it offered, but its location was perfect. I went immediately to the temple, just two minutes by foot from my hotel. I removed my shoes at the entrance, washed my feet in cold water, and covered my hair with my long Laotian scarf, the only obligations to enter the sacred temple of the Sikhs, which houses their holy book, the Guru Granth Sahib. Sikhism is a religion founded by Guru Nanak (1469–1538) during a period of conflict in India between Hinduism and Islam. It was developed by ten successive gurus whose teachings are contained in its holy book. Its main characteristics are the idea of one God and human equality regardless of race, religion, caste, gender, and social status. Furthermore, compassion and generosity are very important in its system of values. It is estimated to have over twenty–five million followers worldwide, making Sikhism the fifth largest organized religion in the world.

Once inside, the view of the Golden Temple surrounded by a broad pond was spectacular. Not many people were visiting on that cold afternoon. Most walked clockwise around the pond and entered the golden building along a walkway that connects it to one side of the large pond. I joined them. Mystical music sounded from the temple speakers, creating a unique atmosphere. Some people joined their voices to the songs emanating from the speakers; others sat under the arches of the white buildings that surround the pond. I saw just four other tourists; the rest were Indian Sikhs with their families or alone. I sat down to wait for the end of the day, the sun reflected on the Golden Temple's walls. The flu still resided in me, but I barely noticed it in that wonderful building, that serene oasis.

The temple, whose real name is Harmandir Sahib, was started by the fourth Sikh Guru, Ram Das, and completed by the fifth, Arjan Dev, in 1604. It was rebuilt in 1764 after being repeatedly damaged during battles between Sikh and Mughal forces. Like every Sikh temple, the Golden Temple offers free food to visitors. In the Golden Temple, the kitchen doesn't stop a moment and serves thousands of guests daily, reaching 80,000 meals on the busiest days during one of the main festivals. I climbed the stairs to one of the dining rooms and grabbed a metal tray before sitting on the floor with my legs crossed, waiting to be served. Several men came with buckets, serving boiled rice, lentils, vegetables, and curds. After dinner, I took the tray down from the dining room to where several volunteers cleaned and cut vegetables, and gave a donation to fund the incredible task of feeding such a large number of pilgrims daily.

I returned to the temple the next morning. I walked around the pond and sat under the arches to observe the Sikh visitors. The men were tall, some incredibly burly, broad-shouldered, their noses aquiline, their beards long, and their long hair covered by the traditional turban (Sikhs do not cut their hair or shave). The turbans were of all colors. I saw several blue, yellow, and green but always of a single color, without patterns. Some men carried intimidating, curved swords at one side, like warriors ready to decapitate the enemy. I saw some who, after taking off most of their clothes (though never their turbans), walked down the steps into the pond while holding on to chains attached to the steps, so as not to slip. The contrast with the surrounding neighborhood was much more pronounced than in Delhi. The streets were narrow and dirty and seemed to host a totally different population from the one visiting the temple. How was it possible that the temple was so clean and well painted while the city that surrounded it was so dark and filthy? The definition of an oasis was definitely suited to the Golden Temple, and I even thought such an extreme contrast might be on purpose in order to appreciate even more highly the sacred enclave.

I didn't like the idea of going to the border with Pakistan, twenty miles away, to observe the stupid confrontation each evening that Indian and Pakistani soldiers represent in front of hundreds of tourists during the closure of the border, so I took a bus to Chandigarh, the city designed by the Swiss architect Le Corbusier, and the joint capital of Punjab and Haryana states. After the Labour victory in the British parliamentary elections of July 1945, the idea of an independent India took center stage. Mohammed Ali Jinnah, leader of the Muslim League, demanded an independent Islamic state. In August 1946, Direct Action Day took place in Calcutta, which led to violent riots between Hindus and Muslims, resulting in more than five thousand dead. On July 18, 1947, the British Parliament passed the Indian Independence Act, which agreed to the partition of the country, creating the independent state of Pakistan, including current Bangladesh, then called East Pakistan. The state of Punjab was divided in two, its capital Lahore on the Pakistan side of the border. With the idea of becoming the capital of Indian Punjab, the creation of Chandigarh was approved by Prime Minister Nehru and initially planned by the American architect Albert Meyer and Poland's Matthew Nowicki; Le Corbusier later took over the project. In 1966, India decided to divide the state of Punjab in two, one with a Sikh majority, today's Punjab, another with a Hindu majority, the new state of Haryana; thus, today Chandigarh is the capital of both states.

The city is divided into sixty rectangular sectors of the same length, each over a kilometer long. The idea was that each sector, each rectangle, would be a small town, providing the inhabitants with all basic needs, such as a market and a school. The sectors communicate with each other via long, wide, tree−lined avenues—a welcome contrast to the urban structure of most Indian cities, and therefore considered the most enjoyable in the country, the cleanest, and the one with the highest average income. However, I didn't like all of it. Indeed, the sense of space and amplitude was welcome, as was the cleanliness compared to Delhi and Amritsar, but in my opinion it lacks character. Sector 17 is considered the city center, with movie theaters and a large number of shops and restaurants, but the rest is just rectangle after rectangle of similar buildings without any personality. Some might consider it an example of efficient development, but to me it was not a city but a set of mutually independent islets. Perhaps it was very nice for the citizens to have everything so close at hand in each gigantic sector, but for visitors, at least for this one, Chandigarh at no time gave me the feeling of being a city with an active street life, an aspect that I find so fascinating in big cities. Its most iconic buildings—the Assembly, the Secretariat, and the Palace of Justice—are certainly interesting from an architectural standpoint, but they represent the domination of concrete from the '50s. I spent two nights in Chandigarh due to my night arrival, two nights that seemed like wasted time.

I got to Rishikesh, on the Ganges River, after more than seven hours of travel in a dilapidated bus. I stayed on the north, less populated, side of the river, home to a few guesthouses on the steep slopes of the mountains that make Rishikesh an attractive enclave. Famous for a visit by the Beatles in the '60s to one of its ashrams, Rishikesh has become northern India's capital of yoga, meditation, ayurvedic massage, and spirituality. Very New Age. The town itself is disappointing. I'd imagined it full of cute houses and streets with cozy cafes and restaurants, the style of those seen, for example, in Pokhara, Hoi An, or Ubud. However, Rishikesh is in India: its streets and buildings were in poor state, and the first restaurant I went to eat in wasn't very clean (at least it offered free Wi−Fi). The first tourists I met were as expected: the hippies of the twenty−first century, with their long hair and baggy, colorful clothes; tourists in search of spiritual experience. The nights were cold, and despite the good blankets, they were so heavy they crushed you in order to warm you; in the absence of heating, I felt the cold in the room with every inhalation.

After my first week in India my sensations hadn't been as expected. Perhaps the flu had prevented my regaining my normal energy levels. Sitting on the terrace of the hotel, facing the high mountains, I wondered if I was overstretching my trip, if I needed to return home to a routine. I started worrying about my future, about what to do if my plans to sell the script and the book didn't bear fruit, which, I realized, despite my natural optimism, would probably be the case. Going back to a corporate life wasn't attractive at all. The theme of loneliness resurfaced again in my mind, not because of feeling desperately alone, but because I was tired of having been unable to establish a long−term relationship with a woman in years. Would there be people who, like me, didn't have the luck to meet a being with whom a shared life would be more interesting than a solitary existence? I thought of my friends, confused by the relative ease with which most of them had found their soul mates, with whom to start a family. What is it in me that makes it so hard for me to fall in love? What am I looking for that, despite having met many women in London and New York, I had only found them interesting for friendship or a casual relationship?

I thought maybe it was time to settle down in a nice, small city by the sea where I could find a job without too many complications and abandon myself to a routine life, to escape the distractions of the great metropolis and its constant stimulation, in order to take root in a simple life focused on work, reading, writing, sport, and meditation. Maybe I was not yet old enough for this, or maybe I was aging faster than I thought. Not that I considered my life in New York a failure, on the contrary, but perhaps it was time to return to Spain, although I didn't know where, and I even loathed the idea, or at least it didn't fully convince me. But where to go? Cold northern Europe is not for me. Italy would be a new language and a tough start. Many Latin American cities are risky to live in. New York is still the best city, but for how long? Asia is certainly interesting, but I didn't know if I would have the strength for such a drastic move. I was at a crossroads.

During my brief stops in New York and London some friends ironically asked me if I had found myself during my trip, but it seemed I had gotten lost. Life doesn't have to be a linear journey, rigid and predictable in its entirety, but it must possess some direction. Sometimes I seemed to have lost my way; I felt I was wandering with an itinerary but without a direction, dreaming of a life as a writer without even being sure I had the ability for it. When I read some recently published books, I thought I could do it better, but I didn't know if that meant I could make a living by writing. Photography seemed even a more difficult challenge, with so much competition and the commoditization of digital imaging. Setting up a business could be a way forward if my artistic skills were insufficient. I feared that I would lack the discipline and energy, the determination and ambition needed to succeed in such a dramatic life change. Without these, without dedicated daily effort, success is not possible. Until now I'd had an easy life guided by my ease in acquiring knowledge and using it, but never, or almost never, had I worked intensely for long periods. I had never given passionately of myself to anything, except when I was a soccer coach for youngsters in San Sebastian and during my travels. In the rest of my challenges I had done just enough, and perhaps it was now time to employ my bad temper, the positive one, to bang my fist on the table, and once and for all become who I really wanted to be: stop being the introvert, thinker, and follower and become the extrovert, the doer, the leader of my own existence.

I thought vipassana meditation would help me get there (since one of its benefits also is to help meditators realize their life goals) so I felt the need to return to it with discipline, to fully surrender to it daily, to give it the chance it deserved. But it must also be accompanied according to my own intellectual determination, by an unequivocal decision that this was my way forward. I had to stop just living, existing with passive inertia, like a drop of water in a wild river. I had to become the river itself, with all of its force. It was time to take my mask off, let my guard down, look into the world's eyes, and give everything I had at every moment. And above all, to see in myself what I wanted to be, to invent each day of my existence, and sculpt a rich, active, and unforgettable life. Every moment is precious in itself. That afternoon, at last, I managed to meditate for an hour, the first time in a month. During my stays in New York and San Sebastian I had all but stopped meditating, and was quite disappointed with myself because of it. The cold in my rooms over the past days hadn't made the idea of sitting in meditation attractive, but during the afternoon, before the cold came down the mountains, I was able to focus without much difficulty for an hour. The first few minutes were tough, not the concentration itself but the ability to feel the different parts of my body. It was as if lack of practice had desensitized my body. But I persisted without feeling disappointed, according to vipassana technique, and gradually became aware of body sensations. I felt really happy to return to my meditation practice.

The flu had completely gone by then, but I hadn't yet regained enough energy to take yoga classes. So I just walked around and enjoyed the beautiful views of the Ganges valley from the balcony of my hotel. I was about to stay another night in Rishikesh, so wonderful had been the first half of the day, but I wanted to get to Agra to visit the Taj Mahal on Thursday, as it closes to visitors on Fridays. I caught a bus at noon to Haridwar, six miles south of Rishikesh, and one of the seven sacred cities of Hinduism, the others being Varanasi, Ayodhya, Mathura, Dwarka, Kanchipuram, and Ujjain. Located on the banks of the Ganges, where the river descends from the Himalayas, Haridwar is, with Nasik, Allahabad, and Ujjain, one of four sites where drops of amrita—the nectar of immortality—fell from the jug of Garuda, the mythical bird, half man and half eagle, and the vehicle of Vishnu. (My ignorance of Hinduism was almost total, and I wanted to use my trip to India to at least understand a religion that seemed as complicated as it was old. The first thing I learned was that even though, for many, Hinduism may seem a strange, polytheistic religion due to its many gods, they are actually no more than representations of one god, Brahma, eternal and infinite.)

After finding a rather expensive but spacious room overlooking the Ganges in Haridwar, and more specifically the *ghats* of the city, I went with my camera to capture the activities taking place on them. *Ghats* are steps leading down to, and into, a river, lake, or sea, commonly used by Hindus to descend to purify themselves in the water. The Ganges is considered the sacred Hindu river, and runs from west to east for more than 1,550 miles from its source in the Himalayas to its mouth in the Bay of Bengal. For a couple of hours until sunset, and despite the cold weather, I saw the clear waters of the Ganges receive visits of numerous Hindus. I had witnessed Sikh rituals at the beautiful Golden Temple, but until Haridwar I hadn't entered a Hindu temple in India nor had I witnessed any of its rituals. Men took off their clothes before entering the Ganges in their underpants; most women simply approached the river and poured water drops on their heads and drank the Ganges water. In an area to one side, I saw a couple of women take off their tops, leaving their breasts exposed, a fact that surprised me in a country as prudish as India. Some collected holy water in plastic containers. Numerous men asked for money for various charities, handing out receipts to donors as proof of their generosity. Given the numerous requests, I donated a few rupees to one of them and used the receipt to scare other collectors off. There were several flower stalls where flowers were sold in trays of palm leaf so that pilgrims could deposit them on the surface of the river. Several children tried to place the traditional red dot on my forehead in exchange for a donation, but I refused it. I took many pictures, although I was at first shy with my camera. I wanted to make sure nobody objected to being captured digitally. With sunset, the food stalls drew great activity. I had dinner at a restaurant next to my hotel because I had decided to avoid street restaurants so as not to get an intestinal infection, the most common memory of all visitors to India.

The train to Agra would leave Haridwar at 6 a.m., which forced me to wake up an hour earlier, the earliest start since my arrival in India. Under the quiet dark of an incipient dawn, I walked, huddled against the cold, to Haridwar station. The train was on platform number one; I located my carriage, saw my name on the passenger list attached to the carriage door so there was no possible misunderstanding, got into the train, put my luggage on my bunk (the top one down the aisle), and sat on a still vacant bench, feeling somewhat shrunken due to the cold. An American couple sat down in front of me, and we chatted a while about our stay in India and future plans. They had spent two weeks in one of the ashrams in Rishikesh, practicing yoga and meditation. I became interested in the latter and inquired about the type of meditation they'd practiced. They said it was too superficial, nothing like the vipassana course they'd taken the previous year. As I feared, Rishikesh ashrams' meditation is more a relaxation technique to calm the mind than a practice aimed to purify it as vipassana meditation does. The compartment began to fill up so I climbed to my bunk, where I stayed for the rest of the journey, which was slow, with frequent stops—some very long—so many that the train seemed to be static as often as moving. But it wasn't a boring trip, thanks to the vendors constantly offering coffee and chai (the traditional masala tea prepared with tea, milk, and spices), peanuts, sweets, toys, and even socks. A blind man begging crossed the wagon; two youngsters cleaned the dirty floor, crawling, while they asked for spare change for the unsolicited service. With nearly three hours' delay, we arrived at Agra, at night, where the most popular lodges were full and I had to trust a man to find me a room, even knowing he'd take a commission from the hotel that I'd obviously end up paying, but it was too late to do the search myself.

As soon as I got up, I went to the Taj Mahal, whose southern entrance was only 150 feet away from my hotel. It was 8 a.m. A slight haze almost imperceptibly enveloped the magnificent building. The Taj Mahal is the mausoleum that Shah Jahan, the fifth Mughal emperor, built in memory of his second wife, Mumtaz Mahal, who died in 1631 during the birth of their fourteenth child. The main building took eight years to complete, but it wasn't until 1653 that the rest of the complex was completed. An estimated 20,000 men worked on its construction. We've all seen the famous pictures from a distance of the much−admired building, which show it as if levitating in the air. And so I saw it: a white, floating wonder, impressive in its size and shape, in its eternal beauty. I prowled around it for two hours, taking pictures from all the angles that attracted me. It was certainly more stunning from afar than in proximity. It was its elevation above the River Yamuna at its rear that made it seem heavenly. Emperor Shah Jahan said that its beauty brought tears to the eyes of the sun and the moon, and Indian poet Rabindranath Tagore described it as a tear on the cheek of eternity.

I returned to the hotel for breakfast on the roof terrace overlooking the Taj Mahal. Then I took an auto−rickshaw that the hotel had offered me at a reasonable price to visit the Agra Fort, Emperor Akbar's tomb, the tomb of the noble Mirza Ghiya Beg, known as the Baby Taj, and Mehtab Bagh Park, on the shore opposite the Taj Mahal. The fort was in much better shape than the one in Delhi, and therefore much more interesting and beautiful. The emperor Shah Jahan spent his last years at the fort, arrested by Aurangzeb, his own son, who with his men cut off the water supply to the fort from the River Yamuna to force the surrender of his father, who, from his spacious cell, could admire the view of the mausoleum of his beloved wife two miles away. After his death in 1666, Shah Jahan was buried next to Mumtaz in the Taj Mahal. The mausoleum of Akbar is located in Sikandra, more than six miles from Agra, with a spectacular gate. Inside, it is a beautiful place to walk around and admire the stunning Islamic architecture. Akbar was the third Mughal emperor and reigned from 1556 until 1605, a period during which the Mughal Empire spread to most of northern and central India. Akbar was only thirteen years old when his father, Emperor Humayun, died. In addition to the territorial expansion of the Mughal Empire, Akbar is considered responsible for the great development of art and architecture during his reign, which was characterized by a great respect for other religions existing in India (he even promoted dialogue between Hindus, Muslims, Jains, and Catholics). It is for this reason that he is known as Akbar the Great.

My hotel in Agra was excellently located for access to the Taj Mahal, but in an area, old Agra, of narrow streets in poor condition that seemed to have infected the owners of the hotels. I had been ten days in India, and most of the hotels had been rather disappointing. Their quality was much lower than those I had found the previous year during my exploration of Southeast Asia. In India, most hotels and restaurants are operated exclusively by men: cooks and waiters in restaurants, and hotel receptionists and cleaners are all male. Women remain secluded from the public, restricted to a purely domestic presence. In fact, since my arrival I had spoken with only one Indian woman: the one who sold tickets in the National Museum in Delhi. And not only was the maintenance of the hotel poor; their employees' attitude had also proved disappointing. In most hotels I was never greeted with a smile or thanked for my stay, and in a similar way I was treated in most restaurants. Men showed themselves like the weather: too cold, devoid of the human warmth that India boasts of having.

The plan for the next day was to go by bus to Fatehpur Sikri, a town twenty-five miles from Agra and the capital of the Mughal Empire between 1571 and 1585, to visit the mosque and the palace before continuing on to Jaipur. Akbar the Great moved the capital from Agra to Fatehpur Sikri after going there to consult Salim Chishti, a Sufi saint, on the possible birth of an heir, the subsequent fulfillment of the saint's prophecy of the birth of Akbar's son, and in honor of which saint Akbar ordered construction of the host of fabulous buildings in the new capital. Besides the gorgeous mosque, Akbar built three palaces for his three favorite wives: one Muslim, one Hindu, and one Christian, by which Akbar the Great showed his great tolerance, perhaps his great diplomacy.

I arrived in Jaipur on a Friday night, the day on which the Literature Festival began, the most important in Asia, according to the organizers. This greatly complicated finding a place to stay; it took me over an hour to find a room. My exploration of Jaipur was on foot, as I like to discover cities. My Lonely Planet suggested a walking tour of old Jaipur, within the walled area, whose buildings are painted pink for the most part, the reason the city is called the Pink City. Jaipur was painted in that color, associated with hospitality, in 1876 at the behest of Maharaja Ram Singh to welcome the Prince of Wales, later King Edward VII, on his visit to the city. I visited the Palace of Jaipur, where I ate on the terrace of its cozy cafe. After that, I approached the most famous building in the city, Hawa Mahal or Palace of the Winds, an extremely unusual building in both its structure and its use. It is a seven-story screen, without any structure behind it apart from stairs, a facade to the street full of tiny windows through which the women of the court, after climbing the stairs to the windows, could follow activity in the street without being seen; a palace of voyeurism rather than of wind, I thought. I used the rest of the afternoon to take pictures in the old streets of Jaipur, now full of the debauchery of Saturday afternoon activity.

As I was walking through the streets, a man in his fifties asked me where I was from, and as soon as I replied Spain, he asked for a favor: to write for him in Spanish a love letter to a Madrid woman he had met in Jaipur the previous year. I agreed willingly to such a romantic request. He took me to one of the narrow alleys nearby, got a stool, a piece of paper, a pen, and a newspaper for support, and began to dictate in good English a love letter to Carmen. The letter wasn't very original, full of cliches like "I think of you twenty–four hours a day," "Now we are away but our hearts remain close," "I dream of the day when you come back," "Please come back to Jaipur as soon as you can, I would go to Delhi to meet you at the airport," "All I do is work and think of you," "Our love is eternal" . . . As a postscript he added: "I hope you haven't forgotten my special massage." I wrote it all in capitals because my handwriting is somewhat chaotic and I didn't want Carmen to miss any detail of that man's love message. While writing it I felt like the Brazilian writer of letters for illiterates in the beautiful film *Brazil Station*. Having finished the letter, the man offered to do something for me in return for my services. I told him it'd been a pleasure to be his scribe and wished him good luck with his distance romance before continuing my walk through the Pink City.

I traveled by bus from Jaipur to Ajmer, and from there to Pushkar, a small town built around a sacred lake where it's said Brahma dropped a lotus flower onto the earth. It's a special place because of the *ghats* surrounding the lake, fifty–two in all. At one of them were spread some of Gandhi's ashes, in another it is said that Vishnu appeared in the form of a boar, in another that Brahma himself had bathed. To get from the bus station to the guesthouse, I had to walk through a procession of women who were following a band of musicians in the direction of some temple. The women collected donations from people. A cow, aware of its privileged status, tried to cut through the crowd. Stubborn it was; it pushed down violently a little girl, who began to cry, terrified of the sacred animal. Finally I got a decent room. More than that, it had a narrow balcony, was immaculately clean, and well decorated, with a four–poster bed, a small sofa with a coffee table, and a spotless bathroom. It was about time.

The afternoon was Hindus' favorite time to descend the

ghats to the lake for the rite of purification. I was surprised to see for the second time several women shed their tops to bathe with their naked breasts. I recognized several Brahmins, like my Nepalese guide in the Annapurnas, by a thin string wrapped diagonally around their bodies. Guesthouses and restaurants offering views of the town and the lake from their rooftops occupied the rest of Pushkar, which was quite touristy. There were also numerous temples, the most important being the Brahma Temple, painted in bright orange and one of the few in the world devoted to him despite his being the creator god of the universe. Inside there was a donation box for cows; I imagine to buy them food.

At night I saw the first of the many weddings I came across during my journey in Rajasthan. More than the wedding itself, I witnessed the procession of the groom, dressed in a traditional costume, very ornate and colorful, to the bride's house, on top of a white horse. Ahead of him, a band enlivened the procession while family and friends merrily danced while collecting money for the couple. To light the congregation, several men carried lamps fed from an electrical generator loaded on a wheeled cart. *The Times of India*, in its Sunday edition, includes an extensive section called *Matrimonials* where Indian families seek partners for their children. The supplement is divided into sections by caste, religion, profession (doctors, engineers, etc.), and language. Apart from physical data (height, skin tone, etc.), many ads inform the reader of the candidate's salary level, and others specify that a dowry is not expected. The ads often use the word alliance rather than marriage. The following is an example of one:

"Industrial Sunni Muslim family, highly respected and internationally known, living in posh area of South Delhi seeks alliance with girl of good family, exceptionally beautiful, well−educated and family oriented, for dynamic handsome son, 34 years and 173 cm, with an MBA in the UK, dedicated to flourishing family business. Please respond with photo."

After Pushkar, and continuing in Rajasthan, I reached Bundi, another small town, famous for its blue houses (painted indigo because the color is believed to scare off mosquitoes) and the fabulous palace built on the side of the mountain protecting the city. It's a magical place that hooked me as soon as I saw it from the window of the bus bringing me from Ajmer. The palace is an imposing building of several floors and asymmetrical structure. Above the palace, on the top of the mountain, sits the fort from which spread the city's protective walls. Bundi's streets are labyrinthine and narrow, with many houses over 250 years old and having tiny windows and cozy courtyards. Walking around Bundi, crossing its high, arched gates, visiting the palace and being dazzled by its fabulous frescoes, all as subtle as they were colorful, was a journey back to medieval times, when Bundi had its glory. On the city's outskirts, near the lake, is Suk Mahal Palace, where Rudyard Kipling wrote part of his novel *Kim*.

People in Bundi were really nice, throwing you a hello often, the children asking for a picture for the pleasure of seeing themselves on the digital display. Unfortunately, the streets were poorly maintained, and dirt, as always in India, was too present. Much worse was the state of the fort, almost totally neglected and occupied by many monkeys, its current guardians, so many that it was recommended I visit it with a stick in case they became aggressive. Bundi could be much more beautiful if it were as well maintained as a similar historical European town would be, but this didn't hinder my enjoyment one bit. I liked it so much I extended my stay there to three nights.

My accommodation was a modest room overlooking the lake in a *haveli*, a mansion of Indian Islamic architecture over two and a half centuries old. It had a beautiful garden next to the lake where breakfasts and afternoon teas served in the sunshine were glorious. January weather in Rajasthan is similar to early spring in Spain, neither cold nor hot. Gone were the low temperatures in the north, and absorbing the rays of the winter sun in Pushkar and Bundi was one of my daily activities, as was meditation. My room in the *haveli* was ideal for the latter, with its elevated sitting area by the windows, with cushions where I could sit. The combination of the sun and daily meditation practice had calmed and warmed my mood. For the first time since arriving in India I felt really happy to be traveling there. I thought I'd really love to take a second vipassana course of three to five days, and began to investigate options in India and elsewhere. There was one of three days in Chennai in March and one in Malaysia in late April. I filled out an application online, thinking of going a second time to the Dhamma Malaya center.

After Bundi, it was time to visit Udaipur, known as the Venice of the East and considered by many the most romantic city in India. Halfway there, in Chittor, I used the five-hour wait for the Udaipur train to take an auto-rickshaw to Chittor's fort, the largest in Rajasthan, the size of a small town. In the fort's capacious interior I admired its palaces, several temples, and two towers, all spectacular in their architecture and carvings. At the entrance to one of the temples a poster asked menstruating women not to enter, to maintain its sanctity. Udaipur is located next to Lake Pichola, which gives the city a spacious feeling, something so rare in Indian cities. Its palace is 800 feet on each side and 100 feet high, the largest in Rajasthan, so much so that two-thirds of the structure has been converted into two luxury hotels. I stayed a couple of nights in a beautiful *haveli* with a rooftop restaurant and one of the best views of the city. Dining one night at one of the nice restaurants by the lake, the owner told me a dam was being built to ensure the lake would always have water. Apparently, three months before, it had been almost dry; he told me he had played cricket with his friends in the lakebed in front of his restaurant.

The next morning, a girl approached the group of tourists waiting for the bus to Jodhpur and asked for a handout. A young Dutchman gave her a few rupees at the same time loudly proclaiming that if the other tourists gave the kid a rupee, she'd have enough to eat for the day. Many think that giving money does nothing but perpetuate the condition of thousands of poverty-stricken children who need only a few rupees a day to survive. Despite the difficulty of not sympathizing with child poverty, I agreed with that position, and although a few times I showed my generosity, I tried during my trip not to promote the begging of children.

Jodhpur is less beautiful than Udaipur, but its fort and palace are truly impressive. Another two nights were enough to visit the city, one to rest after the long journey by bus, another to explore it. Jodhpur market, next to the clock tower, gushes with life at sunset, and that afternoon I shot my Nikon with ease, especially at Indian women wrapped in their colorful saris like sweet candies in amazing combinations. I never thought orange could go together with pink and yellow. Daring Indian women taught me that any light color can be combined with another; the only thing needed was audacity. I thought it might have been the jealousy of a husband who, due to his wife's beauty, decided to wrap her in beautiful saris to hide her from other men's eyes.

I arrived at noon in Jaisalmer, the Golden City, named for the sandy color of its fort and its houses. On leaving the station we were greeted like soccer stars by young fans, in this case men holding signs offering free transportation to particular hotels. I took the opportunity to ride on a motorbike, my first time in India, something I had been missing after it being my favorite transportation in Southeast Asia. Lonely Planet's latest edition didn't list any hotels inside the fort (the only inhabited fort in Rajasthan) because of serious drainage problems it was experiencing. The fort hadn't been built with a proper drainage system, and the tourism boom was causing the collapse of the fort on the hill; so most tourists, faithful to the traveler's bible, found lodging outside the fort. And so did I.

After eating on my hotel's roof, enjoying the magnificent views of the south side of the fort, I entered the fort and walked through the narrow and winding golden streets. I then booked, through a specialized agency, a two–day camel trek through the desert, one of Jaisalmer's attractions.

The next day, a jeep picked up two young Australian couples, a young Swiss who spoke good Spanish, a young Chinese guy from Shanghai, a woman from Buenos Aires, a man from Santiago de Chile, and me. After less than an hour, with all of us squeezed into the jeep, we got off where our guides were waiting with the camels. Desert men were physically quite different from the Indians I'd seen until now. Their faces and eyes were larger and rounder, and they spoke a local language that, as the young Chinese said, with its strong pronunciation of certain consonants, sounded like Spanish. My camel was called Jokal, a tall male, fifteen years old, in fact the tallest of the group, so much so it seemed impossible to climb up him. Each time I had to get onto his back, I dreaded tearing my pants or my hamstrings. Despite the animal's imposing size, he was docile and obedient. I enjoyed riding him even though the sitting position I had to take was not the most comfortable I've ever experienced. The first couple of hours were very uncomfortable, my abductor muscles having to open up more than usual. Since the camel saddle had no stirrups, my legs dangled and swayed freely with Jokal's walk, and since my legs are very muscular, the weight of them increased the pressure impinging on my groin. I was grateful for the first break at a well to hydrate the camels, when I was able to relax my legs.

The second part of the day was more pleasant, my body slowly getting used to Jokal's movements. I protected my skin from the sun with a long shirt and pants, my head with my Laotian scarf, and my eyes with sunglasses. We visited a few desert villages of only around twenty houses with tiny windows and low, smooth walls of golden sand. Children came up to us, asking for pens, chocolates, or rupees. Sometimes they allowed us to take pictures of them, at other times they hid or a parent would order them away. Several times we heard "no photo" when trying to take pictures of their homes, especially if one of their daughters would have been by the lens. As people, we sometimes aren't aware of what we actually do. If someone came to our gardens or balconies, and began taking pictures of our children, we would surely show some anger, and might even hurl an insult at the intruder. That's what we were: intruders in the desert.

What we saw was not the typical image one has when one hears the word *desert*—an endless Sahara of great, barren dunes—but rather an arid land of dry shrubs. We camped before dark. There we admired the desert sunset and later one of the most beautiful skies I had ever seen, with a density of stars hard to beat. We had dinner around a campfire. One of the guides took one of the empty plastic containers to carry water and placed it in front of him with the bottom up to use as a percussion instrument, and set the pace for his colleagues as they all sang a beautiful song that I recorded with my video camera; such was the song's beauty, I played the video several times over the following days. It was a song about a woman who sometimes loves, sometimes doesn't love, a man. We slept in the open, under warm blankets and, especially, under a starry sky.

After breakfast, the group split in two. The Australians and the Swiss departed for Jaisalmer (they had booked the trek only until that morning); the rest of us continued on our camels through the desert, this time trotting, which, although it may seem contrary to common sense, was more comfortable than just walking, as if the camel's fast movement was more natural than a slow pace. Camels surprised me for their incredible strength. We were told they were capable of carrying between 660 and 880 pounds and of going for a week without water. When they knelt so we could get off them, they did it with smooth movements, but when they got up, it was best to lean back and hold on tight to the saddle, otherwise the sudden lift of their back legs seemed to want to throw the rider over the camel's head.

During another stop at one of the barren villages we passed a woman carrying a metal pitcher with water on her head. Dressed in a sari of intense red, she covered her face with it as soon as she saw us, an example of the practice of *purdah*, the custom of not only Muslim women but also Hindus in northern and central India, to hide their face in the presence of men who are not direct relatives.

Just outside the village, we came across the schoolteacher, a woman who in English told us that, because the Indian government provides free meals to children in the area, these come without fail to the school daily. It's a smart practice adopted by many countries in their poorest areas to ensure children's school attendance. What "grew" in the desert were windmills. The Indian government had planted hundreds of them, and although some tourists might surely regret this, I loved to see their tall, thin shapes and smooth, silent motion. I was surprised there weren't solar panels in the desert. Solar power may not be as economically viable as wind power, but I found it somewhat ironic to attempt to capture the intermittent wind rather than the ever—present sun.

I loved the desert. I really enjoyed it from the height of such an elegant and strange animal, and especially for its silence. Sounds barely existed—like wildlife here—which endowed the desert with an atmosphere disarmingly quiet and relaxing. I dreamed of going to one in Africa for a longer visit. This was my first desert, and I found it a distant cousin of my beloved sea. In both, men are outsiders, our existence seems in danger, but our fascination with their sense of eternity is such that we are constantly drawn to them, to their infiniteness.

RITUALS, TIGERS & PLASTIC

"The first condition of understanding a foreign country is to smell it."
—Rudyard Kipling

"One always begins to forgive a place as soon as it's left behind."
—Charles Dickens

Before leaving Jaisalmer I bought two books: *Seven Years in Tibet*, a fabulous travel book by Heinrich Harrer, and *Midnight's Children*, by Salman Rushdie. On the last day, I visited Jaisalmer's magnificent *havelis*, its palace, and the seven Jain temples near the palace, beautiful temples with stunning reliefs on their walls. I didn't know much about Jainism, but had time in the coming days to read a little about this religion since my next stop, already outside Rajasthan, would be in one of the holy sites of Jainism, Palitana, in the state of Gujarat. To get there I had to take an overnight trip by bus from Jaisalmer to Ahmedabad. My bunk, above the seats of the bus, was accessed by opening a sliding glass door that reminded me of the top of a cabinet where the crockery that is rarely used is kept. Once in the bunk, I opened the window to allow the evening breeze in. Through the night I closed the curtains on both sides to try to sleep, something that seemed impossible in the incessantly jiggling bus. For a moment, I thought I was in a hearse.

I arrived alive in Ahmedabad at 4 a.m., found a hotel, with difficulty due to a medical convention taking place in the city, and slept until morning. The hotel took my fingerprints in the logbook at check—in as in a prison. I didn't object because there was barely a room available in town, and I noticed all the guests, almost all Indians, also had to blacken their right thumbs to get a room. During the morning I visited a couple of mosques, some of the oldest in India, before boarding another bus to take me to Palitana, the dusty town at the base of the mountain on whose heights sit the celebrated Jain temples. I stayed in a modest hotel opposite the bus station, and walked around the long and crowded main street, where I bought some fruit at a street stall before dinner. I had a *thali*, a combination of various Indian dishes served on a metal tray.

Next morning, I got up really early and began the ascent of the 3,200 steps to the top of the mountain of nearly 2,000 feet where the Jain temples stand. It was Sunday, and many buses with pilgrims had already arrived. I was glad it was that day of the week, which would bring more visitors and with them a better chance to experience the Jain rites. The rise of 1.6 miles (according to the guidebook) took me forty−five minutes without stopping more than to photograph the fabulous views and the ascending pilgrims. Some, too old or too obese to climb by themselves, were ported to the top in *dolhis*, a chair hanging like a swing from a wooden pole carried by two men. The effort two men had to make to transport a person who sometimes may have weighed as much as both carriers combined was difficult to imagine. They helped themselves by leaning against a rod with each step, a thick cane also used to rest the *dolhi* before alternating shoulders. They rested from time to time, but after reaching the top descended immediately to find their next customer, offering their services on the way down to anyone tempted by the luxury they offered more than the virtue of the climb.

Jainism is a nontheistic religion founded by Mahavira, a contemporary of Buddha, in the sixth century B.C. Its basic principles are nonviolence, adherence to truth, non−stealing, chastity or control over the senses, and detachment from the material world. Jains are strict vegetarians, and Jain monks usually go naked as a sign of their indifference to possessions, and sweep the floor before each step to avoid killing insects. Mahavira is considered the last Tirthankara, the twenty−fourth. A Tirthankara is a *Jina*, a conqueror who has not only achieved enlightenment but is also dedicated to preach to the community. Jain temples contain representations of the twenty−four Tirthankaras in sitting or standing positions, very similar to the images of Buddha.

Although these temples were originally built in the eleventh century, Muslims destroyed them in the fifteenth, and the current buildings date from the sixteenth. When I was there, men came out of the locker room after changing into white robes similar to the togas of the Romans, garments used for the offerings (*bids* in Hindi), clean clothes without seams that are not used to eat or to go to the bathroom in while being worn. I watched men go into the temples carrying flowers, sandalwood paste, and saffron, which were placed on different parts of the statues of the Tirthankaras. It was part of the Svetambara ceremony or *puja* of eight offerings, in which the pilgrim walks clockwise three times inside the temple, three times as a symbol of the three jewels of Jainism: right faith, right knowledge, and right conduct, and then performs the eight offerings: pouring water over the image to purify it, spreading sandalwood paste on it as a symbol of the cooling of the passions (based on the belief that sandalwood cures fevers caused by colds), placing flowers on the image as a symbol of forgiveness, burning incense to eliminate ignorance and desire, waving the light of a lamp to symbolize enlightenment, with the last three offerings being rice, sweets, and fruit.

After witnessing the rites of Buddhists, Hindus, Sikhs, Muslims, and now Jains (besides the ones of my Catholic culture), I could not help but think how much they share with each other. To cross oneself after dipping the fingers in water, baptize a baby wetting his head with water, light a candle, kneel to pray, dip into a river, touch a cow and then one's head, cover the hair or never cut it, burn incense, offer flowers or food, ring a bell or hit a gong before entering a temple, dress in certain way—these rituals mostly represent purification, sacrifice, and a humbling sense of belonging to each group.

The journey from Palitana to Diu, a small island connected to the mainland by a bridge, that along with Goa and Daman was a Portuguese colony until 1961, took about five hours. The second half of the journey was along a road in very poor condition, the frequent potholes so deep that I feared that, by the end of the ride, my kidneys would be entangled with each other, my heart would have tilted to the right, and my stomach would have traded places with my liver. I arrived so late and tired from the long trip that I decided to stay in Diu to rest for a few days without going to visit Junagadh, the second of the holy sites of Jainism, at the top of 10,000 steps. At least I got a room in the most interesting accommodation in Diu, the old church of Sao Tome, whose nave has been converted into a museum and the former priest house and offices into guest rooms. Thanks to its location on a hill, and to the terrace along the roof, Diu's views were unbeatable.

I was glad to be once again facing the sea, drunk with its blue smell. But I was in a place that didn't seem to be Indian. Diu is not densely populated (including its cattle population), and its people are of Portuguese descent, as corroborated by their names, the crucifixes hanging from their necks, and the white Catholic churches. Diu was the first place in India where I was served by women. First, at the Sao Tome church it was a woman, of Portuguese looks more than Indian, who showed me to my room, then in a restaurant run by a young couple both of whom served the customers, which was repeated at another restaurant two days later, both with Portuguese names. In Diu I also found the first soccer field I had seen in India, with only a few patches of dry grass and young players kicking the ball around.

One afternoon, while reading on the church terrace, I chatted with an Englishman whose wife was in bed suffering from severe diarrhea. He told me that, since many Diu residents have Portuguese passports, many locals study and work in London, so they make enough money to keep their homes in Diu, the reason the island continues not being marketed to tourists, as home prices in Diu are quite high. This explained the lack of heavy tourism in Diu, and I remembered when, after my visits to beautiful Hoi An and Luang Prabang, I had wondered if there was a place somewhere that had decided not to succumb to mass tourism. It seemed that I had found it.

I stayed four nights there. I visited the fort, wandered the narrow streets, walked along the beaches, biked to Vanakbara, a fishing village at the western end of the island, meditated, wrote, took pictures, and recharged my batteries before the toughest stretch of my trip to India, the one that would take me across the country from west to east at its widest part, from Diu to Kolkata, visiting, along the way, Bandavgarh Natural Park, Kajuraho, and the holy city of Varanasi.

I left Diu by bus at 7:30 p.m. and got enough sleep in the bunk so as not to feel too tired when I reached Ahmedabad at dawn. I rode another bus at 7:30 a.m. to Indore, a long journey of more than thirteen hours. As soon as I arrived in Indore, I found a hotel, ordered dinner in my room, and went to bed exhausted after a refreshing shower. I had to get up early to catch the 6:55 a.m. train to Bhopal. I could not believe that, being Sunday and so early, the train was totally packed. I had to stand in the aisle for an hour until several passengers got off at an intermediate station. We arrived at Bhopal, the state capital of Madhya Pradesh, at 10:30 a.m. and, with some difficulty, I got an emergency overnight train ticket to Umaria for the following day, a town twenty miles from Bandavgarh National Park. Each train in India has a few seats in each class reserved for emergencies. Only available when all tickets have been exhausted, they are sold at an additional cost: I was delighted to avoid a long bus ride.

In Bhopal, I spent part of the day planning the rest of my trip, and bought online airline tickets from Kolkata to Mumbai, from Trichy to Bali, from Kuala Lumpur to Chiang Mai, and from Kuala Lumpur to Hangzhou (China). I got a confirmation email of my acceptance to the three–day vipassana course in late April in Malaysia. The only thing left to do was to buy the flight from Beijing to Tokyo and from there to London. In the afternoon I visited the city with the highest percentage of Muslim population in India, about 40 percent. India, with more than 160 million Muslims, is the country with the fourth largest Muslim population in the world, after Indonesia, Pakistan, and Bangladesh. The contrast in Bhopal between the colorful saris of Hindu women and the Muslim women in black was staggering. The next morning, a bus took me to Sanchi, just thirty miles from Bhopal, which has some of the most important Buddhist monuments, not only in India but in the world, and is one of the country's fifteen places listed as World Heritage Sites. The numerous temples and monasteries, some now in ruins, others in good condition, in Sanchi were built during the reign of Ashoka (270–232 B.C.). The town stands high on a hill and is very quiet and peaceful. A group of Thais came in a bus and, led by four Buddhist monks wrapped in mustard–colored robes, sat in the shade of a leafy tree in front of the main stupa to meditate.

The reign of Ashoka (known as Ashoka the Great) marks the apex of the Maurya dynasty (317–189 B.C.), the first great Indian empire. During the first years of his reign, Ashoka was known for his cruelty, which had its peak during the conquest of Kalinga, a war that left tens of thousands dead. Ashoka, after observing the devastation caused during the conquest, the brutality and violence, decided to adopt Buddhism as his religion and for his kingdom in 262 B.C. From then until his death thirty years later, his empire established nonviolence as one of its pillars and spread the Buddhist message, both in his empire and beyond. His new model of rule involved changing the concept of a divine king for that of a king who legitimized his rule through his relationship with the Buddhist authorities (the *sangha*), specifically by actively seeking their support. The new model became an example for Buddhist kingdoms such as those of Bagan in the eleventh century and Chiang Mai in the eighteenth. The conversion of Ashoka, which was somewhat similar to that of Buddha, had a profound impact not only on the expansion of Buddhism in India, Sri Lanka, and Southeast Asia, but in the subsequent relations between kings and Buddhist authorities, a pattern that continues today, as in the case of Thailand. Without Ashoka, Buddhism may not have spread beyond India.

Back in Bhopal, I went to the mosque Taj–ul–Masjid, the largest in the city. It was nearly 6:30 p.m., and speakers called believers to prayer. Muslim men arrived, some approached the pond at the center of the mosque to wash; others went directly, after removing their sandals, to the main building to begin with the recitation at dusk. I sat on a bench at the mosque entrance to listen to the verses of the Koran floating from the speakers in a flowing, songlike chant. I doubt if there is another religion with a more beautiful sound.

The simple purity of the human voice was enough to get you into a deep trance. I thought about the power of the collective ritual. In just a few hours I had witnessed a group of Buddhists meditating in front of a stupa, and now Muslim men reciting the Koran, and in both cases, and excluding the real meaning of each ritual, I couldn't doubt the emotional force of sharing a belief or tradition, the irresistible attraction that a sense of community created by such rites. Other modern manifestations of the same force are sport teams' fans, and their sometimes almost irrational passion for them, or heaps of youth dancing to music in clubs (as the song of the electronic group Faithless says: *God Is My DJ*).

My night journey to Umaria was in sleeper class, the cheapest and least comfortable bunk available on Indian trains. First, second, and third class AC (air conditioning) are extremely popular and almost impossible to get a few days before the day of travel. I had to put my two backpacks on the bunk, leaving enough space for my head, and lie with my legs slightly bent. It was difficult to get enough sleep in such a restricted posture. A bus from Umaria to Tala left me at the gates of the national park that has the highest density of tigers in India. And that's why I had come so far: to see a tiger. Visits to Bandavgarh are made by jeep, which, in addition to the driver and a government guide, can carry a maximum of six visitors. The entry price is per vehicle, so I had to find some tourists if I didn't want to pay $70 per entry. The park opens early in the morning for four hours, is closed during the midday heat for three hours, and reopens late in the afternoon for three hours. The price is per visit, the afternoon illogically costing as much as the morning despite being 25 percent shorter. I met at my hotel a young English couple from Newcastle, an Italian guy from Florence, and a French woman from Calais, and we hired a jeep for 1,000 rupees for the next morning. We went to bed dreaming of running into the most beautiful creature of nature. Since childhood I have always considered the tiger that. No animal approaches the beauty of its skin, the grace of its imposing gait. Hunted almost to extinction, only the timely intervention of the government and NGOs has managed to preserve it. Almost impossible to spot free in its environment, Bandavgarh might be the only place on earth where a few visits almost ensured an encounter.

The jeep came to pick us up at 6 a.m., and we headed to the park's main entrance, Gate 1, which admitted only thirty-two jeeps at a time. When we arrived we learned the quota had been filled by tourists who had booked in advance, so we had to enter the park through Gate 2. The morning was cool and beautiful, with the sun gently awakening and lighting the park's vegetation. This was predominantly forest and jungle, with several areas where trees disappeared in wide-open areas of grass, dry and golden at this time of year, with the aspect of an African savannah. Despite being winter, many trees still kept their yellow and red leaves, giving the park a more fall-like atmosphere than winter. I immediately thought how much I would have enjoyed crossing it on a mountain bike. We sighted deer, lots of them, plus monkeys, wild boars, vultures eating the remains of a deer killed by a tiger, beautiful and colorful peacocks, and many other birds. We passed a jeep with four Italians who had seen, in the distance, a tigress with two cubs. We didn't find her. We returned somewhat disappointed but amazed by the beautiful natural scenery that had surrounded us for almost four hours.

In the afternoon we walked over to Gate 1, hoping for a last-minute cancellation so we could visit the area of the park I'd been led to believe was more conducive to encountering tigers. No cancellation. We decided to wait just in case. When almost all of the authorized jeeps had entered, a man approached us saying that an Indian couple would be willing to share their jeep with four of us. The English couple, remaining in our jeep, allowed the rest of us to accept the Indian couple's offer. Once inside the park, we went up a steep hill and down the opposite side to an area with the greatest number of animals, especially deer. We saw a couple of wild boars eating the remains of deer hunted by a tiger that had maybe not been very hungry, perhaps chased away by a jeep, since the deer was almost in one piece, about fifteen feet from the road. Our presence didn't alter at all the wild boars' concentration on their feast.

On the way out, for the second time crestfallen by the absence of a tiger, we observed about a dozen jeeps massed along a ridge, all the tourists staring at something. We arrived and looked in the same direction, and there it was: a tiger, coming down the steep slope towards the cars. It walked slowly, calmly, with firm, smooth steps, and brimming with the confidence that characterizes something that knows itself the master of its surroundings. The emperor of cats (in this case empress) wasn't surprised by the arrival of more jeeps, the voices of tourists asking their drivers to get closer, the constant clicks of cameras capturing her beauty. I expected the tiger to veer and go back from where she had appeared or to border the hill on one side, but the magnificent animal continued descending towards the nearby track. The first jeeps moved forward to leave room for her to pass. The tiger crossed the dusty track like a beautiful woman crossing a city intersection, aware that drivers would stop their vehicles to admire her beauty. Our jeep was the third vehicle from where she crossed, and therefore we could enjoy her proximity. After crossing she turned to her left, toward us, through the high grass, and then turned to her right when she was in front of us. She was only ten feet away, and to see her so close, so beautiful, was a vision I will never forget. She went towards the creek, crossed it, then pulled herself up to draw deep furrows in the trunk of a large tree with her front claws, marking her territory before disappearing into the woods a few moments later.

Unforgettable, unsurpassed, seeing a tiger so close. A completely surreal experience that a wild animal, a predator of such size, would be unafraid of humans and cross between fifteen jeeps as if they were so many trees. It seemed a dream. When she descended the hill and crossed the track between the cars, and when I spotted her ten feet away, what impressed me the most was her walk, her soft and sweet moves, strong and elegant, a walk of great confidence and presence that mesmerized me by its power. I knew then why I had always been drawn to the tiger. Actually I wanted to be one, to be the holder of that natural force, the elegant beauty of its unforgettable presence. We left the park stunned, happy, and smiling. My purpose had been achieved, the long journey completely justified. As I washed off the day's dust in the shower, I replayed in my mind the sight of the tiger walking, which produced a gratifying smile of admiration and incredulity.

I had booked a drive to Satna, nearly four hours by bus from Khajuraho, a World Heritage Site for its splendid temples. A driver had to pick up some tourists arriving by train in Satna, and he offered to take me for 500 rupees (first he had asked for 2,000). It was a great deal. In three hours I could reach Satna. Without a car, as there was no direct connection by road, the only alternative was a bus to Umaria, a train to Katni, and a second train to Satna. I showed up at 7 a.m. in front of his home; a young man came out and handed me his cell phone. His father informed me that the tourists had missed the train and cancelled the pickup at the last minute. Disaster. I remembered that a Dutch couple had hired a car to take them to Katni for a mid—morning train, but when I got to their hotel they had already left. Second disaster. I adopted my Buddhist attitude: *anitya, anitya, anitya*, everything passes away, and resigned myself to waiting for the first bus (at 8 a.m.) to Umaria. It was already 8:20 a.m. and I was still waiting, thinking I would miss the 10 a.m. train to Katni, when a car stopped and the driver offered to take me to Umaria. I offered him fifty rupees, and he accepted. Fortune.

The Katni train was packed and dirty, and I had to suffer it for two hours to cover just forty miles. It was cheap, only ten rupees, reflecting its quality. In Katni I got on the train to Satna at 2:30 p.m. and enjoyed a window seat in a nearly empty train. Fortune again. The two—hour trip turned into three due to a couple of long stops. Another disaster. I reached Satna at 5:30 p.m. when I should have arrived at 10:30 a.m. if I had come by car as planned. I was physically and mentally exhausted. I thought of looking for a hotel in Satna and going to Khajuraho in a bus at 6 a.m., but decided to get to the bus station and see if there was still a bus to Khajuraho. There was one to Bamitha, just seven miles from Khajuraho, and I gathered some strength to continue my long journey, thinking that at least I would not have to get up early for a fourth day. It took three hours to reach Bamitha, where an auto−rickshaw carried me to Khajuraho. In total, it had taken more than fourteen hours to cover a distance of approximately 250 miles.

I hated India for its lack of investment in infrastructure, its slow and crowded trains, its inefficient and trembling buses. More than once I'd heard about India, that you either love it or hate it, but that day I realized the correct conjunction wasn't "or" but "and": India, you love it *and* you hate it, you go back and forth between these feelings several times a day, sometimes several times in an hour. You love its colors as much as you hate its dirt, you fall for its temples and shy away from many of its hotels, savor the food while abhorring the street odors, love its cheerful music and hate its noisy cities, you are dazzled by the friendliness of its people as well as rejecting their uncivilized behavior when they constantly pollute their country or don't allow you to get off trains and buses in their eager hunt for a seat. In India there is no respite, indifference is impossible, balance nonexistent. Perhaps that is why Buddhism disappeared, unable to find the Middle Way there.

In Khajuraho I enjoyed its calm and especially the incredible temples that make it so famous. The reliefs on the walls are spectacular, and not just the popular erotic reliefs of acrobatic positions that make them known as the Kama Sutra Temples. From there I went by night train to Varanasi, the holy city, one of the oldest in the world, the religious emblem of India, the place where every Hindu wants to die, where the cycle of life and rebirth is broken. I took an auto−rickshaw from the station to the old part of the city, which throngs the west bank of the holy Ganges. The streets are so narrow that auto−rickshaws can't fit; bicycles and motorcycles are the only ones able to negotiate the maze of buildings piled on top of one another. I got off the auto−rickshaw at the gates of the labyrinth, and the driver told me the way to go, advising me to ask in stores for the whereabouts of my hotel, since I'd be unable to find it by myself. And so I did, I asked for my hotel not one or two but so many times I lost count; so many that I thought I was the victim of a joke and did nothing but go around the same alleys. It was impossible to get oriented, once trapped between the confining verticals of the buildings.

When I finally escaped the maze, I found myself peering into one of the *ghats*, Scindia Ghat, with the breadth of the Ganges before me. A young man asked what I was looking for; I gave him the name of my hotel, and he kindly walked me to it, passing the famous Manikarnita Ghat, the main cremation site of all India, where pyres never stop burning during the night. It was encircled by woodpiles. Several men weighed large timber on scales as it was sold by weight and priced according to its quality. We met the next corpse coming to be cremated. Wrapped in an orange robe and adorned with flowers, it was carried on a wooden stretcher by four men, followed by the family.

In my hotel, situated only seventy feet from the *ghat*, I ate at the restaurant on the fourth floor with expansive views of old Varanasi and the Ganges. As I looked across the city, the buildings themselves seemed to be coming down to the river, fighting to purify themselves, jostling as many Indians do when they try to get on trains and buses. It was as if the whole city wanted to fall into the river, some houses pushing others to get to the holy water first, as if venturing into the Ganges was Varanasi's only purpose; the religious river a magnetic force that has attracted millions of pilgrims for thousands of years. I went to the *ghat* to observe more closely the rite of cremation. Several tourists and some Indian men witnessed the ritual close by, while a man stepped out of his tiny stall, offering *chai*. The remains of several pyres, still hot, showed how the two that had just been lighted would end up in a few minutes. A couple more bodies arrived. The stretcher of one of the deceased was taken to the river and lowered onto the river's surface. Then the relatives poured holy water over the body to purify it. Wood vendors piled logs where the inert body would rest for the last time. I looked at two bodies already burning. One looked like the body of a small woman, but as it was covered from head to toe it was impossible to determine. The other was a man; he was uncovered, his feet sticking out at one end of the pile, his head at the other. The fire consumed the bodies more slowly than one would imagine. As the center of the fire consumed most of the body; I saw the woman's legs collapse, the heat melting death's rigidity. A little later it was the man's turn: his feet were wrapped in flames, his head grew blacker and blacker. I was strongly impressed by the vision of a human body being devoured by the flames. Nobody was crying. Death for Hindus is another step in the cycle of life and birth, and the rite of cremation is done quietly, respectfully, without showing pain in public.

After my second episode of arrhythmic tachycardia, I informed my cardiologist back in London about what had happened during my vacation weekend in San Sebastian. My cardiologist glanced at the electrocardiogram, and told me that my heart had reached 300 beats per minute. How can a heart contract at that speed, five beats per second? Such was the risk I was in that I was asked to come to the hospital in a couple of days to carry out an electro–physiological study of my heart. This involves inserting a wire to the heart through the femoral vein by way of a hole made in the groin. I lay awake during the procedure, only my pierced right thigh having been anesthetized. I felt the wire reach my lower abdomen and especially the turn it took to get into my right atrium. Small shocks delivered through the wire are capable of altering the heart's beating rate. The objective is to identify anomalies in the conduction of electrical impulses through the heart wall. The cardiologist warned me each time before altering the rate of my heartbeat, yet it was the strangest sensation, to feel such a blatant manipulation of my heart. My heartbeat quickened and decreased as if at the mercy of a knob that controlled the speed of my heart's contractions.

The study found out the anomaly in my "engine": I had an accessory pathway, a second "highway" capable of connecting my left atrium and ventricle, a path that allowed the electrical impulses to travel without the surveillance of the control center, generating a loop that had caused those two severe episodes that had got me so scared. It's called Wolff–Parkinson–White syndrome, a rare congenital condition estimated to affect 4 out of 100,000 people that usually goes unnoticed. The next step was to destroy the accessory pathway by ablation, which involves using radiofrequency to burn the tissue through which the electric impulse can travel, thereby interrupting any potential heartbeat loop. Having the accessory pathway on my left side had its advantage and disadvantage: the advantage was that it is far from the natural pathway, which therefore could not be hurt by the radiofrequency; the downside was that, to access the left side, it was necessary to pierce the membrane separating the two atria, which entailed the risk of clotting. They had to cut to a vein in my left thigh too, to introduce a second wire that would pierce the membrane and reach the left atrium. The earlier process would then be repeated: electric shocks to locate the accessory pathway before burning it with precision. I was told I'd feel something like a pinch in my heart. And that's exactly what I felt: an intense pinch of short duration. It turned out to be a repairing pinch: the short circuit had been removed.

The whole process was surreal, from the fact that doctors could access my heart from my groin to being fully conscious throughout the procedure, but also that they could alter the rhythm of my heartbeat in order to study it and burn part of my heart's muscle in order to repair it. Actually, the worst part of the process, aside from the tension (I was sedated), was the healing of the two holes in my thighs. I returned to my room and had to push with my hands to make sure both holes would close by themselves, without any sutures. Two days later I was discharged, and, since each step I took pulled the tender skin around my groin, I had to walk with very short steps, like a hundred–year old man. I had to stay home for a week before regaining a natural stride. I was cured; I just had to take aspirin for a few weeks to avoid the risk of clotting. I could not believe it: I had gone in just a few days from panic to euphoria.

Once I had witnessed the rite of cremation, I walked south past the *ghats*. After the rainy season you can walk all along the Ganges. Each *ghat* has its name painted on the building's wall. Most are not wider than seventy feet. One of the most popular is Dasaswamedh. Thanks to its easy access it is frequented by hundreds of Indians who every day go down the steps and into the holy, but filthy, Ganges to purify their souls, if not their bodies. The Ganges water not only takes ashes and dead corpses (the bodies of children under a certain age are not incinerated but simply buried or dumped into the river), but also carries fecal remains in an amount that far exceeds the limits of hygiene. Some not only bathe in these waters but also drink them, another example of the predominance of emotion (or superstition) over reason. Not only is the Ganges severely polluted; Varanasi has dirt in abundance. Cows roam the streets and the *ghats* they share with dogs, goats, and buffaloes, undermining the Old Town with their feces and smell. I ran into a dog playing with a skull, an entertaining bone ball. It was not just animals that littered Varanasi; men peeing almost anywhere (every wall was a urinal) and garbage deposited in the streets to be eaten by stray animals contributed to the filthiness of the city. In a supposed competition between Varanasi's spirituality and its filthiness, the last would win handsomely.

Kolkata, formerly Calcutta, the old capital of British India, is an interesting city, its streets full of colonial vestiges and the iconic Ambassadors yellow cabs coloring the city, teeming with life in every corner, with food stalls feeding fast—eating, standing eaters, its rickshaws pulled by men on foot, many of them barefoot and so poor they sleep in their vehicles, and groups of workers waiting at street corners looking for jobs with their tools in hand to get hired by the day. There are four major castes in India: Brahmins (priests and teachers), Kshatriyas (kings, warriors, and aristocrats), Vaishyas (merchants and artisans), and Shudras (farmers, servants, and laborers). Dalits, the untouchables, are a class so low that they are not considered a breed, and were responsible for carrying out tasks such as cleaning impure excrement and sewage, and collecting dead animals. The caste system is the result of a hierarchical professional division rather than a religious concept, and probably was due to the arrival in northern India of Indo—Aryan groups who dominated the indigenous population at the time, mainly the southern Dravidians. Therefore, the upper castes are lighter in skin tone, the skin tone darkening as you descend the hierarchy.

I really enjoyed my three days in Kolkata, where I visited the magnificent Indian Museum, with its archeology section of wonderful Buddhist and Hindu sculptures; the Victoria Memorial, built to commemorate the death of Queen Victoria in 1901, an imposing neoclassical building surrounded by gardens and near the Maidan, Kolkata's Central Park; and the Palace of Justice and the Post Office, both splendid examples of British architecture. In Kolkata I clipped my beard for the first time since my departure from Spain fifty days earlier. The beard gave me respect in India; sometimes I was even taken for Indian.

I flew from Kolkata to Mumbai, where I chose to stay not in the city center but in the suburb of Bantra, a residential area where a good portion of Mumbai's upper middle class lives. A former Indian colleague had recommended it if I wanted to enjoy restaurants, cafes, and bars without many tourists. Since accommodation in Mumbai is very expensive, perhaps the most expensive of all Asia in terms of the ratio of price to value, I chose to pay more to be in an interesting area than to stay in the tourist part of Mumbai. Luckily, Fernando, the brother of a Spanish friend I had met in New York, resided in Bantra with his girlfriend. I contacted him, and we met up for a drink that night.

During the day I went to the Colaba neighborhood, where I saw the famous bay of Mumbai, formerly Bombay (the Portuguese christened it Bon Bahia in 1534), although I didn't see it clearly, given the air pollution, and walked down to the city center to appreciate the excellent architecture of the university, the Palace of Justice, the art deco apartments, and the fabulous Victoria Station. I also went to the synagogue Keneseth Eliyahoo, which is heavily guarded by police after the horrific terrorist attack of November 2008, when eleven Pakistani terrorists spread fear in the city, killing over 160 people and injuring more than 300. Near the synagogue, I ate fish at a nice restaurant, not too big, a place without windows, hidden behind an opaque door; very common in India. Restaurants for the upper middle class are not only unattainable for most of the population from a purely economic point of view, but also visually. When they have windows, the windows are opaque; the restaurant hides from the outside behind curtains (and the outside is hidden from patrons). Many, like the one I was in, are entirely indoor oases, converted into caves to escape the noise and dirt of the streets.

Fernando sent his driver to pick me up at my hotel. How different is the life of the expatriate from that of the backpacker! Residences with servants and car service paid by the company—that's the way much of the upper middle class lives in developing countries. From a purely economic standpoint, the professional classes in many countries in Latin America and Asia enjoy a standard of living well above their colleagues in developed countries. The driver took me to a bar with a roof terrace where Fernando waited for me. We had dinner there and then went to another place to have a few beers; a Portuguese friend of his joined us there. Young Indian women enjoyed the bar in groups without making eye contact with the rest. Fernando and his friend told me social life in Mumbai was based on the closed group of friends as a social center; it was hard to get into one without being introduced, especially if you were a foreigner.

On my last day in Mumbai I went by train to the city center and walked to Gateway of India, where I boarded a boat to take me to the island famous for the Elephanta Caves, a series of caves with large spectacular sculptures of Hindu deities, some over thirteen feet tall. In the afternoon, I went by train to Mahalakshmi where I saw the largest laundry in the world, a huge open space dedicated to washing clothes brought from various parts of the city. The workers were all male. The views of the giant laundry from the bridge over the train tracks make it a popular tourist spot for taking photographs. From there I walked to the coast to visit Haji Ali Mosque, built on an isthmus overlooking the Arabian Sea, an isthmus covered with beggars, many of them mutilated, asking for money. From there I went by taxi to Mumbai's famous Chowpatty Beach, whose sand was full of plastic brought in by the tide; once again, pollution spoiling what should have been a beautiful place. In all my train journeys I saw with sorrow how both sides of the tracks are littered with plastic containers thrown out by shameless travelers. There's so much plastic stacked along the tracks that if, at a stroke, the extensive Indian railway network disappeared, it could be re–laid merely by following the permanent trail left by the thrown–away plastic. Despite the existence of waste bins at train stations, it's customary to throw trash and garbage onto the tracks and wait for the station janitors to pile and burn it to get rid of it. On the outskirts of most towns, plastic forms a multicolored mountain nobody has an incentive to remove.

To return to Bantra I took a commuter train at rush hour, at the end of the workday. As in Jakarta, it had some carriages only for women. The doors of the carriages were always kept open, which was taken advantage of by those who got on the train early but failed to get a seat; they travel holding the entry bar and enjoying the freshness of the wind. The rest stood standing, following a tacit order: first they filled the aisles, then the area between the doors. Here, the first to arrive rested on the backs of the seats; once these had been taken, men lined up, one after another, all facing the same direction, glued and compressed despite having enough space to not do so, human domino pieces lined up in neat rows. I've traveled in packed trains both in London and in New York, but there everyone takes a place in no particular order. In Mumbai, however, that precise order seemed to be necessary; obviously they were anticipating what was about to come. Within a couple of stops, the train overflowed, and then I understood it was because of that perfect placement that so many human beings were able to pack into the train and return to their homes after work. I'd have loved to shoot a video with my compact camera, but my backpack was between my feet (luckily I was leaning against a backrest in the seating area), and it was impossible to get it. I was glad the density of my carriage went down significantly before my stop; otherwise it would have been somewhat difficult to escape from that prison–in–motion.

On my last night in Mumbai I went out with Fernando,

his girlfriend, his Portuguese friend, and a Spanish couple who had just arrived in Mumbai to inspect it prior to a career move. They took me to one of the hottest clubs in Mumbai, Trilogy, located in Hotel Sea Princess in front of Juhu Beach. Inside, two glitzy floors shone: the dance floor with a DJ on the top floor, a quiet bar on the bottom. The place was just three months old, but it had already become one of the favorite destinations for Mumbai's wealthy youngsters. We got in thanks to Fernando's Portuguese friend who managed to put our names down on the selective guest list. As soon I got in I felt like I had landed in another country, on another planet, not because anything I saw there surprised me, but because, after having traveled through India for almost two months, Trilogy seemed to be totally oblivious to all that I had experienced hitherto in India. No doubt this was the other India, the one that was taking advantage of economic growth, enjoying stratospheric incomes compared to the average citizen, showing that rapid economic development was happening somewhat unevenly.

Some of the male customers wore T—shirts at least a size smaller than appropriate to make their tanned muscles clearer, and some women wore miniskirts and heels, and displayed cleavage, showing the skin that was always hidden on the street. Some young men walked alone down the dance floor, looking at women, but these never responded; lonely men were completely invisible to them. Female eyes didn't travel the dance floor, preventing any flirtation between the sexes. Each group remained isolated from the rest in the tumult. We had a couple of drinks, one upstairs, the other in the quiet bar downstairs, while I missed the accessibility of Southeast Asian women.

From the dark cave where goddesses in high heels and short skirts reigned to the ancient caves of Ajanta and Ellora, where the ones idolized are Buddha and Hindu and Jain gods: both of the latter caves are located near the city of Aurangabad. Few places have impressed me as much as Ajanta and Ellora. The former, the older, from the second century, is composed of thirty caves along the gorge of the River Waghore. Buddhist monks retreated there during the rainy season, which was an unpropitious time to propagate Buddha's message, where they excavated temples in the caves, painted scenes from Buddha's life wonderfully on the walls, and carved serene sculptures of Buddha in an unparalleled combination. Ellora, however, includes not only Buddhist caves, but also caves devoted to Jainism and Hinduism. The star of the complex is Kailasa Temple, a temple excavated from a basalt cliff, from top to bottom: the temple was carved into the rock from the roof down, removing about 200,000 tons of stone. Viewed from the front, one can see the gigantic temple carved into the rocky hillside cliff; inside one can see, not only the delicate building itself, but also full-scale elephants and splendid reliefs and towers. It's a stunning building.

To reach Goa the journey took two trains, one from Aurangabad to Mumbai and another from there to my destination. I had a lower bunk on the side, ideal to enjoy the views from the window. In the next compartment was a young Canadian couple. I spoke with the man briefly while his wife read a book. They were coming from Varanasi. It's possible to take a train at one end of India's vast country and finish at the other. Perhaps the longest is the one that connects Kanyakumari, at the southern tip of India, with Jammu Tawi, in the northwest of the country. It's the Himsagar Express and makes a total distance of 2,300 miles in more than seventy hours. During my twenty-hour journey, I read, wrote, and slept quite a bit. I was struck by the Canadian couple's relationship. During every long train journey in India, food and drink vendors pass constantly through the carriages, particularly the air-conditioned ones. During the breakfast, lunch, and dinner hours they offer hot food; between meals they bring all kinds of snacks, as well as *chai*, coffee, juices, and carbonated drinks. When the Canadian woman wanted something, which was often, she requested it of her husband, who stopped a seller to place her order and paid for it. Once consumed, he picked the garbage up and threw it away in the trash area between the carriages. She never talked to any seller or picked up and threw away what she'd consumed. He always did it for her, with a servant—like, or gentlemanly, attitude.

I thought about the evolution of relationships that I had experienced lately and about that couple, which, perhaps unfairly, represented the opposite of what probably happens in most Indian households. It was March 8, International Women's Day, and newspapers printed numerous articles on the status of Indian women. In India, on average, every hour a woman is raped, every ninety minutes a woman is killed as a result of domestic violence, and every thirty minutes there is a death related to a bride's dowry. Maternal mortality is one of the highest in the world, and the ratio of abortions of female fetuses in areas of the north and west of the country is outrageous (in some states only 75 girls are born for every 100 boys; the normal rate in Europe is around 95). Sixty—eight percent of Indian men think women should tolerate domestic violence, 40 percent that it is women's responsibility not to become pregnant, 47 percent would be upset if they were asked to use a condom, and only 16 percent of men share tasks at home. News of sexual abuse and rape comes daily, from teachers who abuse their students (including little girls) to policemen who rape women of the lower castes, to parents who kill their daughters after they are discovered in a relationship with a boyfriend. I wondered where the Indian spirituality so much talked about in the West was.

The train left me at 6 a.m. in the south of Goa, in Margao, where I went by bus to the coast, specifically to Palolem. Immediately I noticed that most women were of Portuguese descent, with their uncovered hair in a ponytail or covered with a scarf that was tied under the chin, as my grandmothers did in Spain. In Palolem I stayed in a cabin on the beach, and my days were devoted, after the recent intense traveling, to relaxing by walking along the beautiful beach, swimming in the warm waters of the Arabian Sea, kayaking, reading, and meditating. I finished the wonderful *Midnight's Children* and changed it for *The White Tiger*, a hilarious novel by Aravind Adiga about India's corruption. I was enjoying breakfast on one of the terraces in front of the beach when I read the daily newspaper bringing the terrible news of the violent and tragic earthquake in Japan with its consequent tsunami. I'd been about to buy a flight from Beijing to Tokyo a few days earlier. Given the seriousness of the situation in Japan, I began to fear for the desired final destination of my journey across Asia. I decided to go online daily to follow the evolution of the situation, hoping it would quickly improve and I would not to have to alter my plans.

After my beach days, a morning train took me to Hubli, where a half—empty bus transported me to Badami. The views from the train as we pulled away from Margao were of precious tropical scenery reminiscent of what I'd witnessed the previous year in my travels through Southeast Asia; it was evidence that I was already in southern India. In Hubli, in the state of Karnataka, Hindi disappeared from information signs, shop names, and newspapers to be replaced by Kannada, the local language, whose characters are more like Burmese than Hindi. In Hubli I noticed that saris didn't cover women's heads, which were adorned with flowers, and many men wore skirts. In southern India, it was not just the clothes that differed from the north but also people's faces, which seemed more relaxed, especially those of women. In addition, the literacy rate is higher in the southern states, corruption levels are lower, and women are treated better (the ratio of female births is almost normal). I started drawing an imaginary dividing line diagonally from Kolkata to Mumbai, above which lie the parts of India that have received the greatest Muslim influence, and with it, unfortunately, the development of a very particular Indian culture that clearly underestimates women.

In Badami I visited the caves, wandered through the city's narrow streets, taking pictures of the cute kids that came my way, and early the next morning, I went to Pattadakal, a World Heritage Site, to see its fabulous series of temples. On the train to Hampi two Indian transvestites, *hijras*, appeared, asking aggressively for money from travelers, which they did by clapping their hands loudly twice or thrice, the right hand against the left, before extending the right hand in demand. I was ignored, but not so each Indian person in the carriage. Anyone who wasn't generous got a series of aggressive words I would have loved to understand. Some *hijras* are gay, others have been castrated (for reasons unknown to me); to earn a living they often appear uninvited at weddings and births to ask for money in exchange for not casting spells on the couple or the newborn.

Hampi has one of the most wonderful architectural sites in India and is one of the country's fifteen World Heritage sites. In 1336 Prince Harihararaya chose Hampi for his new capital; then called Vijayanagar, by the sixteenth century it had half a million inhabitants. Besides the Virupaksha Temple and the Royal Enclave, the star is Vittala Temple, excellently preserved and at whose entrance stands a huge chariot carved in stone—truly spectacular. The village of low houses along the Tungabhadra River is very enjoyable, and its inhabitants are extremely friendly. Both on the banks of the river and in the areas around the temples, gigantic rocks adorn the rolling hillsides, forming a striking landscape.

After two days in Hampi that felt too short, a night train took me to Bengaluru, the new name of Bangalore, the Indian capital of information technology services. Because of its altitude, 3,000 feet above sea level, Bangalore's climate is very pleasant, dry, and even cool at night. The city center is also agreeably urban, the result of British design, whose legacy still remains in places like the Palace, inspired by Windsor Palace; Lalbah, the botanical garden, whose pavilion is reminiscent of London's Crystal Palace before it caught fire; and the beautiful Cubbon Park, ideal for walking or taking a nap in the middle of the city. In the afternoon, walking back to my hotel I heard shouting coming from the stadium where a world cup cricket match between Australia and Canada was being played. My two urban days led to a dinner at Pizza Hut and another in a burger resto (I needed a break from the daily Indian food), and coffee in a modern cafeteria full of businessmen, some Westerners, with their BlackBerrys in hand, devices that seemed more interesting than the conversations taking place at their tables.

Another overnight train took me to Chennai, formerly Madras, but I opted for not stopping there and proceeded to Mamallapuram, two hours south by bus. It's a town on the coast next to a beach which that day showed very rough seas resulting from a strong wind. Besides its beautiful temple overlooking the sea, the city is famous for its five Rathas, large sculptures made from a single stone, dedicated to Durga (the goddess of femininity and fertility), Shiva, Vishnu, Indra, and Dharmaraja. Splendid is the gigantic relief called "Arjuna's Penance," one of the largest and best preserved in India. In Mamallapuram I fell for the luxury of staying in a hotel with a pool. In the morning, a group of Indian men went for a swim and took advantage of their wives' absence to fix their eyes on three Russian women sunbathing in their bikinis. When the sight of female skin is so elusive, these men's visual fixation on the undressed Slavic women wasn't a surprise.

Continuing my journey southward, I reached Puducherry (formerly Pondicherry), a city that was French territory until 1954. It's another coastal town, but Puducherry's citizens and visitors look toward the sea not from a beach but from a long, raised walkway made of rocks, a promenade that fills up every evening with food stalls and walkers, as well as crows (the only "gulls" of Puducherry are of black plumage). The streets of the French Quarter still contain colonial buildings, such as the *hotel de ville* (city hall), the *douanes* building (customs house), the old lighthouse, the French consulate, and the churches of Our Lady of the Immaculate Conception, Sacre Coeur, and Notre Dame. I stayed at the ashram of Sri Aurobindo, by the sea, a beautiful building with a garden, a dining room, a meditation room, and spacious and clean rooms with balconies overlooking the ocean; it was one of the best accommodations I had during my trip in India. I liked Puducherry, especially its architecture; however, I could not but regret it wasn't like Vietnam, where the promenade would have been full of restaurants offering fresh grilled seafood instead of the simple Indian snacks. At least Puducherry had several excellent restaurants, some, of course, French. One evening, on the way to one of them for dinner with the intention of having beef (so elusive in India), I met a group of young Indians speaking in French. *Très chic.*

As couldn't be otherwise in India, the tranquility of the days in Puducherry disappeared abruptly with the horrible journey from there to Kodaikanal, on top of the Palni Mountains, 7,000 feet above sea level. I woke up at 5 a.m. to catch the bus from Puducherry to Trichy, where I jumped onto a second bus to Dindigul. From there I caught the 4:30 p.m. bus to Kodaikanal. Shortly after leaving Dindigul, the vehicle stopped at a garage because of a mechanical problem requiring urgent attention. Back on the bus, our next stop brought hysteria with a horde of humans trying to get into the vehicle as if their lives depended on it. Later on, in sweltering heat because of the crowd, the driver stopped because of a noise coming from one of the rear wheels. After inspecting it, he returned to the garage to try to fix the second mechanical problem of the day. We got off and waited, sitting on the ground outside the garage, for the mechanics to solve the problem. Next to us was a small shrine dedicated to the god Ganesha, half man, half elephant, one of the most popular among Indians because he is responsible for removing obstacles. That day it seemed Ganesha had taken the day off. An Indian man offered me marijuana; he was completely stoned, and said, "This is India, man," which sounded to me like our "Spain is different." I finally arrived in Kodaikanal at 10 p.m., fourteen hours after my departure from Puducherry, for a journey of about 250 miles. Lacking the energy to find a hotel I liked, I went to the first one I came across in the town center, desperate to lie down and sleep. The next morning I went to the Greenlands Youth Hostel, where I got a simple room with fabulous views of the valley. The glorious views and mountain climate immediately erased the previous day's nightmare. Once again: *anitya, anitya, anitya.*

The road between Kodaikanal to Munnar was built in 1942 by the British in response to the Japanese bombing of Madras (Chennai) during the Second World War, bombing that inflicted little harm but caused the evacuation of the city. The British plan was to facilitate movement from the city to Munnar, and from there to the port of Cochin (now Kochi), in case of an eventual thrust by the Japanese into the Indian Ocean; this, however, didn't happen. After my last experience with Indian state buses, I chose to go to Munnar in one of the private cars offering group journeys, because the only other option would have been to take three buses to get there. My companions were, besides the driver, a retired Norwegian man and two Indian couples. The state of Kerala greeted us with the magnificent Munnar tea plantations, miles and miles of rolling hills carpeted by thick tea bushes. We were also received by many billboards of political parties seeking the vote of the people of Kerala in the state's local elections; many were for the Communist Party, which has a strong presence and history in the state of Kerala. Communists won in the first legislative elections in Kerala in 1957; it was the first communist party to win a democratic election not only in India but in the world. Kerala is presently the Indian state with the highest literacy and lowest corruption rates.

I had booked accommodation in a cottage in the middle of a cardamom, pepper, and coffee plantation that also offered yoga classes. The house driver picked me up in a jeep at the entrance to Munnar to take me five miles to the south, where the beautiful plantation was located. The guesthouse had been recently established by a couple of Indians who had returned after several years working in Tokyo, to fulfill their dream of having a retreat in Munnar. The place was beautiful, if somewhat pricey, though the quality of both the rooms and the vegetarian food justified the daily rate. The first afternoon I went for a walk in the vicinity though I was somewhat anxious about getting lost for a few hours between the tea bushes. These are planted close together but leave enough space for plantation workers to move between them to prune the leaves. From a distance, in an unparalleled visual spectacle, the hillsides appear to be completely covered with comfortable green cushions that, if it weren't for their height, seemed to invite one to sit on them. During the walk I paused on a small terrace beside a stream for, of course, tea.

Back in my room I put on the television to watch the movie *Up in the Air* on the HBO channel. Movies in English are released in India in the original version with subtitles in English to facilitate understanding. When an actor says a dirty or prohibited word (fuck, shit, sex, orgasm, etc.), it's substituted in the subtitle for another or simply removed from the text. For example, orgasm would become climax, sex turns to making love, and fuck would be removed completely. In *Up in the Air*, George Clooney plays an executive who spends his life traveling the U.S. from city to city, firing employees of large companies. He lives in the air, hence the title, without a sedentary life as most people have, or important personal relationships (he is not married, has very little relationship with his family, and doesn't seem to have any friends). I thought that, while he was "up in the air," I was "closer to the ground"—both of us unattached, constantly moving, and traveling light. Clooney's character did it for work and was completely satisfied with his solitary traveler lifestyle, so much that when the company considers introducing dismissal by videoconference, he almost sickens at the thought of working from an office and living in his empty apartment instead of bag in hand, going from city to city, hotel to hotel, accumulating air miles (his dream is to reach ten million). Traveling is a constant stimulation of the senses; endless new sensations appear in front of you every day, an antidote to the routine that most people experience, that some suffer. I have often wondered how some people who have never left their place of residence deal with their daily lives—not those who have not had a chance to do so; I mean those who could have moved to another city, even in their own country, but hadn't even considered it. In a world as connected as we have today, as open and accessible to many, especially to Westerners, it seems to me that residing in one place for a lifetime wastes endless possibilities. You learn so much traveling or living outside your city or country.

Kochi, the new name of Cochin, is a port city with a long history in international trade. Occupied by the Portuguese from 1503 to 1663, subsequently by the Dutch until 1814, and finally by the British, the old town offers a wonderful and diverse group of colonial architecture. Saint Francis Church, founded in 1503, is considered the oldest European church in India. There, Vasco da Gama was buried after his death in Cochin in 1524. His tomb inside still remains, even though his body was taken to Lisbon in 1539.

Kochi also has an old Jewish district in which is located the beautiful Paradesi synagogue, built in 1568 by Jews who had fled from persecution in Spain. In Kochi I bumped into Pier, the retired Norwegian man I had met on the way from Kodaikanal to Munnar. We went out for dinner and beers a couple of nights and enjoyed together India's victory over Sri Lanka in the final of the World Cricket Championship. The young Indians who followed the final with us soon started to dance happily to celebrate the victory in their main sport. Cricket is for Indians what soccer is for Brazilians, and their star player, Sachin Tendulkar, one of the best hitters in history, is their Pele. Sachin is indeed more than a king of the sport: he is called the God of Cricket.

Before reaching the far edge of India, where I would finalize my three–month journey through the country, I stopped to spend a couple of nights in Varkala, a village that faces the sea from atop a stunning cliff. A few hours by train from Varkala is Kanyakumari, the Indian Finisterre and the southernmost point of the country. The sun fell slowly over Indian visitors crowding onto the tiny beach, soaking their feet, or washing thoroughly (the women fully clothed). Three men wearing only the typical southern skirt went down the steps leading to the sea east of the beach to bathe and fill several jugs of water. It must be that the seawater here was also holy. Every so often, a wave stronger than others stalked the shore, and shouts of anticipation rose in volume as it approached. With its arrival some women lost their balance and fell to the sand, totally surprised, and got fully soaked, to the amusement of family and friends. Others simply watched the scene from the dry zone of the beach, having an ice cream or some dried fruit purchased at one of the many stalls nearby.

I sat on the wall of the small balcony–like structure that stood above the country's end point, beyond which everything was sea, and spent a few moments reflecting on my three months of intense travel through India. I remembered the beginning in Delhi with the flu, and my short journey to the north, cold and not very cozy (except the Golden Temple in Amritsar), the men in hotels and restaurants unfriendly and even ungrateful; my interesting exploration of Rajasthan, with its magnificent forts and the beautiful blue Bundi; my first breaths in cute Diu, my amazing encounter with the wild tiger; my enchantment with, and repudiation of, Varanasi; my fascination with the colorful streets of Kolkata; my curiosity about the modern Mumbai; my admiration for the genius of the caves of Ellora and Ajanta; my enjoyment of the sea in Goa; my pleasant urban life in Bengaluru; my taste of France in Puducherry; my feelings of relief in high Kodaikanal; my delight in Munnar's tea plantations; and my embrace of the ocean from the cliffs of Varkala.

In ninety days I had traveled approximately 8,000 miles (only 1,400 by air, the rest by bus and train) and had achieved my initial goal: to get to know, however briefly, much of India. Some areas had been excluded because of their remoteness (the northeastern states) or their climate in winter (the Indian Himalayas on both sides of Nepal), many for lack of time (Orissa, for example), which gave me a perfect excuse for a future visit. I felt satisfied and grateful for having spent three intense months traveling in India, but I also acknowledged that I had only been able to discover a minimal part of its culture, complex and strange for a rational Western atheist like me. I thought how well chosen was the slogan of the country's tourism ad campaign: *Incredible India*. It certainly is a unique country, a really amazing one. One needs to experience it with time to appreciate its uniqueness within its considerable cultural variety.

FRIENDSHIP, LUXURY & RESPITE

"I have found out that there ain't no surer way to find out whether you like people or hate them than to travel with them." —Mark Twain

"A journey is best measured in friends, not in miles." —Tim Cahill

Following the resumption of my trip in India, I had come to consider not attending my London friends' reunion at Easter in Bali, thinking, instead, of taking advantage of the time available to travel and discover new places like Borneo, Flores, and Sulawesi in Indonesia, or Malaysia, of which I only knew Kuala Lumpur. However, the possibility of seeing some of the great friends I had made in London beat my explorer's temptation. Traveling through India, especially following my ambitious plan, had been exhausting, and, although my last two weeks had been quite enjoyable, I really felt like being sedentary for a while, especially while being surrounded by great friends—a welcome contrast to the lonely days of the last three months.

By then I had planned the whole rest of my trip. After Bali, I'd spend ten days between Malaysia and Singapore (including the three–day course in vipassana) and then fly to Chiang Mai, in the north of Thailand, where I wanted to enjoy such a pleasant city writing, meditating, and practicing yoga for two weeks before tackling the last part of my Asian trip in China and Japan. Following the catastrophic earthquake and ensuing tsunami, visiting the latter was still uncertain. There were still two months before my arrival in Japan, which I expected would be sufficient time for the situation to improve. However, the confusion about the radiation emitted from the damaged Fukushima reactor forced me to be cautious. I fervently wanted to see Japan; an exploration of Asia would be incomplete without a visit to Japan.

My friends had rented a villa in Bali with five bedrooms, a swimming pool, and a huge garden, which had, at its far side, hidden among plants and flowers, a Jacuzzi, a kiosk with two massage beds, and a yoga studio open to the garden. The price included breakfast and the availability of a minivan and driver for the day. When they booked the villa several months before, I considered the price too high for me, and told them if I was to come to Bali I'd stay nearby according to my budget. A coveted pregnancy made David and Lisa cancel their trip, leaving an empty room and a higher cost to be shared among the rest. My friends, extremely generous, insisted on my taking the vacant room and contributing what I could to its cost; it was really stupid to pay for a hotel instead of staying with them and helping cover the price. The villa was spectacular. My mouth dropped when I arrived. It was certainly the most luxurious place I had ever stayed in, and the contrast with the usual lodgings during my trip couldn't have been more extreme. I had moved from a dirty cave to a luxurious palace in just a few hours.

I was the last to arrive, and was really happy to see all my friends together with their smiles of excitement over our next two weeks together in Bali. From London had come Dave and Stephanie with their two children, as well as Tony and Maria, and Will; from Hong Kong, Marc and Ivy with the two girls; from California, Steve and Monique. Fred would come from Singapore to spend a weekend. Besides David and Lisa, we also missed Gerry and Lucy, Mathieu and Emmanuelle, and Joaquin and Francesca, who all, for various reasons, couldn't attend the reunion we intended to organize every two years now that many of us no longer resided in London. The group is called La Familia, in Spanish, because for all of us this is what it had represented in London: our family, a group of people, very different, from different backgrounds, and yet not only naturally congenial but above all made of individuals who didn't judge the others and accepted them as they were.

The first day was one of total relaxation in the villa. They were recovering from their long trips to Bali; me from my intense Indian travels. The following days we alternated tours of Bali with days in the village practicing yoga, enjoying the pool, playing with the kids, tasting the local cuisine, and drinking Bintang beer in the warm evenings. We set up a net on the pool to play volleyball, and almost every morning I became a spontaneous yoga teacher for the group. The day trips were to Seminyak, the luxurious town on the south coast, to Ubud (the same town I had visited recently), to the Tana Lot temple, to the surfing beach of Echo, to the rice fields in Jatiluwih and the nearby Pura Luhur temple, and to Danau Bratan Lake. We also went out on Saturday evening. Unfortunately, that day Dave didn't feel well and stayed home resting. At my suggestion we went to KuDeTa for a drink, and then to Hu'u to dance a little. We couldn't remember the last time we'd all been out together dancing. We had a great time. When I woke up late Sunday morning, Steph told me Dave had been admitted to the hospital with a suspicion of having contracted dengue, a disease transmitted by the bite of a mosquito that is spreading worldwide and for which there isn't a vaccine yet. Aware of dengue's risk, I worried a bit, but fortunately Dave improved immediately and after three nights in the hospital was discharged, to the delight of all.

I flew from Bali to Kuala Lumpur, a city of contrasts, and now, thanks to AirAsia, perhaps the most important air hub in Southeast Asia. I had been in contact with Lani sporadically through Facebook. Once in India, and after I had concretized my travel plans, I told her I'd stop by Kuala Lumpur, and since then she became more active commenting on my photos on Facebook. She had asked me to buy her a silk scarf in India, and I had promised to do so. I acquired it in Kochi, one of colorful pastel tones I imagined would go perfectly with her complexion and dark hair. Two nights before arriving in Kuala Lumpur we saw each other on Facebook and chatted for a while. The conversation turned a bit serious; she seemed too glad about my arrival, perhaps understanding my visit as motivated by her. I feared she would be disappointed once she found out about my vipassana course over the weekend and my plan to visit Singapore.

After checking in at the guesthouse where I had stayed the previous July, I went to the restaurant where Lani now worked as a waitress. When I got there, I saw her from the back while she waited for the bartender to prepare her tray: her straight black hair, her sexy curved figure sculpted by tight black trousers at the hips, and a white shirt belted at the waist. She turned, saw me, and came over to give me a hug (no kissing while working, I was warned in Facebook). I ordered some food and chatted with her at intervals while she served other tables. She was a little nervous, which surprised me since in our first meeting she had seemed confident at all times. We agreed to meet at 8 p.m. at a nearby bar. I took the rest of the afternoon for a short nap, to buy a toothbrush and some new flip–flops, and have coffee at Starbucks while reading my emails and news on the Internet.

I found Lani wearing an elegant black dress with red patterns and sitting at a table on the terrace outside with a glass of sangria. As expected, she was quite disappointed to learn of my plans. She'd thought of taking me to a concert by a Canadian rock band on Saturday. She loved the silk scarf. We dined nearby and had a drink. I found out she was seeing someone, nothing serious she said, just going out occasionally together. She was feeling much better emotionally than when we first met, but she continued to insist on her caution with men. When she mentioned it, it was like a warning, a powerful invisible barrier that stood in front of anyone she could become romantically involved with. My expectations for a few days of fun were vanishing. During drinks, her leg touched mine and she didn't pull it away, and she took my hand briefly, naturally, several times. However, despite physical attraction on the surface, she insisted on going home with the excuse of having to get up early the following day. She tried to console me by saying Thursday was her day off, so Wednesday could be her crazy evening.

The next day, I went to the office in charge of processing Chinese visas. Mine would be ready the following Wednesday. I walked to KLCC mall under the impressive and famous Petronas Twin Towers, Kuala Lumpur's architectural emblem. Late in the afternoon the extreme, humid heat resulted in an intense rainstorm so common in Malaysia. I stayed in my room until the evening. A message from Lani asked about my plans. I replied I had none and invited her out for drinks. She responded with a terse "Maybe later." My attempt to clarify the meaning of later didn't get an answer. I went out for dinner and had a couple of beers on the balcony of The Social. I didn't hear from Lani. I figured she'd be enjoying her wild evening with her new man. Nevertheless, I saw her the following day. We met for a drink at The Social. She apologized for not having responded to my message. Apparently she had got drunk at a colleague's apartment. We ate some tapas with a glass of Ribera del Duero at Pinchos, a Spanish restaurant. She was tired, so she chose to go home without accepting the invitation to spend the night with me. Maybe when you get back from meditation, she said.

The first day of the course was devoted exclusively to anapana meditation, the next two to vipassana. Although I'd planned to ask for a chair if my legs couldn't tolerate long periods sitting on the floor, I decided against it and tried to survive the three days of chairless, ground-based meditating. The first day was not too hard, and with the help of different pads and changing position regularly, I managed not to suffer too much. However, on the second and third day, after the accumulated hours in such an unusual posture, my knees and ankles protested strongly. On a couple of occasions I was about to concede defeat, but my determination prevailed. Like everything in life, the value of any experience depends on our expectations beforehand. In my case, I wanted to get some intense meditation sessions, to feel deeply devoted to my meditating, to completely abandon myself during the three-day course. But my determination to stay with my legs crossed on the ground became a serious obstacle to succeeding at this. The constant discomfort, the pain in my joints and my back, the constant search for the perfect position (which doesn't exist; an excellent metaphor for life itself), precluded the fulfillment of my desires. I then realized that my expectations and my attitude towards the course were themselves the problem. I had to take each session as it came, without specific hopes, and observe reality and experience it as it appeared at each moment. With this new attitude, in a couple of sessions I learned to let my previous expectations go, not to seek a solution to my suffering, but to accept it and live it, not listening to it constantly but hearing it as a background noise, and concentrate on observing all of my body sensations and not only the most intense (*anitya, anitya, anitya*), and thus I went into a deep meditation—at times too pleasant, so much that I had to stay poised and not cling to it, as vipassana meditation shows us.

Buddhism teaches us that the important thing is to learn through experience, and certainly the three days were very productive, because I went quickly from discomfort to pleasure thanks to accepting the former, and for a few moments I managed not to cling to either by either rejecting or longing for it. Experiencing that feeling of abandonment, of acceptance of reality as it is in every moment, however brief it is, just experiencing it, showed me the way to go in my life. In comparison to the constant search for immediate gratification that today prevails in developed societies, which I think is tearing at and damaging new generations, Buddhism, with the help of meditation, brings us closer to freeing ourselves from the heavy armor with which we restrict our lives in complicity with the pressures of society.

I returned to Kuala Lumpur in a car owned by Chan, a retired Chinese Malaysian, with Viola, a Chinese–Canadian woman who, like me, was traveling through Asia. It rained with violent intensity, and as it was the end of a long weekend, the traffic back to the capital was dense and we suffered from long traffic jams. In Kuala Lumpur, Chan invited us to dinner at a local restaurant famous for its *bak kuh the*, a dish created by Chinese immigrants in Malaysia consisting of a pork broth with vegetables, tasty and rich, and very welcome after the vegetarian food at the meditation center. After dinner, I went to get a foot massage to ease the tension accumulated in my legs during the past three days. The young Chinese masseur did his work with the necessary pressure to make me forget all the hours I had fought against the strain in my legs during the course.

The next day, Tuesday, was a day of waiting, as it wasn't until Wednesday that my passport would be available with the

Chinese visa. All day I felt deeply and pleasantly relaxed, not only my muscles but also all of my organs. It was a magical feeling that tended to disappear gradually with the daily routine (although sometimes I managed to recover it during short intervals), with sometimes impure mental activity, with small tensions and desires that camp in our mind without our realizing it, and perhaps also with the inadequate food, including alcohol intake. I had dinner at a street restaurant: squid *sanbal* (spicy sauce) served with sauteed bok choy with garlic, and had a couple of beers on a terrace in Changkat, passing time until the start of the return leg of the Champions semifinal between Barcelona and Real Madrid. While waiting I saw Lani with a girlfriend enter Reggae Bar accompanied by two blond men. The match was better than the first leg, but once again Barcelona's technical and tactical superiority was enough for a 1–1 draw that put them in the final at Wembley. After sleeping no more than four hours, I took a taxi to the visa center and picked up my passport with the Chinese visa before going by bus to Singapore, where I stayed at my friend Fred's apartment.

My first day in Singapore I went by bus to the city center, to the famous Orchard Street, full of shops and malls. I walked the long street, constantly admiring the beautiful local women, ate a bowl of rice with roast duck, followed by a coffee, on a terrace, and took the subway to Little India, a neighborhood of small houses where the Indian community had settled. From there I went to Arab Street, the Arabic equivalent of the Indian neighborhood, dominated by the imposing Sultan mosque. After wandering around the modern luxury of Orchard Street, I was thankful for the modesty of both neighborhoods, although by merely looking up, I could feel the presence of the high skyscrapers in the distance, a reminder that Singapore is, perhaps with Shanghai, the leading exponent of the new Asian modernity.

Singapore was taken by Thomas Stamford Raffles for the British in 1819 with the express intention of turning it into an international port. In five years its population totaled 10,000 people, 3,500 of them Chinese immigrants, and in 1845, 61 percent of the 52,000 inhabitants of Singapore were from

China. Local people always considered the Chinese immigrants to be temporary, a vision also shared by the Chinese themselves. After the Second World War, their situation took a drastic change. The new Communist China formed in 1949 left the Chinese immigrants distanced not only geographically but also politically, making their return impossible. This not only affected the Chinese immigrants in Singapore but also those who settled in Saigon, Jakarta, Phnom Penh, and other cities in Southeast Asia.

That evening I met with Fred and his French friends to attend the opening of a Spanish tapas bar, where I was disappointed to see only Western expatriates. Their number was high in Singapore, a city where nearly a quarter of the population is foreign. Fred and his friends told me they had no friends from Singapore, since according to them it isn't easy to mix with Singaporeans outside professional life. If true—and I had the same feeling when I visited Hong Kong for work in 2007—I found it really sad to live in an Asian city if one had to mingle exclusively with Westerners.

The next day I toured Chinatown, with its low houses with wooden shutters painted in bright colors, before going to the marina area, surrounded by modern office buildings and luxurious hotels. I waited patiently for the evening to arrive to take some pictures of the city lights. Later I met with Fred and his friends to go drinking, and we finished with a visit to Orchard Towers, which they consider a must–see for every visitor, a commercial building with many bars and clubs spread over four floors so much frequented by prostitutes that it is known as "The Four Floors of Whores." On the first floor we went to Naughty Girl, where a live band played and a few young women clung to poles contouring their bodies on top of several tables. A young woman started talking to me. She was Indonesian, from Jakarta. I invited her for a drink and regretted it the moment I saw the bill: $30 Singaporean ($22 U.S.), one of the most expensive drinks I'd ever bought. I tried to amortize it by chatting with the girl, who openly told me she made a third of the price of each drink (I saw the waitress immediately handing her $10 that, according to the bar's style, she then stored in her bra) and that on a good night she could get ten drinks, five being the usual. Simple math gave me $50 to $100 Singaporean ($35 to $70 U.S.) for one night of work coaxing drinks from stupid men. I was not surprised that women all over Southeast Asia, attracted by Singapore's wealth, traveled as tourists to work the night this way and finance their lives and the lives of their families in their countries of origin. After the drink, Fred and his friends invited me to go to Ipanema, a larger and more popular bar, also with live music, where a beautiful young Thai offered to spend the night with me and disappeared as quickly as she came when I told her I didn't pay for sex.

Prostitution is legal in Singapore, though selling chewing gum, or even bringing it into the country, is not. And the fines for littering the streets can be severe in a city where cleanliness is an obsession. After my three months in India, I loved this puritanical attitude despite its making Singapore too aseptic for my taste, without the underground atmosphere I like to discover in every big city. Perhaps this is what "The Four Floors of Whores" represents, and hence its importance, not only because Singapore is a port city, with the thousands of sailors who arrive every day in need of venting, but by offering a place, although hidden, where vice runs free.

Besides its cleanliness, I liked Singapore's religious diversity. Buddhists account for about a third of the population where there are also Christians, Muslims, Hindus, and Taoists. Its calendar celebrates festivals of all religions, an example of fairness and integration. Its festivities include Chinese New Year, Good Friday, Labor Day, Vesak Day (Buddha Day), Singapore's Independence Day, Hari Raya Puasa (End of Ramadan, or Eid), Deepavali (Festival of Lights, or Diwali), Hari Raya Haji (Celebration of Sacrifice, or Eid al−Adha), and Christmas Day.

After leaving India and returning to Southeast Asia, only a few days in Bali, Kuala Lumpur, and Singapore were enough to bring back my idea of living in Asia. Either my literary adventure would be fruitful or it would not be; if it wasn't, and I had to seek employment, Asia presented a unique opportunity. It was an ideal time to experience both its culture and its economic potential. The energy and optimism prevailing in Asia would be an effective antidote to the pessimism and anxiety prevailing in the developed world, with its deep economic crisis prompted by a lifestyle, both private and public, founded on excessive borrowing, a standard of living too high to be maintained over the medium and long term.

Chiang Mai is so nice and quiet that you feel immediately relaxed as soon as you arrive. The airport is only ten minutes by taxi from the city center, a convenience hard to beat. I stayed in the same guesthouse I had on my first visit to the northern Thai city. Its location is perfect, near the Sunday market street and next to restaurants, cafes, and bars, and its rooms are spacious, with a refrigerator, a small balcony, and Wi-Fi, all at a reasonable price. My two weeks there were spent as I had imagined: taking some morning yoga classes, daily meditation, reading and writing, enjoying the tasty and spicy Thai food, relaxing with excellent Thai massages, and drinking a few beers in the cool of evenings. Although I hesitated, in the end I contacted Khae, who now worked in a restaurant. She invited me to come over for a drink. After completing her shift, we went to a bar to play pool before spending the night in my room. The only difference from our first meeting was that now she had to go to work at 10:30 a.m.; the rest was identical, including the excellent sex. However, I didn't intend to see her much. We didn't have much to talk about, and once my sexual urges were satisfied, our appointments weren't that interesting. We saw each other a couple of times.

Despite the confusing news about the levels of radiation in Japan, I bought an airline ticket from Beijing to Tokyo for early June. Fukushima is many miles north of Tokyo, and my plan was to visit the capital and head south to Kyoto, so I didn't think my brief exposure to Japan could have negative consequences for my health. Inevitably, I ended up also thinking about what to do immediately after finishing my Asian adventure. I decided to take a ten-day vipassana course in Massachusetts after returning to the U.S. and thought about renting an apartment in Brooklyn for three months (August through October), and devoting myself to finishing and selling the script and the book. The date 11–11–11 was the fiftieth birthday of my friend Kellie, who had thought of celebrating it with her best friends in Seville. Therefore, I brought forward my flight to Spain, where I intended to spend Christmas with my family in San Sebastian and probably the winter too, because I wasn't ready to suffer it in New York after having skipped the last two.

That was my plan for the following months: to finish my two current projects, select and edit my best photos, and think how to give all of these a commercial exit to the world. I had to put a time limit on this, and early 2012 seemed sensible. Beyond that, everything was up in the air. What might fill many with panic I saw as a challenge. I felt no apprehension at all, didn't fear the possible failure of my creative dreams. If these didn't come through successfully, I had no doubt I'd keep trying with other projects. At the end of the day, we regret much more what we don't do than what we try to do. When we try, even if we fail, we at least learn something; inactivity hardly produces anything useful. Happiness dwells in those who act, not in those who don't.

REDS, GASTRONOMY & TAO

"I travel not to go anywhere, but to go. I travel for travel's sake. The great affair is to move." —Robert Louis Stevenson

"Travel makes one modest. You see what a tiny place you occupy in the world." —Gustave Flaubert

The AirAsia flights from Chiang Mai to Kuala Lumpur and from there to Hangzhou were on time. The latter flight landed in Hangzhou at 10:30 p.m. On our approach I saw from my window several neon signs in Chinese on different buildings, as expected, all in deep red. Already on Chinese soil, as we taxied to the airport building, I saw one of the employees on a bicycle, something I had never seen at any airport. Maybe Chinese modernity wasn't as advanced as I had expected and the bike was still the main means of transport of the Chinese people even at their airports. Hangzhou's was definitely modern, and going through immigration and claiming my backpack were very quick. The excellent initial impression was adversely affected when I couldn't find an ATM in the international arrivals terminal, which until then had been so easy in any airport I'd flown to. I was told there was one in the domestic terminal, just five minutes away. After obtaining local cash, I bought a bus ticket to the city center. In my inquiries to find an ATM and the bus departure time, and the available stops in Hangzhou, I saw how little English was spoken in China.

I got off at the first stop in Hangzhou, which was separated from my hotel by over a mile. Despite the late hour, several women carrying picture brochures approached as we got off the bus, trying to get customers for their hotels. All spoke to me in Mandarin. I took a taxi to my hotel after showing the driver the hotel's address in Chinese. The receptionist didn't speak English either and had to ask for the help of a colleague, who at least was able to communicate in the language of Shakespeare to proceed successfully to complete my registration and give me the room I had booked online days earlier. This was on the sixth floor of a sixteen—story building with hallways and doors painted in bright colors. The doors to the room were so low I almost knocked my head on my way in. The room was simple, small, clean, and functional, plastic being the most abundant material. It was a cheap city hotel. It was very late so I went to bed right away.

Even though I tried to get up early, I stayed in bed until midmorning. When I got up and looked out the window the views were horrific. The neighboring building had been demolished and the rubble was lying on the ground. Several adjacent buildings were under construction; the ones already built were as tall as they were ugly, which in the mist, or rather the severe pollution, depressed my first daylight vision of China. I left the hotel after buying a map of the city, all in Chinese, to show taxi drivers and ask for directions in the streets. On the one hand, I wished I had bought a guide of China in English; on the other, I thought it would be more adventurous and fun to travel without one.

I got into a taxi and, using the Chinese map, showed the driver where I wanted to go: the eastern shore of a beautiful lake that makes Hangzhou one of the country's top tourist destinations. "There's paradise on earth, Hangzhou on earth," goes a Chinese saying. As it was too late for breakfast, I decided to have lunch early in a restaurant overlooking the lake, where I ordered boiled rice with barbecued pork and tofu in soy sauce accompanied by a lemongrass tea. After the delicious meal, I began to walk around the lake. It was spring in Hangzhou; I mean spring as we know it in Spain, perfect weather for a long walk. Along the side of the lake closest to downtown, I saw a row of Armani, Versace, Zegna, Hermès, and Cerruti stores, plus Ferrari, Aston Martin, and Porsche dealerships. As in Vietnam, communism survives only in the political sphere and not in the economic, which in theory should be its true center of attention. The only thing remaining "in common" was the one political party allowed to exist.

The lake and its surroundings were stunning, so much so I could not recall another city lake like it (only a Swiss one might match it). With gardens and trees adorning the lakeside, cycling tracks, pagodas strategically located around its shoreline, boats to explore its waters, restaurants, cafes, and teahouses, silent in its entirety, all well–maintained and clean, it was a wonderful place to spend an entire day. So quaint and idyllic was it that I saw more than a dozen wedding couples being photographed on its shores. I continued experiencing the beauty of Asian women from my first day in China, a fact somewhat unexpected because I'd had the impression that, the more I traveled north, the less beautiful the women would be, an impression that perhaps came from my observation of women in the Chinatowns of London and New York, clearly insufficient samples for such a blunt opinion, one that a few hours walking around Hangzhou had been enough to destroy. In the evening, looking for a restaurant to have dinner, a woman came up and offered me a "massage." I was surprised to receive an offer of intimacy on my first evening out in China. A few minutes later, as I was about to enter the restaurant I had chosen for dinner, another woman, this one old and unattractive (I deduced that she was seeking customers for her girls), came up to me with the same offer, this time with a somewhat aggressive tone, as if not willing to accept a negative answer.

The next day I visited the Six Harmonies Pagoda on the banks of the Qiantang River, a seven–story pagoda 200 feet high with magnificent views of the river and its opposite bank, where several new buildings seemed empty, and a wide two–lane avenue, plus one for bikes, with trees on both sides, was completely deserted. As it had seemed in the ride from the airport, and as I'd read repeatedly, the Chinese real estate bubble was real. While I was admiring the views, a young Chinese woman came up and asked me to pose with her for a photo. I agreed, and a man and another woman followed her. They thanked me in their language, "*xiexie*" (thank you, in Mandarin), and with their smiles. Then I took a taxi to the village of Mamjouelong, on the hills south of the lake. I sat at a restaurant with tables outside, and three young waitresses came up with a menu only in Chinese (none spoke English). One invited me with gestures to follow her to the kitchen, where I saw some meat dishes of not very appetizing organs. I returned to the deck and looked at the tables around to see what they were eating. Then the restaurant manager came to my rescue with his limited but sufficient English. He suggested my ordering roast duck with vegetables and rice. Perfect. I ordered some tea too and savored the delicious duck with boiled cabbage in a spicy sauce with immense satisfaction.

Back in another taxi, I again pointed to my destination on my map: Linying Temple, one of the oldest in China. The entrance runs along a beautiful walk by a stream where you can see several statues of Buddha and of bodhisattvas carved into the rocks. The temple appears to have been remodeled several times and consists of several buildings with large statues of Buddha inside. It was packed with Chinese tourists, most offering incense to Buddha. Once having lit bundles of incense sticks, and before placing them in a container, some of the worshippers repeatedly bowed forward, others bowed then turned, four times in all, as if to the cardinal points of the compass.

The impression that Hangzhou made on me was unbeatable. All the locations I visited were in pristine condition, as were the roads to them. Women constantly swept streets and sidewalks, and cleaned the interiors of the sites. The foliage of the trees, with its intense green, made the whole trip and the surrounding pagodas and temples seem more beautiful. I couldn't recall having visited another place as well maintained as Hangzhou during my trip to Asia (with the exception of Singapore, of course). Inevitably, I remembered the dirt of India, not inside its monuments, which are very well maintained and clean, but in the streets. I'd just arrived in China, but the differences with the other emerging great power on the continent were obvious. China was far advanced over India in both infrastructure and maintenance.

After my relaxing two weeks in northern Thailand, which is almost entirely Buddhist, and the friendly reception I was receiving in China, besides my fantastic visits to Myanmar, Cambodia, Vietnam, and Laos, I began to see the demise of Buddhism in India, its country of origin, as a tragic fact—terribly tragic. While their neighbors to the east, from Myanmar to Japan, appeared to have benefited profoundly from the arrival of Buddhism, India seemed to have buried some, if not all, of the values of Buddhism, especially the value of equality. Maybe I was wrong, but other Asian countries seemed to me more socially enjoyable, their people more relaxed, without the tension I saw in India, especially in the north. I thought that, in India, the class struggle is more acute than in any other country I visited, and the status of women (perhaps this was the most negative aspect of all) was the worst.

Hangzhou is 117 miles and forty-five minutes from Shanghai, the time it takes the high-speed train to travel between the two cities. An electronic display informed passengers of the train speed at all times; we reached 210 miles per hour, but the ride was so quiet and smooth that the speed left no impression. It seemed that centuries separated China from India, whose trains run an average of twenty to thirty-five miles per hour. At Shanghai Honquiao station, I connected with the subway to the city center where I went to the Marriott apartment Marc and Ivy had rented for the weekend. I was the first to arrive, got the key card, and noted that the apartment was on the thirty-third floor. After entering the apartment, the first thing I did was drop my bags in the entrance hall and go up, stunned, to the huge glass windows and admire the fabulous view over People's Square up to Pudong, the city area on the other side of the Huangpu River. Marc, Ivy, and the girls would arrive from Hong Kong late in the afternoon; until then I strolled along Nanjing Road, one of Shanghai's commercial arteries.

I went back to the apartment before my friends' arrival. I was glad to see them again. Since Marc had moved to Hong Kong from London two years after I did to New York, we'd seen each other on only a few occasions, and the distance between us meant the frequency wouldn't change in the short term. Janet, a Taiwanese friend of Ivy's residing in Shanghai, came to pick us up and took us to dinner at a fine Taiwanese restaurant. After dinner, the four of us (the girls stayed in the apartment with a babysitter) went to a spa for a two–hour massage. I had returned to luxury, and how easy it was to get used to it. The next day, to complete our urban weekend, we ate dumplings at an another magnificent Taiwanese restaurant, walked through the Old French Quarter, the French Concession, visited the fairground at People's Square with the girls, had dinner at an art deco restaurant specializing in Shanghainese food, before walking along the river, along the Bund, Shanghai's promenade famous for its colonial architecture, to the Peninsula Hotel bar where we had a few drinks. That night was the final of the Champions League, between Barcelona and Manchester United. Marc, a Manchester United fan, went to bed after David Villa scored the 3–1, amazed at Barcelona's superiority.

Marc returned to Hong Kong with the girls; Ivy stayed in Shanghai for work and flew to Beijing on Monday. Thanks to a tremendous coincidence, Marc and I were to arrive in Tokyo on the same day (he on a business trip). We agreed to get in touch as soon as we landed in Japan. I returned to my backpacking life, leaving behind the luxury and the heights of the Marriott, to go to a hostel near the Bund. In the afternoon I met with Chandler, the young Chinese I'd shared the camel trek with in Jaisalmer's desert and with whom I'd remained in touch since. We walked to the old part of Shanghai, near Yuyuan Garden, where we tasted some delicious dumplings and egg rolls. We had dinner at a restaurant serving Sichuan, a region famous for its spicy cuisine. We had prawns, mackerel, pork, and vegetables, most of them accompanied by red chilies, but without being excessively spicy or killing off the original flavor of the ingredients. Chandler insisted on paying for dinner; I was a visitor and in China it wouldn't be appropriate to reject the invitation. When he asked for the check, he explained that to force restaurants to pay taxes, the government had introduced a lottery using restaurant checks as tickets. The checks come with a number to scratch and attractive prizes for the winners. Therefore, customers always ask for the check and the government ensures collecting taxes on the tab; an excellent idea. I promised to invite Chandler to dinner on my return to

Shanghai after my two–day visit to Suzhou.

Before getting to Suzhou, I spent a day in downtown Shanghai, eating at a terrace in Xintiandi, a new pedestrian area full of restaurants and shops, and strolling through the French Quarter. I went to a bookstore with a good selection of English books and bought *Tao Te Ching* (Stephen Mitchell's version), *Confucius from the Heart* (by Yu Dan), and two issues of the magazine *Beijing Review*, the only national news magazine in English. I started with the magazines while having a coffee. One article was about women's employment status. It said that many companies fear hiring women who may become pregnant, so candidates are asked directly if they are married, if they have boyfriends, and their future family plans. Another interesting article was about the social phenomenon known as *hazuzu*, something like "Renting Clan." These young people, in order to pretend to a certain social status, rent all sort of things, even just for a few hours, from clothes, cars, computers, televisions, and cell phones to children's toys. Apparently the rental business was booming due to the huge consumer pressure prevailing in Chinese cities.

Suzhou, famous for its gardens and canals, is located just fifty–five miles and twenty minutes from Shanghai by high–speed train. I visited five gardens: the Lion Forest Garden, the Humble Administrator's Garden, the Lingering Garden, the Canglang Pavilion, and the Garden of the Master of Nets. I enjoyed the first two under "British summer" weather (an intermittent light rain). The Lion Garden consists of a series of passages between rocks. Part of it is like a labyrinth; as soon I thought I was going in one direction, it made a drastic turn, bringing me the opposite way. I had to be careful not to hit my head when going under some of its passages. The rain intensified for a moment, and I went to the tearoom to savor green tea by a window, watching the rain and the wet vegetation shine. In the afternoon I visited the nearby Humble Administrator's Garden, huge and spectacular. Like the other three, which I visited the following day, its main components are ponds, pavilions, rooms, and balconies, all harmoniously designed, perfectly adapted to their environment. Each pavilion and room has its own name, many of them inspired by ancient Chinese poems, and therefore as evocative as the House of Rice with Sweet Odor, the Hall of 18 Camellias, the Fragrant Island, the Pavilion to Listen to the Sound of Rain, the Gate of the Moon, the Temple of the Waiting Cloud, the Pavilion of the Lotus Breeze, the House of Pure Fragrance, the Pavilion of the Blossoming Lotus, the Tower of the Reaching Beauty, the Reciting Pavilion, the Room of the Stairway to the Cloud, the Pavilion of the Moon That Comes With a Breeze, the Bridge Leading to Silence, and my favorite name, the Pavilion of Who Should I Sit With?, a small room with a balcony overlooking a pond that invited me to think who I'd have liked to share a chat, or maybe a silence, with. I missed having someone by my side that day.

In addition to the gardens, I went to the Confucius Temple, beautiful in its tranquility, so deserted it was. I had started reading the book by Yu Dan, *Confucius from the Heart*, a book that had sold over ten million copies in China and explains the main concepts of Confucianism in the context of modern life. Before reading it my only knowledge of Confucianism was one of its slogans: Do not impose on others what you yourself do not desire. I always thought this must be the only commandment of human social behavior. Why have Ten Commandments when one is enough? That simple message has always seemed to me extremely wise. It was time to expand my limited knowledge of the ideas the ancient sage had given to the Chinese people. The book was an excellent introduction to the basic principles of Confucianism. It was divided into six chapters: "Heaven and Earth," "Heart and Soul," "The World," "Friendship," "Ambition," and "Being."

The first chapter discusses the harmonization necessary between heaven, earth, and mankind. The sky represents idealism, earth realism; people, living between idealism and realism, must hold the two in balance; he who shows ambition without realism is only a dreamer, a workhorse who just lives on earth without looking at the sky. The second chapter addresses the importance of attitude in life: we should not have fears or worries, or blame others (including God) for our luck. Be brave, calm, and confident ("The enlightened are free from doubt, the virtuous from anxiety, and the brave from fear." said Confucius). The third deals with the right attitude with which to face the world: the duty of everyone is to become a loyal citizen, educated and cultured before finding one's place in society, to be the best version of oneself at all times. Talk less and act more, avoid criticism in your speech and regrets in your conduct and you will have less regrets in life, advised the Master.

The chapter on friendship (extremely important to Confucius because, according to him, of all possible relationships our friendships are the ones that reveal what kind of people we are) states that to have good friends, first we must have a good heart, be open to others, and then know how to choose them. Our friends are a mirror in which to see what we lack. We should choose them, not for their money or status, but as they can help us refine our character, enrich our personalities. The chapter on ambition touches on the need of every human being to have a direction, some objectives. It should come from within, not so much from external sources, to find our real way. The calmer, more objective, and firmer our mind is, the easier it will be to reject external grandeur and to focus on our particular nature. The action of a man is his legacy. Finally, the chapter on the being affirms that life runs as does the water in a river. We should focus on learning to live this life, already complex, rather than strive to understand death and what comes after life.

Confucius describes the periods of life: "At fifteen I set my heart upon wisdom; at thirty I stood firm; at forty I was free from doubts; at fifty I understood the laws of Heaven; at sixty my ear was docile; at seventy I could follow the desires of my heart without transgressing the right." From adolescence to adulthood, it is important to learn, to gain experience to understand both the society we live in and ourselves. It is then time to take a stand in life. The perfection of childhood and the turbulence of youth give us the wisdom to start understanding our place in the world and decide what and how we want to be. At forty we reach our social position and doubts vanish. We have begun to subtract instead of accumulate; we can clearly discern the important from the superfluous.

In a way, despite having been postulated 2,500 years ago, Confucius's stages of life, at least the first three, still seem valid today, because it is at about fifteen, past puberty and at the equator of adolescence, when one begins to really learn what happens around us, to face the outside world more dramatically, primarily through love. When we fall in love, we lose control of ourselves, we feel fragile and dependent on reciprocity, and when this doesn't occur, we feel devastated, our ego tragically damaged. Our awareness of ourselves, our wishes and desires, explode with violence and cause us to constantly re—evaluate our place in our society, which we can't find at such a young age without the maturity and accumulated experiences necessary to place reality, both our inner and our external realities, accurately. Today, with an extensive academic education that sometimes doesn't end until well into our twenties, our adulthood is delayed, our youth lengthens, and with it our learning period. In many cases, especially in countries like Spain where young people remain in the family home until even beyond age thirty, the stages of Confucius should be lengthened accordingly, because many won't take their position in life until they become independent. Obviously, all cultures don't follow the same pattern. Youth is usually short, if it exists at all, in developing countries, especially in rural areas where family formation comes immediately after puberty. Sotriana, the beautiful Mentawai indigenous girl, would marry as soon as she turned fifteen, with no time, or perhaps need, to learn as Confucius advised. We shouldn't forget that the stages Sotriana would live have been the norm during most of mankind's existence. The recent economic development is the cause of the lengthening of both human life and its intermediate stages.

As today youth is being extended, some experts talk of another period: emerging adulthood. I read about this in an article in the New York Times. In it, the psychologist Jeffrey

Arnett defines the main features of this stage: identity exploration, instability, self—focus, the feeling of being at a crossroads, the sense of different possibilities for the future. According to him, these are the common characteristics of people in their twenties and thirties. I think that this analysis, like many taking place in the developed world, focuses exclusively on the Western urban population, who have never had so many possibilities, which itself naturally brings potential instability and sometimes a feeling of lack of direction. The extension of the learning period, the use of birth control, the delay in family formation, the long and healthy life that many have, seem to be creating a new stage between youth, in the traditional sense, and adulthood, a stage with specific psychological attributes. Thus, perhaps for many learning extends even past thirty, and doubts remain beyond forty.

I was about to turn forty when I quit my job and started this adventure. At no time had I doubts about what to do or fears for the future. At least in that respect I seemed to have followed the instructions of the Chinese sage. Also, I've always had the feeling that my path has been to accumulate knowledge, a continuous learning (few things in life seem as interesting to me as learning) in preparation for something to come. It wasn't at thirty, however, that I took my position in the world, but rather it was a process that began at thirty—two, when I survived the first episode of tachycardia, culminating with my settlement in New York when I turned thirty—five. If the disease gave me a more transcendental view of my existence and of life in general, overcoming it, and later my arrival in New York, together represented a rebirth, a change that drove me forward, in which the positive aspects of American culture, its optimism, dynamism, and work ethic, soaked me with that stimulating energy that only those who have lived in the Big Apple are aware of.

I decided to spend two last nights in Shanghai, one to invite Chandler to dinner, and then fly to Beijing on Saturday morning. I returned to the hostel near the Bund and went out to eat and have coffee in the French Quarter before meeting Chandler, who took me to dinner at a popular location in Shanghai: a house converted into a restaurant of six tables and the kitchen on the first floor and two more tables upstairs, in what really was the living room of the house. The place was so popular that the line went outside. We had to wait over an hour before getting a table upstairs. We had duck in soy sauce, breaded pork with vegetables, and pork meatballs, all accompanied by steamed rice and stir−fried vegetables. The other table was populated by a group of lively, noisy young Chinese. The TV in the living room was on and showed the French Open tennis semifinal between Maria Sharapova and the Chinese player Li Na, who had won the first set but was behind in the second.

Chandler told me most of his friends had begun to marry. He was twenty−six, and Chinese women, even in cities, when they got to twenty−five began to become impatient and looked for a husband or pressured their boyfriends to marry. Although the average age of marriage has been increasing in recent years, it still remains below thirty. I asked him if his friends were happy, and he thought so, although he had his doubts. For him, marrying at his age was too early, but his parents were pushing him to do it (he didn't have a girlfriend at the time). For them the life cycle was clear, and now that they were approaching retirement, caring for a grandchild would be a blessing. Chandler told me the divorce rate had soared due to the speed at which some young people were getting married and the one−child policy, which had created a generation of spoiled youngsters, too focused on themselves, too selfish, so they found great difficulty in the challenges that marriage brings. Again, the law of unintended consequences was raging. We usually look at the economic and demographic consequences of the Chinese family policy and ignore the psychological ones.

There's so much to see in Beijing that I decided to stay in the Chinese capital until my flight to Tokyo in five days and miss one of China's big attractions, the Great Wall. I didn't like the idea of spending one full day to see it; I preferred to enjoy Beijing's variety. While not as modern as Shanghai, Beijing seemed much more interesting. I stayed in a simple hotel in a *hutong* near the downtown shopping area of

Dongcheng. *Hutong* is the Chinese name of the narrow streets of old Beijing, whose old houses have a patio and communal bathrooms. Unfortunately, due to the drive towards modernization of the communist authorities, many homes in the *hutongs* have been demolished and only a few survive in the city.

My first visit was to Tiananmen Square, where a small army of cleaners in their blue overalls were scratching the ground to remove the chewing gum stuck to it. Security for access to the square was worthy of the entrance to the Pentagon or the C.I.A. On October 1, 1949, the Chinese leader Mao Zedong proclaimed there the new People's Republic of China. His face, painted on a large mural like Big Brother, looms over the entrance to the Forbidden City, which is as immense as it is magnificent and one of the most visited tourist attractions in the world. Both the Temple of Heaven and the Summer Palace by themselves deserve the trip to Beijing. As in Suzhou, the Confucius Temple was practically empty, which I appreciated after the crippling congestion at the rest of the main attractions. One of Beijing's surprises was 798 Art Zone, which has been developed in the abandoned electronic components factory Dashanzi, built by East Germany in the fifties. The industrial complex now houses numerous art galleries, art studios, design companies, and, of course, attractive cafes and restaurants. It is an interesting place to spend a few hours or a full day.

A couple of nights I went for dinner and drinks at the popular tourist area of *hutong* Nanluogu Xiang, a busy street as full of bars and restaurants as any street in the old part of San Sebastian. The range of dishes on Chinese menus is so large and diverse it is sometimes difficult to choose what to eat, especially when you are eating alone. No doubt Chinese cuisine is meant to be shared. On Saturday the Roland Garros women's final tennis match between Li Na and Italy's Francesca Schiavone was taking place. Every bar and restaurant showed the final on their televisions, and young Chinese flocked to the windows of the premises to try to see the action happening on the Parisian clay. The Chinese player won in straight sets and became the first Asian player to win a

Grand Slam.

While drinking coffee I devoured, in one sitting, *Tao Te Ching*, which consists of eighty–one poems attributed to Lao Tzu, the father of Taoism. Immediately I found it one of the most beautiful books I have ever read, as well as becoming aware of the great similarities between Taoism and Buddhism. As had happened with Buddhism and Confucianism, I felt sorry for having known nothing about Taoism before that passionate reading, for not having been informed, during my compulsory education in Spain, of such wise philosophies, ignored to a great extent in Europe and America. Then I learned that *Tao Te Ching* is, after the Bible, the world's most translated book, which left me even more puzzled and dissatisfied about my ignorance. *Tao Te Ching* means "The Book of the Way and Virtue," but it's usually referred to as "The Book of the Way." Little is known about Lao Tzu, though some believe he may have been a contemporary of Confucius (both contemporaries of Buddha, by amazing coincidence). The main themes of the book are surrender to Tao, to nature, to the balance of the universe; the complementarity of opposites (non–duality); female values (yin), flexibility, and adaptability; and the concept of non–action, of emptiness, of not using the intellect but acting instinctively, naturally, without selfishness, removed from prejudices and desires.

Stephen Mitchell, a scholar and practitioner of Zen Buddhism, says that his version is more an interpretation than a translation of the book, because he doesn't speak Chinese. He used various translations into English, French, and German, according to him too literal and therefore lacking the right spirit, to interpret the message and give each poem a sense more in line with the original idea. Since its publication, it's considered by some one of the best versions of *Tao Te Ching*, although his flexible approach has also been criticized. After reading the message of simplicity of this book, expressed in such beautiful words, I felt I understood life better. Reading it was like shedding accumulated layers of confusing interpretations of reality, and it lightened the pressure of preconceived ideas that burden and hinder us every day. I felt such an immediate sense of closeness to the text and its message that I couldn't comprehend how this book had been so long in the dark for me. Immediately I thought it ought to be compulsory reading in secondary education, as well as being one of the most important books for every human being who wanted a more pleasant and balanced life. Until the end of my trip, I went back to read it at least four times.

SILENCE, GARDENS & ZEN

"I'm not the same after having seen the moon shine on the other side of the world." —Mary Anne Radmacher Hershey

"Travel is more than the seeing of sights, it is a change that goes on, deep and permanent, in the ideas of living." —Miriam Beard

I landed in Tokyo midmorning, and the first thing I did at the airport was get some cash at a Citibank ATM (in Japan the use of credit cards, surprisingly, is not as widespread as it is in most developed countries, and foreign cards are not accepted by Japanese bank tellers). Then I went by train and metro to the north of the city, to Ueno, the neighborhood where the *ryokan* where I'd stay in the Japanese capital was located. On the way I noticed immediately the silence that dominated the carriages in the train and the metro. The few who spoke did so in such low tones they looked as though they were communicating by reading lips. The rest quietly played with their phones, read, or just slept. The only sound came from the speakers announcing the next stop in Japanese and English and asking passengers not to talk on the phone in the area reserved for the elderly. During my two weeks in Japan I didn't hear a single cell phone ringing; a blessing, a miracle today.

A *ryokan* is a traditional Japanese guesthouse, usually run by a family, with rooms with tatami mats on the floors, a futon, sliding doors, a low table with a tea set ready to be used, a *yukata* (a kimono usually worn in the bathroom), and slippers available for each guest. My room had no indoor bathroom, just a sink. There was a common toilet in the hallway and two traditional Japanese baths downstairs. Each bath had two showers to be used by a couple at the same time and a large bath with hot water and a small window overlooking a tiny garden, all extremely clean and tidy. The man at the reception greeted me with the famous Japanese ceremoniousness before handing me a brochure of Tokyo, including a map of the metro and trains, another map of the area around the *ryokan* indicating the location of restaurants, shops, and places to visit; he then showed me the bathroom, my room, and the area with the washing machine and dryer. Without a doubt, it was the best reception I had experienced in nearly eighteen months of travel. What seems logical and simple to provide had been inexplicably unusual; an exception to applaud. The only fault I could find was the excessive formality, somehow lacking a bit in human warmth.

As soon as I got in my room, I put on the *yukata* and slippers and went to try the cozy bathroom that had been shown to me just a few minutes earlier. First, I showered while sitting on a low stool just ten inches high; a very practical position, as my hands were so near my feet, making it easy to reach them without bending or struggling to maintain balance. Cleaned of the sweat from the journey, I dove into the hot tub, which was so hot that after a few minutes immersed in it I had to leave to cool off a bit. As we had planned over the weekend in Shanghai, I met Marc for dinner. He had arrived in Tokyo that same afternoon, and I went to pick him up at his hotel in the Roppongi area before going to a bar to have a beer and some dinner. Marc was going to be a couple of days in Japan visiting Sendai, the area affected by the horrific tsunami, with an NGO his company cooperated with.

The next day, after breakfast, I walked through the Ueno neighborhood, one of Tokyo's oldest, towards Yanaka cemetery, stopping at several Buddhist temples and the bare cemeteries next to them. I continued with my walk to Ueno Park, where the Tokyo National Museum is located. I visited the museum before my appointment with Chiharu, a Japanese woman who studied in England with my friend Gerry, who had passed me her contact details. We met at the entrance of the Senso temple in Asakusa, another old part of Tokyo. In the temple, Chiharu encouraged me to perform one of the typical rituals: I took a cylinder filled with wooden sticks and shook it vigorously until one burst through a hole in the lid. She read the number written on it, number four, and we went to the corresponding drawer to open it and take out a paper inscribed with my "luck." "Good Fortune," it said. There was even a paragraph in English for gullible tourists. It stated categorically that I'd get good fortune repeatedly, that my wishes would be fulfilled, that a sick person would recover soon, that the person I was looking for would appear without delay, that I must be careful with my health during my trip (a little bit late, unless something worse was coming), and that it was a good time to build a house, for a move, for marriage, and for work. Wonderful. Chiharu said "Good Fortune" wasn't the best option (there was also "Great Fortune"), but it was her favorite because it left room for improvement. Then it was her turn to ask about her luck, lamenting that "good luck" was typically alien to her. This time, though, she was glad with the result: it wasn't as positive as mine, but at least better than usual.

We ate at a small restaurant with tables on the sidewalk of one of the narrow streets of the neighborhood, one of the most visited in Tokyo. Chiharu was lovely and had a beautiful smile that flowed effortlessly. Besides living in the U.K., she had studied Spanish briefly in Valladolid and worked in Tanzania for an NGO. She had been several years back in Tokyo, but was planning to live abroad again, although she wasn't certain where. After lunch, we went by boat up the Sumida River to the Detached Palace Garden, a gorgeous island in the river not far from the Imperial Palace (hence its name). It is a fabulous place to spend a couple of hours walking around and drinking tea in the pavilion overlooking the lake. There I experienced my first tea ceremony.

Barefoot before getting on the tatami, we sat on the floor, the sliding walls open to enjoy the view of the lake and gardens; green tea was served in a bowl with a small cake. The cake had to be placed on the palm of the left hand and cut into two or four pieces with a wooden knife and eaten in its entirety before having any tea. After the delicious cake had been engulfed, the tea bowl had also to be positioned on the left palm, with the drawing on the cup facing us, and then turned ninety degrees to the right twice until the bowl's drawing looked forward. Once this delicate rotation was performed, we proceeded to drink the tea. The kind of tea used in the traditional tea ceremony is *matcha*, a green tea made from a paste instead of leaves. Light foam floats on the surface, and the liquid looks more like a soup than a tea. The park is surrounded by tall, modern buildings, reminding us that we were in a large metropolis, which really seemed impossible there inside the teahouse, sitting on the tatami, surrounded by silence, sipping tea as had been done for hundreds of years.

After tea, Chiharu went to play tennis with her boyfriend and some friends. I went to the Ebisu neighborhood, in the southwest of the city, to meet Minh, a Vietnamese–American who had worked with me in New York. He had spent almost five years in Tokyo, having a good opportunity to work in Japan. He lived with his girlfriend, a young Japanese who worked in finance and whose working hours were up to fifteen hours a day. While the boss was in the office, all employees must be present. I'd never seen so many people nodding in the subway, but with those long hours it was not surprising. Every subway ride was an opportunity for rest, especially since it was so quiet.

I had dinner with Marc again. He had spent the day in Sendai and showed me the photos he had taken with his phone of the tsunami's devastation. Three months after the terrible catastrophe, large areas remained as on the first day. The number of missing persons was so high that the cleanup would take several months. Each morning over breakfast at the *ryokan* I read the daily newspaper in English that included a map of the country and the different levels of radiation, a map that had become as common as the weather map. To save electricity, air conditioning usage was significantly reduced in public transport, shopping centers, cafes, and restaurants, and the brighter areas of Tokyo, where neon lights advertise products and brands, had decreased in intensity by half. In these June days, with the arrival of the hot and humid summer, allowing workers not to wear a tie to their jobs and starting their workday an hour earlier to beat the hot temperature was being considered. In my *ryokan* a sign asked guests not to forget to turn off the air conditioning and lights when leaving the room.

The next morning, I left the *ryokan* with umbrella in hand, as June is a rainy month in Japan, and went by subway to Shinjuku station to buy the train ticket for my trip to Kyoto in two days. The station, which serves long–distance and commuter trains as well as four subway lines, is considered the most active in the world, based on the number of passengers who use it every day, more than 3.5 million, and has over two hundred exits if we include those to the indoor shopping area. Once inside its womb, I felt as if I was in an underground maze. Despite the extensive sign system, I never really knew if I was going in the right direction. It took me a bit to find the fast–train advance ticket office. From there, I went to the Kinokuniya bookstore, near the station, which has an excellent collection of books in English on its seventh floor. Going up the elevator I was surprised to see a Japanese girl in uniform with hat and gloves operating the vertical vehicle. My fellow culture shoppers told her the floor they were going to, and the young lady repeated it while pressing the floor button. Upon arrival to each floor, she announced the floor, and to my disbelief the process was repeated on each floor. The lift was of average size, not a huge one whose floor–button panel would be too far to be reached when full, so the presence of the machine operator wasn't at all necessary. It was hard to imagine the psychological effect that working for hours a day in that claustrophobic cockpit, constantly repeating floor numbers, could produce in that girl trapped there for economic reasons. I acquired *Essays in Zen Buddhism*, by D. T. Suzuki, my first introduction to Zen Buddhism.

In nearby Harajuku I walked under a fine rain and among some beautiful towering trees to the Meiji Shrine, dedicated to Emperor Meiji and his wife Empress Shoken. In 1867 Emperor Komei died in Kyoto, passing the throne to his son Mutsuhito, Emperor Meiji. The new emperor moved his residence from Kyoto to Edo permanently, naming it Tokyo, or Eastern Capital, ushering in what became known as the Meiji Restoration, which lasted until the death of Emperor Meiji in 1912. With him, power returned to the Emperor's hands (hence the name restoration), and the imperial and political capitals were reunited in Tokyo. Meiji means *illustration*. The new period brought the country's drive toward modernization, a period during which Japanese industrial revolution occurred at the same time as Japan developed its military capabilities. Therefore, the beginning of the Meiji period also gave rise to what is called the Japanese Empire, with the imperialist nationalism that would last until the defeat in World War II.

At the entrance to the sanctuary, I watched several Japanese approach a hut where there were small wooden buckets next to a source of water for washing hands and rinsing the mouth, a cleansing ritual before entering the temple. As I stood on the vast esplanade next to the entrance to the main building, I saw hundreds of wooden tablets hung from a metal structure and written with the visitors' wishes. Since most were in Japanese, I couldn't read their contents, but there were some in English and other languages, asking for love and peace. I turned back and saw a procession coming out of the sanctuary headed, under a huge, traditional, Japanese red umbrella, by a woman in a stunning kimono in white with orange patterns, with, beside her, a man dressed in a black kimono, both wearing white stockings and wooden platform sandals. I soon realized that, being Saturday, it was a Shinto wedding. As many visitors did, I took the opportunity to take photos of the colorful procession. Shintoism is the native religion of Japan and practiced in some form by some 85 percent of its population. It consists of a series of practical rites, first written in the eighth century, revering *kami*, the spirits or gods who reside in nature. Admission to every Shinto temple is through a *torii*, a huge wooden gate that marks the border between the profane and the sacred. The one through which I entered the Meiji Shine was not painted, but it is common to see them in vermilion, influenced by the Chinese red, a color that is believed to scare off evil spirits.

From there I walked to neighboring Yoyogi Park, usually very active but which the rain had left almost deserted. After that, I wandered through the streets of Harajuku, particularly the famous Takeshita Street, where the most daring teens buy their clothes, kitsch ornaments, and punk accessories, and comb their hair extravagantly. Lolitas usually walk around the area, and the Jingu Bridge, a nearby pedestrian bridge, becomes on weekends a spontaneous catwalk for the showcasing of such diverse human fauna, entertainment for tourists and photographers. Unfortunately, the wet weather seemed to have scared away those interesting young people.

Chiharu texted me, saying she was meeting some friends for dinner and inviting me to join them. The appointment was in Shimo–Kitazawa, on Tokyo's west side, not far from Harajuku, at a restaurant serving Okinawan cuisine, where I met one of her friends who had also studied in the United Kingdom and her English boyfriend. After the tasty dinner we had a beer at a nearby bar before I ran to catch the last metro back to my *ryokan*. The subway was crowded and reminded me of my nights out in London, although in the British capital, after so many pints, travelers used to be more intoxicated. In Tokyo those who didn't play with their phones just slept during the journey.

On Sunday I visited the Imperial Palace Gardens, the only part of the palace complex open to the public. Despite the day of the week, the fear of radiation (which kept foreign tourists away) and the rainy season seemed to have alienated visitors, so the stroll through the beautiful gardens was extremely relaxing. In the afternoon I went to Ginza, Tokyo's Fifth Avenue, whose main street, Chuo, is closed to traffic on Saturday and Sunday while the luxury shops are open (some even put chairs and tables in the middle of the street for the busy shoppers to rest). In the midst of dense human traffic, I observed a Buddhist monk in walking meditation: at a very slow pace, each inhalation coordinated with the lifting of one foot, each exhalation with putting it on the ground, while he was being challenged by the frenetic speed of the affluent consumers around him. I had dinner at a restaurant near my *ryokan* after enjoying a hot bath. Before bed, I meditated in my room for an hour after having not done so at all during my two weeks in China. Perhaps it was the Japanese silence, and the simple and traditional room that forced me to sit and sleep on the floor, which naturally led me to return to my meditation practice.

I left part of my luggage in the *ryokan* because I'd be back in Ueno after my five nights in Kyoto. At Shinjuku Station, where I arrived with plenty of time to spare in case I had trouble finding my way in such a confusing station, I got on my Shinkansen train (bullet train) after buying a sushi tray to eat while traveling. In two hours and twenty minutes, I arrived punctually in Kyoto, Japan's capital city between 794 and 1868. With nearly one and a half million people, it's very well preserved and has some 1,600 Buddhist and 400 Shinto temples. When I glanced at the map, deciding on places to visit, I felt completely overwhelmed by the possibilities. With only five days available, it was necessary to be selective and ambitious at the same time.

As part of my exploration of Zen Buddhism, I sought the possibility of staying at a Zen temple in Kyoto, and online found Shunkoin Temple, a Buddhist temple of the Rinzai school that offers a few rooms to foreign tourists as well as the possibility of learning and practicing Zen meditation. It belongs to the Myoshinji monastic complex, which consists of forty temples located within an area bounded by stone walls. If silence is one of the characteristics of Japan, it isn't hard to imagine how serene the atmosphere in a Zen monastery complex is. The streets of the complex were for pedestrians, and cobbled; they were also used by bicycles. Gardens and trees adorned the open spaces around the old buildings. The complex is built around the main temple bearing its name, an imposing wooden structure raised off the ground and located at the complex's center. As I entered, carrying my backpacks, I was immediately glad about my choice. What better place to stay in Kyoto than a Zen temple!

I was welcomed by the vice–abbot of Shunkoin, a young U.S.–educated Japanese man whose English was therefore excellent. He showed me my spacious room, a kitchen attached to share with the other guests, and bicycles the temple makes available for the guests to use. After a shower, I went for a walk around the monastic complex, enjoying deeply its harmony and silence. Back in Shunkoin, I sat at a table in the garden outside my room and started reading the book I had purchased by D. T. Suzuki (1870–1966), a philosopher and Buddhist scholar responsible, thanks to his excellent books in English, for the spread of Zen Buddhism in the West. Suzuki moved to Kyoto in 1919, where he began teaching at Otani University, and regularly visited Hoseki Shinichi Hisamatsu, a Zen philosopher who was then residing precisely in Shunkoin temple, where the two held long talks on the future of Zen Buddhism. The azaleas at the temple's entrance had been planted by both men.

One needs to go to China, however, to find the origins of Zen Buddhism, called *Chan* there (from *dhyana* in Sanskrit, or meditation). History points to Bodhidharma, the twenty–eighth Buddhist patriarch, a monk who came to China from India around the sixth century, as the first patriarch of Zen Buddhism. According to Suzuki, Zen is the result of the adaptation of Buddhism to the Chinese mind, which is much more practical than the Indian, without as much imagination or tendency to mysticism. To Zen Buddhism, the central fact is the enlightenment of Siddhartha Gautama, that special moment when he got to see reality as it was, when he freed himself from all suffering. Therefore, Zen can be defined as the art of looking into the nature of oneself. It is an art that can be used every day, in every action we take in our lives, where we must show our nature and be true to ourselves, stripped of masks, prejudices, and fears. Zen, like the Tao, isn't based on the intellect to achieve the solution to our existential problems. The intellect dissects and analyzes, divides and categorizes, and therefore continually dualizes. Zen means to acquire a different point of view, one that is more natural and instinctive than rational and analytical. What is the intellect for when we are hungry? When hunger comes, we eat; to alleviate thirst, we drink. To make it clearer: determination is more important than understanding. The man, according to Suzuki, is more will than intellect, more action than thought.

Satori is the Japanese word for this new vision of life. It's actually another name for illumination. *Satori* is the central idea in Zen; without *satori* there's no Zen. Words are ineffective to explain it; in fact, that is precisely the point. It is personal experience that brings us closer to it. Zen literature is replete with examples of times when monks and scholars acquired their own *satori*. A common analogy is that of a bucket full of water whose bottom suddenly falls out, all the water pouring to the ground in a moment. Sometimes dialogues between a teacher and one of his disciples are used. In one, very simple and therefore ideal for this brief note, the teacher asks the disciple: "Have you had your breakfast?" "Yes, Master," he replied. "Then wash the dishes." With the teacher's response, the monk got his *satori*. Simple. Do what you have to do, do not waste time, don't think about it; all in communion with the Taoist message of doing what you should do and then letting it go.

As I read the exceptional work by Professor Suzuki, the influence of Taoism, and of Confucianism, on Zen Buddhism was evident. At the end of the day, both are an essential part of Chinese culture, and so it is no wonder that both would influence the new philosophy that had arrived there from India. I was surprised to read that meditation doesn't have a prominent role in the attainment of *satori*. In fact, the sixth and last *Chan* patriarch, Huineng, considered to be the true founder of Zen Buddhism, claimed that the truth of Zen itself arises from within and has nothing to do with the practice of meditation. In other words, it shouldn't be only during meditation that one is aware of the reality that surrounds us, but in every moment of our existence. It's called the Sudden Enlightenment School, or Southern School.

Unlike their Indian and Southeast Asian counterparts, Zen monks have always worked in their monasteries. Climate and geography play a crucial role in the formation of people's psychology. Work has always been valued in Chinese and Japanese cultures, and there was no way that Zen Buddhist monks would remain idle, living solely on alms. This is another example of Chinese pragmatism that inevitably filtered into Zen Buddhist concepts, making Zen an experience to live during all of our activities, not only during meditation. It isn't that meditation is of no help in any way, but what Zen emphasizes is the need to show our true nature in every experience. This individual determination is much more necessary than reading the scriptures, analysis, enforcement of moral standards, and dedication to meditation. Its emphasis on the day to day, on each moment of our life, makes Zen, I think, a special force of unparalleled vitality.

However, I doubt if every human being can achieve his *satori* simply by will. I think there are people with an enormous capacity to turn their lives around, but for many, a period of evolution and growth is necessary, and meditation as a learning vehicle certainly has a role. Although I was using it, and would continue to meditate, I also recognized that it must be accompanied by that existential determination so important in Zen. Meditation calms me, centers me, relaxes my muscles and organs; I believe it repairs my body, helps me understand better and faster what happens around me, to see problems more clearly, to solve them more easily; it also helps me be more creative. If a daily shower washes the body, daily meditation does the same with our mind: it cleans it of automatisms and impurities. My personal struggle, to give it a name, is whether to accept my intellectual, analytical, introverted nature, or try to overcome it for the sake of being more intuitive and direct. Taoism and Zen invite us to let go, to focus on our nature—but how can we be sure of what that is? Hasn't that nature developed over a lifetime, hasn't our upbringing molded it in excess and away from what we really are? It isn't easy to answer that question; it is the eternal dilemma *nature versus nurture*: is our identity innate or acquired?

Accompanied by two other guests, a Pole and a Swiss, I went at 9 a.m. to meet with the vice–abbot for a tour of the temple, a brief introduction to Zen Buddhism, and a short meditation practice. Shunkoin was established in 1590 and rebuilt in the seventeenth century by Noriyoshi Ishikawa, lord and master of the temple, who commissioned Eigaku Kano, a renowned painter, to decorate the temple's sliding doors. To admire them, we sat on a tatami in one of the rooms, with the doors open to the rear garden; the vice–abbot explained that the paintings were located on the lower part of the door panels and were meant to be observed from the ground, not standing; he also explained that, when the doors to the garden are open, they form a frame that the designer of the garden believed enhanced the view of the garden from inside the building. Nature outdoors was represented on the door's lower panels: landscapes, animals, and flowers painted in perfect harmony.

Then we were shown one of the treasures of the temple, the Nanbanji Bell, a bell cast in Portugal in 1577 and brought to Kyoto, to Nanbanji Catholic Church, the first in Kyoto and built in 1576 by the Italian Jesuit Gnecchi–Soldo Organtino. The Portuguese arrived in Japan in 1542, bringing Christianity with them. The Nanbanji church was the center of Catholic missionary activities but was destroyed in 1587, only eleven years after its construction, after the Japanese banned Christianity. The bell arrived in Shunkoin two hundred years ago, in the eighteenth century, and was buried in the grounds of the temple during the Second World War to prevent its destruction by the Japanese authorities.

After admiring the panels, the bell, and the gorgeous gardens, we went to the meditation hall where the vice–abbot, after a brief explanation of Zen Buddhism, showed us the meditation technique used by the Rinzai school (he said that he usually only meditated for fifteen minutes once in the morning and once in the evening, and not every day). After sitting us on cushions, with legs crossed, to raise our pelvis, he invited us to close our eyes halfway, look down at the floor, with blurred vision, and focus our attention on our breathing, inhaling, waiting two seconds before exhaling, pausing for two seconds, and inhaling again. He told us that, if we preferred, we could close our eyes completely, and count while breathing to help our concentration: one, two, three . . . ten, then back to the start. Accustomed to the vipassana technique of eyes closed, no alteration of our normal breathing rhythm, and no verbalization during it, it felt a little strange at first, but soon I got used to the new technique. We did two fifteen–minute sessions, insufficient for me, but adequate as an introduction.

I got on a bike with my Kyoto map in hand and started my architectural exploration, ready to be dazzled, with the temples north of the city. I went big, to the well–known Golden Pavilion (its official name is Rokuonji), the most visited in the city because of the intensity of its golden three–story building, located next to the lake on the surface of which it is reflected. I continued with Ryoanji, famous for its lofty rock garden (without any tree, the garden is composed of only fifteen rocks surrounded by gravel), and I finished in Ninnaji, with its delicate panel paintings, its five–story pagoda, and its extensive quiet gardens. Back to Shunkoin, I continued reading the fabulous book by Professor Suzuki before dining at a nearby restaurant on a plate of *gyoza* and fried rice. Before sleeping, I continued with my daily practice of vipassana.

The next day, once again by bike, I went early to the center of Kyoto. I wanted to visit the Imperial and Sento Palaces, which served as the residence of the retired emperors and where the imperial family stays when visiting Kyoto. What caught my attention, apart from the immense beauty of the gardens, was the harmony of the buildings with their surroundings. All of the buildings were just raised off the ground as if not wanting to interrupt too much the natural beauty around them. Before the end of the afternoon, I still had time for two additional visits, the Nishi–Honganji Temple, a temple of the Jodo school of Buddhism, which, crowded with visitors dressed in traditional attire, was in full celebration, and the Toji Temple, famous for its imposing five–story pagoda towering 187 feet, the highest in Japan, but whose real treasure is its collection of sculpture: beautiful figures of Buddha, bodhisattvas, kings, and guardians.

The following day I woke to the sound of the rain, not very strong, steady and light, which forced me to leave the bike behind and go by local train to the neighborhood of Arashiyama, in the west of the city. First I visited Tenruji Temple, the main temple of the Rinzai school in Kyoto, before walking under my umbrella to the Hozu River, over which lies the picturesque Togetsukyo Bridge. I walked along the river to Okochi Sanso, a spectacular villa that belonged to the Japanese silent film star Okochi Denjiro (1898–1962), who took thirty years to build it. The ticket price included tea, so as soon as I entered, I went to the teahouse to shake the rain off and enjoy a *matcha* green tea. What made the country house worthy of visiting was not the building itself but its location at the top of a hill, with beautiful walks through the woods and fabulous views of Kyoto. At the villa's exit stands a magnificent forest of towering bamboo. Back in the center of Arashiyama, I ate rice soup with a tasty salmon. The rice, the salmon, and the hot broth were served separately, with an empty bowl. The waitress told me I should put the desired amount of rice, salmon, and broth into the bowl to make a soup to my liking. I bought a Japanese cloth fan as a gift for my mother. The end of my trip was getting closer.

I returned to Shunkoin, freshened up, as the day had been extremely wet, and went by bus to Gion, Kyoto's old neighborhood, famous for its narrow cobbled streets, traditional buildings, and fine restaurants and where the curious can see geishas go to work every afternoon. As soon as I arrived I saw a geisha leaving her house, protected by a traditional umbrella. A black cab waited for her at the door. Too fleeting was the vision, but incredibly colorful, and I managed to capture it with my camera. For dinner, I chose one of the restaurants that line the streets (one of the few with a menu in English at the door), so hidden behind curtains and closed doors. A woman dressed in a traditional kimono came out to greet me upon entering: "*Konnichiwa.*" "*Konnichiwa.*" We said hello in Japanese to each other before she invited me to take off my shoes and enter the dining room. She slid open one of the doors and asked me to enter a private room with a long table for eight people, which seemed longer in my solitude. Before disappearing behind the sliding door, she handed me a menu and asked me to push a button on a small device on the table to call her when I was ready to order. I had a sashimi salad, grilled chicken with vegetables, and green tea. Once I was alone, with the dining room all to myself, jazz music of trumpet, bass, and drums barely broke the silence: I felt I was at an exclusive club. Dinner was delicious, as was everything I tasted in Japan.

The rain took a day off, so the next day I was back on the

bike to ride to the northeast of Kyoto, to distant Kamigamo Shrine and afterwards to its brother, Shimogamo, one of Kyoto's oldest, built before the city was declared the country's capital, both with imposing *torii* in vermilion. I went down to the city center and hesitated to stop at the Heian Shrine, since I thought it would be very much like the previous two; but, because of my proximity, I parked the bike and walked to its wide esplanade. Suddenly I saw a geisha walking with a woman towards the temple, with that extremely short step the kimono imposes. I took out my compact camera to take pictures of such a colorful and elusive woman before mounting my Nikon with the 85mm lens to shoot with more power. I followed both of the women to the temple and asked the geisha's companion (she had a compact digital camera in hand) if I could take photos of the geisha. She said yes but not inside the temple. I portrayed her while washing her hands before entering. Then I waited for them to exit the temple and, when they did, took pictures of her near the area with the wooden tablets inscribed with wishes. From there they went to the garden. I hesitated to follow them, somewhat ashamed of my paparazzi attitude, but I thought an opportunity like this would not come back so easily. I paid the entrance to the garden and went in search of them.

I reached them by the pond, very beautiful and surrounded by colorful flowers, where the geisha posed for the other woman. Overcoming my embarrassment, I continued pressing the shutter of my Nikon. The setting was amazing. The geisha wore a light blue kimono with red, yellow, and green patterns, her face makeup in the spotless traditional white, her lips painted deep red, her hair pulled up and decorated with flowers. She carried a box–like handbag, her hands always in the same position: the left under the box, the right resting on top of it. In order for her not to feel besieged, I let them get away while I photographed some delicate white and purple flowers. About seventy feet away, they stopped again and the geisha opened her purple umbrella with its spiral pattern. I saw an elderly Japanese couple acting as paparazzi too. I joined them to take some pictures with the umbrella as background. And so I continued visiting the temple's beautiful garden, stopping wherever the geisha stood to be photographed by her companion, who, I figured, was taking photos for some promotion of her services. From my lips came out several *arigatos* ("thank you" in Japanese), including head bows, to thank them for their graciousness. The geisha never looked into the lens or my eyes. Her smile was as subtle as the rest of her movements, which were so soft they seemed not to exist. I spent over an hour taking pictures of her visit to the temple, over 300 in total, in an unexpected meeting with a very special and inaccessible model. I could not believe my luck, especially since I was so close to having skipped the Heian Shrine.

A geisha is an entertainment professional who has received intense training before providing expensive services that include dancing, playing musical instruments, recitation, and talk (sexual services are not included). The one I photographed was actually a *maiko*, an apprentice geisha. Her kimono with red collar and lively prints and open back to show her neck without makeup, and her hair ornaments indicated her position. Formerly, given the longstanding education they received in geisha houses (*okiya*), geishas had to work for years to pay off their debts. These houses have always been managed exclusively by women, and for many (not for others, who consider it an example of male subjugation) constituted a career outside of marriage and male control, and therefore a more feminist option than a marriage of convenience, as many marriages are in Japan.

In the afternoon I cycled the road called Philosopher's Walk, a beautiful pedestrian and bicycle path that runs along a canal, to Ginkakuji Temple, known as the Silver Pavilion and famous for its dry garden. From there, to make the most of my last day of sightseeing in Kyoto, I pedaled vigorously to reach Kiyomizu Temple (as extensive as it is popular, with fabulous views of the city) and, before it closed for the day, Kenninji Kodaiji. This is the oldest Zen temple in Kyoto, founded in 1202 by Eisai, who traveled to China twice and from there brought to Japan Zen Buddhism and green tea. One of the gardens, the Garden of the Sound of the Tide, an evocative name, is a simple and refined Zen garden with three rocks in the center representing Buddha and two Zen monks. With just twenty minutes until its closure, I sat on the tatami of one of the rooms overlooking the garden, to rest my legs from the long day, remembering and feeling grateful for my encounter with the *maiko* a few hours earlier, and all of the incomparable temples and gardens I had enjoyed in Kyoto. Besides the usual epithets used to describe them, I thought that perfection was, without a doubt, one of the features of them all; there was no way to improve them. We often say perfection doesn't exist, but after experiencing Kyoto's Zen temples and gardens, I changed my mind.

On my last day in Kyoto I decided not to leave for Tokyo until early afternoon, so I still had time for one last visit, to Taizoin Temple (1404), the oldest in the Myoshinji complex, where I had resided for the past five days. It's one of those little—visited temples of small size but incredibly charming and well designed. What I liked the most was its garden, through which runs a beautiful stream to a pond in front of which there's a small gazebo with a bench to gaze upon the descending water, the Waterfall of the Dragon King. I enjoyed the bucolic greenery under a light rain. I ordered tea and sat on the tatami with views of the garden and the pond. There I felt so lucky to be living such a simple and beautiful moment.

Once again in Tokyo, I dined with Chiharu at a table—high counter in a restaurant in the west of the city. She asked for sashimi, a chicken dish, and a dish with seaweed and eggplant, plus a couple of beers. After these we ordered sake, the first a bit too sweet for my taste, the second dry and delicious. The next morning I visited the Museum of Photography in Ebisu, where an exhibition showed the winning photos of *World Press Photo 2011*. An adjoining room projected the *Tsunami Photo Project*, bringing together a total of 120 images taken by fourteen photographers of the devastation from the brutal tsunami. The magnificent musician Ryuichi Sakamoto had composed a song, *Kizuna World*, to accompany the installation. I went into the small room; the few chairs available were already occupied so I sat on the floor. I was the only Westerner there. I could feel the pain of my Japanese neighbors as we witnessed the visual horror of those great images. My favorites were a piano surrounded by water and lying in a jumble of tree branches— the music stopped abruptly with the tsunami; the hand of an elderly woman removing mud from an album of black–and– white photographs—she had kept many of her memories, but how many others were lost forever; and a child reaching for his muddy school bag—a symbol of hope, that life goes on and the only thing left is to march ahead with the memory and pain.

My father fell into a coma five weeks after the tumor had been found. He would die in a few days, the result of liver failure. The murderer tumor had advanced without respite and affected much of his liver. His abdomen had been swollen for days and the fluid that accumulated around his liver had to be drained daily. His skin was painted that unpleasant yellow caused by hepatitis. The morning of his death I had spent the night with my mother in his hospital room. It was with the dawn light that he began to make some noises with his mouth and his body began to shake briefly, announcing his end. We called the nurse, who said he was leaving. My mother couldn't stay in the room and left, crying out painfully; I didn't want to leave my father to die alone. I stood next to him and held his left hand, and watched his last sounds and his final motions, crying, until both simultaneously stopped.

In Shinjuku I bought a Hakone Pass, a three–day pass that covers the return journey by train to Hakone, all buses in the Hakone area, the Hakone–Tozan cable car, and a boat cruise on Lake Ashi. Hakone is a popular tourist destination in Japan, particularly for a few days away from the urban pressures of Tokyo. It's part of the Fuji–Hakone–Izu National Park, a collection of attractions that include Hakone, the Izu Peninsula and islands, as well as lakes and *onsens* (Japanese natural hot springs) and the famous Mount Fuji. In Hakone I stayed in a guesthouse with its pair of own *onsens*, one outdoor, one indoor. It was a large house with rooms on the ground floor. Mine was at the back, at treetop height, overlooking the slope that the river had carved over the years.

It was raining lightly when I checked in, but I was so eager to walk in the mountains that, after browsing the various possible routes, I decided to climb Mount Kintoki (3,980 ft). As I went up, low clouds heavily laden with moisture surrounded me. The steep path was well marked, and I felt energetic despite the difficulty. To my mind came a verse by Antonio Machado: *"Se hace camino al andar"* ("Paths are made by walking"), which, together with another of my favorite quotes, from the Irish poet W. B. Yeats ("In dreams begin responsibilities") make up perhaps one of the most valuable life mottos that may exist. You have to be true to your dreams—they show us the way in our life—and once known, there's nothing more to do than to start walking, the only way to chart our own path. It takes nothing more than dreams followed by decisive and courageous action. And since happiness is not a destination but a way of traveling, the essential thing isn't the result, on which we fix our gaze stupidly, but how we make the journey.

As I approached the top, which was nearly naked of vegetation, the wind shook me fiercely. Visibility was scarce, only a few feet. At the mountaintop, a building I could barely see through the fog stood to my right. An old woman stuck her tiny figure out the door and, with gestures, invited me in. Protected from the wind, I sat at a table, grateful to be indoors. Without being asked, the old lady served me tea and cookies. She spoke in Japanese; we couldn't understand each other. She brought an old atlas so I could tell her where I was from. I searched Europe, then Spain, and pointed my finger at San Sebastian. She read the name of my hometown in Japanese. Then she showed me a book whose cover in English said: *Mt. Fuji's Daughter.* Inside, the book was filled with black—and—white photos. She pointed at a girl in a photo and then to herself. I realized then that the book was about her, who seemed to have lived in that place all her life. The text was in Japanese so I couldn't read it. Some photos showed her as a teenager, some with her children. The old woman didn't let me pay for the tea and cookies, and handed me a rice cake for the descent. Wonderful kindness from the old mountain woman.

As I went out the clouds began to open up, and miraculously, like a surprise apparition, I spotted Mount Fuji, a towering cone of 12,388 feet. Perhaps it was his daughter, the old woman, who had made it appear. I weathered the strong wind still reigning to enjoy such a magnificent sight. Gradually I could see as far as Lake Ashi. The clouds traveled at high speed, driven by the strong wind, covering Mount Fuji from time to time. During the descent I was glad to have defied the weather and climbed Mount Kintoki. The easiest thing would have been to remain in the guesthouse, drinking tea, reading or writing. Sometimes our efforts bring us valuable rewards. I remembered the beginning of my long journey, trekking in the Himalayas. The mountains of Hakone would put an end to my Asian tour; a great close to a wonderful adventure.

The plan for the next day was to go to Lake Ashi. But first, immediately after getting up, I took a warm bath in the *onsen* before breakfast. Despite an overcast sky, it was not raining. I went by bus to the funicular station, then by cable car to Lake Ashi, more than two and a half miles away, making the Hakone cable car the second longest in the world, after the Kriens Bahn in Switzerland. The trip takes half an hour in cabins with space for thirteen people. Unfortunately, visibility was almost nil from the cabins, and the wind was so strong the cabins swayed from left to right enough to cause concern among the occupants. Half the journey is uphill to Owakudani, where I disembarked briefly to see and smell the volcanic sulfur spouting from the mountain. At Lake Ashi, the cruise service to the other end of the lake had already been suspended due to poor visibility. On the lakeshore visibility barely went beyond thirty feet. I had been told it was possible to walk around the lake, so I went for a long hike through the forest. Lake Ashi is a crater, with a perimeter of more than twelve and a half miles, formed after Hakone volcano's last eruption more than 3,000 years ago. My hike was to Moto Hakone, a little more than halfway around the lake. It took me about three hours to get there, a walk in the woods and through the fog, without rain but breathing in the omnipresent moisture, and lonely as I didn't see a soul. It was really pleasant and relaxing to enjoy an atmosphere so familiar to a Basque. I ended the day as couldn't have been otherwise: in the *onsen*, this time in the outdoor pool.

The next morning I woke up at 5:30 a.m. in one of the most beautiful awakenings I can remember. The sun, so absent over the last few days, came directly into my room, its rays filtering through the high tree branches, giving me its good morning. I opened the windows wide to invite it without barriers. Birds sang from the trees. A glorious sunrise; the sky finally deep blue. I soaked myself in the *onsen* before breakfast, and decided to take advantage of the clear sky to repeat the previous day. The weather gave me a second chance. I rode on the cable car, enjoyed the crystal clear views of Mount Fuji in the distance, and at Lake Ashi boarded the ship to cruise to Moto Hakone. What a difference in just few hours! It was a beautiful day, and the views of Mount Fuji from the cable car cabin, of the surrounding mountains, and of the lake were spectacular.

I returned to Tokyo, to my Ueno *ryokan*, at 3 p.m. with time to do laundry before meeting Chiharu in Shinjuku for my last evening, not only in Japan but in Asia. Chiharu invited her girlfriend Aiko to join us, and first we went to Golden Gai, an area of narrow alleys of old buildings full of tiny bars. I thought the bars of the Old Town in San Sebastian were small, but nothing like the ones in Golden Gai. We went to one that had a low table with two seats and seven stools along a short and narrow bar. That was all; more than a dozen drinkers struggled to find space for their feet on the floor of that bar. We ordered beers, and the friendly waitress offered us some Japanese tapas. We had dinner in a typical restaurant of Shinjuku: a place located on the third floor of what from the outside seemed to be an office building. We shared squid, Japanese tortillas, *yakitori*, and a salad, everything delicious. I love the lightness of Japanese cuisine. One always feels fabulous after Japanese food, satisfied in the palate as much as in the stomach, without any heaviness at all.

During the conversation, the topic of holidays in Japan

came up, and they told me of some very curious celebrations. Later I researched them and learned that apart from the common ones such as New Year's Day, Constitution Day, Emperor's Day, and Labor Day, Japan also celebrates a few that I wouldn't hesitate to import to Spain and the U.S.A.: Coming of Age Day, Greenery Day, Children's Day, Ocean Day, Respect—for—the—Aged Day, Health and Sports Day, and Culture Day. Due to the secularity of the state, there aren't any religious celebrations in Japan. All holidays seemed worth commemorating, especially if they came with sincere celebrations. My favorite was Ocean Day, although not the most urgent to import; that honor, in my opinion, would have to go to Respect—for—the—Aged Day, as old people seem so forgotten today in many Western cultures. I was glad I enjoyed the last evening of my trip in Tokyo with Chiharu and Aiko, both of whom were intelligent, interesting, and very nice. They missed living outside Japan and were considering a change of scenery. How difficult it is to return to your own country after living abroad!

WRITING & LOVING

"Once you have traveled, the voyage never ends, but is played out over and over again in the quietest chambers. The mind can never break off from the journey." —Pat Conroy

"Remembering that you are going to die one day is the best way I know to avoid the trap of thinking you have something to lose. You are already naked. There is no reason not to follow your heart." —Steve Jobs

The physical journey had ended, but a journey so vast in time and space will travel with me every day into the future. The experience of living like a nomad, exploring a continent like Asia, so different, distant, and interesting, didn't end with my flight from Tokyo to London but will remain with me for life. I returned not the same person as when I left. Everything changes, nothing is permanent (*anitya, anitya, anitya*), every thing has an end. In no way was I saddened by the end of my wonderful adventure. By then I had perfectly learned and embraced the concept of temporality. I remember the words of the Zen vice—abbot in Kyoto: "Every present moment is the moment when we are the youngest, when we have more opportunities in front of us." This is why we must seize the present and not let it slide away with constant mental wandering, nostalgia, and daydreaming. Once continuous change is accepted, one has to look forward to the next stage in life, which in my case was to complete my book and my script, as well as edit the thousands of wonderful pictures I had taken during the trip, with the intention of pursuing a life as independent as possible—a challenge that was full of uncertainty.

I spent a few days in London with friends before going to San Sebastian to see my mother and my brother, and then flew to New York. It was mid—July, and I'd decided to take a second ten—day vipassana course in the U.S. as a prelude to my landing in the Western world. I found a place for the course at Dhamma Dhara in Massachusetts during late July. The center, one of the first S. N. Goenka centers outside

India, has been offering courses since the early '80s. During the summer, tents are installed to accommodate the overflow from the large numbers of meditators who come. I was fortunate to be housed in a tent just for myself. The course was as intense as the first one, yet different. You are calmer in your second course (the third in my case, if I include the three—day course in April), you already know what to expect regarding the conditions and how you react to each day's experience. However, just as every working day is different, every day and every meditation session is unique, as is every moment that we live, and therefore the course wasn't without novelty.

The center has meditation cells for individuals, and senior students (those who had already completed a ten—day course) were each assigned a cell where they could meditate from the afternoon of the second day. This facilitated my daily meditation because I was able to concentrate more easily in the solitude of the cell, as well as change position on the floor without worrying about disturbing other students. Despite the usual pain endured in my back and knees, I managed to complete the course meditating on the floor, although on a couple of occasions I was tempted to ask for a chair. The course went quite pleasantly until the eighth day when, perhaps motivated by the accumulated fatigue, I began to wonder what the hell I was doing there, spending my days exclusively sitting for over ten hours feeling body sensations. Once I had overcome my rebellious period, intense in its negativity, I returned to the serenity that vipassana provides.

During my walks in the nearby forest I crossed paths with several rabbits. As happened to me during my course in Malaysia, meditation makes your mind so calm, but fully awake, that any manifestation, any stimulus, becomes extremely interesting. It could be a beautiful butterfly fluttering its colors against the green background of leaves or grass, or a bird brightening our inner silence with its singing, or a cute rabbit eating by the side of our path; any vital event seemed extremely beautiful, a miracle in itself. I thought that our evolution has endowed us with a brain capable of anticipating and planning for the future, a key to our survival, yet fears and desires still live in our minds, trapping us tight. I saw the rabbits eating peacefully, without fear, until my proximity made them hide; but soon, once the danger had passed, they returned to their task, stress–free. Animals, as Taoism recommends us, do what their instinct dictates and once the job is done, they let it go. When they are hungry, they eat, if it's time to sleep, they do so, if they perceive danger, they flee. They never remain in the situation longer than necessary; there's no animal that rejoices for hours after having gobbled a prey, lingers for hours after waking up, or is trapped by panic after escaping from its pursuer. They continue with their lives doing what they have to do at all times, without the slightest worry about the past or the future. They live only in the present and therefore are happy, because neither the past nor the future exists for them. Much of humanity is stuck in the past and trapped in the future, slaves of their memory and their expectations. There was no doubt I'd continue practicing vipassana meditation (maybe not daily, but I'd try), but I was also more than determined to have a Zen attitude in my daily life, to focus on what I'd be doing at any time, to abandon unproductive distractions, and to lead a more simple and intuitive existence.

I spent three months in New York. For two months I stayed at my friend Heidi's apartment on Union Square while she enjoyed the summer in Italy; in October I shared with two roommates I didn't know a spacious and beautiful loft in Brooklyn that I found online. During the hot and humid New York summer I wrote and sorted out and edited my photos. I also reconnected with yoga; during my two months on Union Square going several times a week to Om Yoga studio. I continued, as well, with my study of the Tao and Zen, and bought *An Introduction to Zen Buddhism* by Professor D. T. Suzuki, and *The Second Book of the Tao* by Stephen Mitchell, both essential for the Zen enthusiast.

November came quite fast and I flew to London, where I stayed a week at my friends Dave and Steph's home, before going to Seville to celebrate Kellie's fiftieth birthday with her sister and a group of friends coming from New York. We spent a whole week in beautiful Seville, with a couple of day trips to Cordoba and Cadiz, ending with a few days in Madrid, where I stayed with my cousin Javi and his girlfriend Alenda for almost three weeks. I've always liked Madrid, a city where I had tried to do my last two years at college (though that had proven impossible under the rigid regional university system in Spain) and where I'd planned to go after my first year in London.

Before the arrival of Christmas, which I'd spend in San Sebastian with my family, I had to decide what to do in early 2012. My two projects were being delayed. The constant traveling and changing places of residence wasn't helping me find the routine necessary for giving the finishing touches to my script and my book. It seemed I wasn't far from completing them; however, it took me a while to realize that, for a virgin writer like me, polishing phases is far more complicated than I had expected. I didn't want to go back to New York during the cold winter, having dodged the previous two (as well as New York being too expensive), and neither did I want to remain in San Sebastian. I considered three options: Candeleda, my mother's village in the southern foothills of the Sierra de Gredos, where we have a house; a cheap beach apartment on the Cadiz coast, which was unknown to me; or an apartment in Madrid. The Spanish capital was chosen over the others because, since my college days, I'd always wanted to live there for a while. I found online a simple attic with balcony near La Latina that I rented for two months.

I arrived in Madrid after Epiphany, and settled into my new temporary home, wanting to devote my working time to writing, my leisure to enjoying the city. In addition to four cousins and an aunt, I had three friends I had met in New York living there: Claudia, a Mexican married to a Spaniard; Sara, a painter who had returned to Madrid after a long period in America; and Martin, a professor who had spent time in New York on a research project. One of the advantages of living in London and New York is that you can meet people from around the globe.

I met with Martin on a Sunday afternoon in late January. We had a couple of beers before going to El Junco, a popular jazz club in Plaza de Santa Barbara. The jam session was to begin at 11 p.m., but, since this was Spain, it wasn't surprising that the musicians didn't start playing until almost midnight. The American trombonist Norman Hogue led the session. Martin had to get up early on Monday so he left soon after the beginning of the concert. I decided to stay and enjoy the good music and a whiskey on the rocks. Around 1 a.m. I saw a woman come in and stand in front of me, a little to my right. With very black hair, she wore dark jeans and a tight black top with red floral patterns that marked her curved and attractive figure. From the side, with her complexion and slightly slanted eyes, I thought she might be Latina. The lively jazz made her dance slightly without moving her feet off the ground. I thought about talking to her as soon as the musicians took a break. When the break came, the woman started talking to someone sitting on a stool to her left. I didn't like to interrupt them. I hesitated between going home to sleep so I could get up early to write, or extending the musical night with another shot and trying to meet the woman with the black hair.

I went to the bar to order a beer, but there was no one serving. I asked a woman seated on a stool where the waiters were, and she replied that the closet was behind the bar and, with the stampede of customers to get outside to smoke, the waiters were there in search of customers' coats. Ignorant of the closet, I had hung my coat on a hook on one of the ledges in front of the stage, and fearing someone might steal it, I went to pick it up. While waiting for a waiter to serve the thirsty patrons, the black–haired woman appeared on my left.

"It looks like we're gonna have to wait," I said, to start a conversation.

"I just want my coat to go outside to smoke," she added.

"They're quite busy in there. I can lend you mine," I said, offering her my black winter coat.

"Do you really mean it?" she asked, surprised.

"Sure, as long as you bring it back."

"Of course. I have mine in the closet."

After I removed my wallet and cell phone, she took my

black coat, somewhat surprised by the generous gesture of a stranger. Beer in hand, I headed toward the stage, waiting for the resumption of the concert and the return of the attractive woman with my coat.

Smokers returned to the premises, and with them came my coat on female shoulders. Her name was Ana, a Coruñesa with a Venezuelan mother who was in Madrid for a few days and returning to Galicia the following day, or perhaps on Tuesday. We listened to the rest of the concert together, chatting intermittently with the jazz background. At the end of it, we left El Junco and talked for a while in the cold night. I felt as if both of us were enjoying the conversation. We would have liked to carry it on, but I didn't suggest extending the evening, and neither did she. We parted without even exchanging phone numbers; I thought I wouldn't see her again. A friend of hers, a musician, had told her Tuesday's jam session would be very interesting, and she hinted at the possibility of extending her stay in Madrid. I told her that I'd probably come to El Junco on Tuesday night.

I arrived at El Junco after 11:30 p.m. just as the musicians began the session. Ana wasn't there. I had a beer while enjoying a young Cuban's trumpet solos. After midnight, to my surprise and delight, I saw Ana descending El Junco's stairs. We enjoyed the concert together. When it ended, around 3:30 a.m. we stood chatting in the bar while customers left the club, musicians picked up their instruments, and waiters cleaned the premises. At 5 a.m. we were asked to leave after having been the only two customers for at least the last hour. Outside, two of the musicians were in conversation at the taxi stop in Plaza Santa Barbara. Ana approached them to ask if they knew of any place still open at that hour on a Tuesday night. One of them, before getting in the taxi, suggested Volta, just five minutes away. The other musician, Antonio, a saxophonist and flutist, joined us, although I would have preferred that the duo hadn't become a trio. When we got to Volta, they were closing. We walked down to Gran Via in search of a cafe, but there was nothing open. We continued our night walk to Sol, where a young

Romanian invited us to go to an *after bar*. We fell into the temptation of a last drink in a gloomy place where just a dozen youngsters danced, including a pair of very stoned French girls and a camp Russian dressed in tight light blue jeans and V–neck red sweater that brightened his blond hair. The bar closed at 8 a.m. We walked to La Latina for breakfast. Antonio took his coffee and bun quickly because he wanted to rest before going to a rehearsal. Ana and I enjoyed our breakfast calmly, with me about to fall sleep at any moment. We exchanged phone numbers and email addresses, before a mid–morning goodbye on a gorgeous sunny winter day. I went home and straight to bed; Ana said she wanted to walk.

I woke up at 5 p.m. with a message on my cell from Ana with the following options: theater, dinner, concert, or nothing. I opted for dinner, and we decided to go to Annapurna, an Indian restaurant not far from El Junco. She told me about her trip to Nepal with a friend in the fall of 2010, exactly a year after my long stay in Kathmandu. My extensive tour of Asia dominated part of the conversation. Nepal had been her first visit to Asia; her second had been two weeks in China last spring. She loved Asia and smiled every time I talked about my backpacking adventure. The conversation flowed as naturally as the previous evening. After the extensive and tasty dinner, we had a drink at a bar in Plaza Santa Barbara. When we finished our drinks, given the late hour and the distance to my place, she kindly invited me to stay at her nearby apartment.

When we got there, she, somewhat tired after having skipped sleeping the night before, asked if I preferred sleeping with her or in the guestroom. Obviously, I chose the first option, aware that conditions weren't ideal for any activity other than sleeping. In bed, and although I did think twice, I decided to use the mattress to sleep, thinking that, if something were to happen beyond sleeping, it would happen the following day. I even preferred that, if it were to occur, it would be with both of us rested. When Ana woke up, she must have forgotten my presence because she turned to me with her left arm extended, hitting me in the face. After her apology, she went to the bathroom, and when she returned, trying to jump over me, we kissed passionately and made love with the energy two fully rested bodies have.

Fortunately—such is life—a business meeting she had in La Coruña on Thursday was postponed, so Ana decided to extend her stay in Madrid until the following Tuesday, a full week that we spent mostly in her room ("*el zulo*" we called it, since her apartment was in a basement), chatting, listening to music, making love, and then taking to the streets under the Madrid winter evenings for dinner and drinks. Days and nights went by, fast and intense. When she parted early Tuesday afternoon, I felt a little put off by the situation. I had intensely enjoyed our days together, but the fact that Ana resided in La Coruña, in the far northwest of Spain, didn't make our meetings at all easy to continue. The farewell was as fast as it was cold on my part, and not because I didn't like Ana—on the contrary—but because the thought that maybe this was a permanent farewell subconsciously resounded in my mind. We didn't even talk about a possible next step. I walked back to my cold attic, feeling a bit lonely, but also expectant about what would happen next.

We didn't hear from one another until Sunday evening, when I sent her an email with a link to the YouTube video of *Where the Hell Is Matt?*, a fantastic video made by Matt Harding during his two-year world tour. Ana immediately replied, surprised by the coincidence of seeing my email arrive just after going online after several days without doing so. I opened the Gmail chat to ask if she had seen the video, and our digital talk lasted from 8:30 p.m. until 3:15 a.m., nearly seven hours of online flirting, with numerous music videos brightening the night. At the end of it, we talked about trying to see each other again because it was clear neither of us was willing to have the intensity of the previous days vanish as a result of the wicked combination of distance and time. Two days later, Ana bought a plane ticket to Madrid for February 23, with a return on March 6: twelve risky days we both imagined would clarify whether the initial fervor had dissipated or whether, on the contrary, it was a symptom of something extraordinary.

A few days later I phoned her from El Retiro Park, where I was enjoying a quiet and sunny winter walk. We talked for a long time, I've forgotten what about, but after hanging up I felt we could have continued talking for hours. On the way home, in one of the narrow streets between Anton Martin Market and Tirso de Molina Square, I suffered from an internal convulsion that shook my body hopelessly. A woman passing by looked almost worried about what was happening to me. It didn't last long, perhaps no more than a minute, but it was extraordinarily intense. It was a feeling of exuberance, of inner joy, that I immediately interpreted as a loving light, a powerful physical confirmation that I was really in love, that Ana was no doubt a very special woman worth keeping.

A fortnight after our farewell, I went to Barajas airport to pick her up by surprise, although she obviously expected to see me there. We kissed passionately as soon as we got hold of each other, even though I think we both suffered a slight uncertainty about how we would react when we met. The bitter cold days of late January having departed, we stayed in my attic, much brighter than the *zulo*, if somewhat colder. If during our first encounter the days had elapsed locked in that loving cell, the dozen days in La Latina brought trips to the theater (we laughed a lot with *The Caveman*), art exhibitions (Juan Gatti, Picasso, Hines), a comedy club, and of course Madrid's culinary offerings, with dinners at Japanese, Vietnamese, Arab, African, Korean, and Chinese restaurants, amongst others. We had a lot in common, not just our passion for travel, food, music, and art, but also our instinctive curiosity about the world. However, our personalities were very different: she much more spontaneous, sociable, and outgoing than me, aspects I hoped would complement each other rather than push us away as we got to know each other closely. Before the end of our second romance in Madrid, we spoke of seeing each other again at Easter. My friends David and Lisa were baptizing their daughter Amaya in Seville on Easter Sunday, and as Ana didn't know the beautiful Andalusian city, I invited her to come along. Everything seemed so fast and natural, just like when we were together, when time flew like our conversation flowed. Our second goodbye couldn't have been more different from the first. Uncertainty had gone, and therefore our hugs and kisses didn't lack ardor this time.

Two days later my mother arrived in Madrid by bus from San Sebastian. I rented a car for a week and picked her up at the station and went to Candeleda. It had been more than eight years since my last visit there, on a weekend after a business trip to Madrid from London. When I told my mother I had met Ana, she thought I was joking. I don't usually tell my mother much, and it'd been years since the last time she had heard of a girlfriend. One of the first things I did upon arriving in Candeleda was to visit my grandparents' old farm, now disused, but when my grandfather was alive, it had grown tobacco, peppers, tomatoes, peanuts, and melons, besides the fruits from fig, orange, and plum trees and grape vines. I entered the barn where once tobacco plants had hung to cure, grabbed a plastic chair, took it outside, and sat near the oak, on the small hill from which I could contemplate the full extent of the farm. Immediately images came to my mind, of my father helping my grandfather during the tobacco harvest, or picking a fresh tomato that he ate immediately after splitting it in half and salting it a little. I could almost see him walking around the farm, still in his bathing suit after our afternoon dip in the Tietar River, with his shirt unbuttoned, enjoying the country life. I became so emotional that I ended up crying, and the first thing I thought of was calling Ana and sharing with her what I was going through. She understood perfectly because she'd also lost her father a few years before.

The end of winter and the arrival of spring is a great time to enjoy the mountains. My first outing was to a lake in the Sierra de Gredos by way of a long but gentle walk along a path deserted except for a number of beautiful mountain goats. On my second outing, I walked up from the village of Guisando to Los Galayos, whose vertical rock faces are ideal for climbing, and La Mira (7,687 ft), a peak with magnificent views of the rest of the mountains and the south valley, including the towns of Arenas de San Pedro and Candeleda.

On both occasions I walked on a thin layer of snow. The winter was unusually dry, and the Gredos peaks seemed hardly painted in white. I also used my four weeks in Candeleda to practice my golf swing. Over the last two weeks in Madrid I'd taken a golf course for beginners, and since Candeleda has a municipal golf course of nine holes, I went there several afternoons to try to give direction and height to the rough ball on that course with its breathtaking view of the Gredos peaks. I loved practicing my swing with the excellent views of the snow–covered Almanzor peak. With my mother we took a couple of drives, one to Trujillo, a beautiful town in Caceres, and another to see the wonderful spectacle that the Jerte Valley offers for a few days in early spring, when its slopes whiten with flowering cherry trees.

Communication with Ana was no longer through chat and phone. We started using Skype to see each other's face; a tool more to my taste than the phone (I don't like not seeing the face of the person I'm talking to), even though having Ana's face on the screen without being able to touch her generated plenty of frustration. The month apart was becoming difficult to bear; both of us eagerly counted the days left until Easter. Since I had to go to New York to keep my green card, I suggested that Ana come with me and visit a city she didn't know and I was sure she'd love, especially if she discovered it with me. Ana worked for herself as a personal and business coach, which gave her unusual flexibility. I didn't have to work hard to convince her, and we immediately planned the trip to New York: I would fly on April 18; she could get away on May 14. We would return together on June 4 with the intention that I would go with her to La Coruña for a few months, for the summer initially, and see where the wonderful romance we were enjoying would take us. I couldn't believe how fast everything was moving, especially after having spent so many years away from that special feeling. It seemed a bit unreal that what I had considered almost impossible was happening with such spontaneity and intensity. *Anitya, anitya, anitya*, once again I thought.

Ana drove from La Coruña and spent a night in

Candeleda, which meant, of course, that she had to—perhaps I should write she was forced to—meet my mother, as well as my uncles and my cousins who had just arrived for Easter. I asked her to stop and wait for me at the edge of Candeleda, with a double purpose: to prevent my mother from being present during our reunion and to hide out in my grandparents' barn so we could kiss without spectators. There we went, and once inside the barn, where once tobacco plants had dried, our bodies became wet before making love passionately. We had lunch with my family, and the forced meeting went smoothly. Ana has a special way with people, very naturally she knows how to navigate any social situation, including meeting my mother so prematurely.

We arrived in Seville the following day. We went to the cathedral to see the famous Easter processions. What I liked most was the profound and moving music that accompanies the pilgrims. The baptism of blonde Amaya was celebrated in a cozy *cortijo* outside Seville. Several of my London friends attended the event, and I was happy that Ana had the opportunity to meet them. David and Lisa invited the group to spend a few days in the house his uncle has in Manilva. They were days of beach relaxation and friendship. On the way back to Candeleda we stopped in Ronda and Grazalema, both beautiful towns, and spontaneously decided to spend a night in Jerez de la Frontera, where we wouldn't have minded staying a couple of days, so interesting is Jerez. After a night of passion in Candeleda before our farewell, Ana dropped me at Avila's train station, where I caught a train to Madrid. My flight to New York was that evening. She continued with the long drive to La Coruña. In three weeks she'd be arriving in New York.

I rented for six weeks an apartment in Brooklyn, specifically in Prospect Heights, a neighborhood near the beautiful Prospect Park, Brooklyn's Central Park, where Skype again became our communication tool. Two days after my arrival we began to look for an apartment in La Coruña. Since her last breakup Ana had lived with her mother. We wanted to find something in the city center for the summer. In the absence of availability of apartments for just three months, I suggested extending my stay to six months, knowing that ninety days would go fast, especially when you're so in love, so I thought I'd stay in Galicia until the end of 2012. Ten days later, and given the difficulty of finding an apartment for six months that satisfied us both, I decided to venture, put my guard down, and committed myself to a full year. I started to count the days since our first evening at El Junco in late January, and my analysis came up with: we had decided to spend Easter together after having seen each other for ten days, Ana had bought a ticket to New York after we had spent twenty–four days together, and I was brave enough to go and live in La Coruña for a year after we had been together for just over one month (counting in days). What a wonderful madness! Two days before her flight to New York, Ana signed a lease on a lovely two–bedroom apartment in the center of her city.

After spending my days in Brooklyn writing and seeing my friends (all expectant to meet and get to know my love), Ana landed at JFK, excited, smiling as always, and full of energy. So much had I longed to see her over the previous two days that I could hardly concentrate on work. I had prepared a long and interesting list of activities in addition to visiting New York's main tourist spots, including live music, outings to explore different cuisines, and also great bars. And to complete the New York experience, we escaped the city with my friends David and Eleanor for a weekend in the Hamptons. These were three unforgettable weeks in which I enjoyed New York in a way I hadn't done in my previous five years of residence there.

We landed in Madrid on June 4. Ana flew to La Coruña the following day; I arrived by train two days later. The long train journey allowed me to go over everything I had experienced since I left my job at the end of April 2009, more than three years earlier. Initially, I had planned a trip of only twelve months, but the two operations on my leg and the time spent on the sideburn cyst in Saigon had pushed me to extend it to eighteen, which gave me more time to explore Asia, a continent I love and to which I will go back many times in the future. On my return from Japan I didn't at all have a clear idea of where to settle. Actually, I didn't force it then, with the hope that the success or failure of my projects would determine the following steps to take. And it was my tardiness in finalizing my projects, my lack of routine after returning from Asia, that were the cause of my encounter with love, ironically in my own country, in Spain, after so much travel, so much fruitless search.

I was on the train with little luggage; I continued to travel light, and was about to arrive at a completely unknown city with a suitcase full of extremely positive experiences. It had been over sixteen years since I left San Sebastian and was now returning to another small city by the Atlantic Ocean with the feeling of the possible closure to an entire life cycle. What would life in La Coruña be like? Unconsciously perhaps, it didn't worry me in the slightest; all I wanted was to live with Ana. Time would clarify everything that still needed elucidating. As always, it was time to live in the present.

Thanks for reading "*The Year I Became a Nomad*"; I hope you have enjoyed it.

In gratitude for buying my book, I'm offering you as a gift the chance of downloading one of my journey's photographs for your personal use.

Just type the following url in your browser:

www.carlospenalba.com/thankyou